How to Be Successful in Your First Year of Teaching Middle School

Everything You Need to Know That They Don't Teach You in School

M.E. GRIFFITH

and

ANNE KOCSIS

How to Be Successful in Your First Year of Teaching Middle School: Everything You Need to Know That They Don't Teach You in School

Copyright © 2011 by Atlantic Publishing Group, Inc.

1405 SW 6th Ave. • Ocala, Florida 34471 • 800-814-1132 • 352-622-1875–Fax

Web site: www.atlantic-pub.com • E-mail: sales@atlantic-pub.com

SAN Number: 268-1250

Kocsis, Anne B., 1965-
  How to be successful in your first year of teaching middle school : everything you need to know that they don't teach you in school / by Anne B. Kocsis and Mary Ellen Griffith.
     p. cm.
  Includes bibliographical references and index.
  ISBN-13: 978-1-60138-336-5 (alk. paper)
  ISBN-10: 1-60138-336-3 (alk. paper)
  1. Middle school teaching--United States. 2. First year teachers--United States. I. Griffith, Mary Ellen, 1962- II. Title.
  LB1623.5.K63 2010
  373.11--dc22
                              2010028231

EDITOR: Melissa Peterson • mpeterson@atlantic-pub.com
BOOK PRODUCTION DESIGN: T.L. Price • design@tlpricefreelance.com
COVER DESIGN: Jackie Miller • millerjackiej@gmail.com

Printed in the United States

Printed on Recycled Paper

We recently lost our beloved pet "Bear," who was not only our best and dearest friend but also the "Vice President of Sunshine" here at Atlantic Publishing. He did not receive a salary but worked tirelessly 24 hours a day to please his parents.

Bear was a rescue dog that turned around and showered myself, my wife, Sherri, his grandparents Jean, Bob, and Nancy, and every person and animal he met (maybe not rabbits) with friendship and love. He made a lot of people smile every day.

We wanted you to know that a portion of the profits of this book will be donated to The Humane Society of the United States. —*Douglas & Sherri Brown*

The human-animal bond is as old as human history. We cherish our animal companions for their unconditional affection and acceptance. We feel a thrill when we glimpse wild creatures in their natural habitat or in our own backyard.

Unfortunately, the human-animal bond has at times been weakened. Humans have exploited some animal species to the point of extinction.

The Humane Society of the United States makes a difference in the lives of animals here at home and worldwide. The HSUS is dedicated to creating a world where our relationship with animals is guided by compassion. We seek a truly humane society in which animals are respected for their intrinsic value, and where the human-animal bond is strong.

Want to help animals? We have plenty of suggestions. Adopt a pet from a local shelter, join The Humane Society and be a part of our work to help companion animals and wildlife. You will be funding our educational, legislative, investigative and outreach projects in the U.S. and across the globe.

Or perhaps you'd like to make a memorial donation in honor of a pet, friend or relative? You can through our Kindred Spirits program. And if you'd like to contribute in a more structured way, our Planned Giving Office has suggestions about estate planning, annuities, and even gifts of stock that avoid capital gains taxes.

Maybe you have land that you would like to preserve as a lasting habitat for wildlife. Our Wildlife Land Trust can help you. Perhaps the land you want to share is a backyard— that's enough. Our Urban Wildlife Sanctuary Program will show you how to create a habitat for your wild neighbors.

So you see, it's easy to help animals. And The HSUS is here to help.

THE HUMANE SOCIETY
OF THE UNITED STATES.

2100 L Street NW • Washington, DC 20037 • 202-452-1100
www.hsus.org

Dedication

"The dream begins with a teacher who believes in you,
who tugs and pushes and leads you to the next plateau,
sometimes poking you with a sharp stick called truth."

— *Dan Rather, American journalist (1931 to present)*

This book is dedicated to all those individuals who have ever taught in a middle school environment. The transition from a child to a young adult is challenging. Thank you for making a difference. In particular, I would like to thank the teachers in the Cumberland Valley School District who took the time to provide their best tips and advice for future middle school teachers everywhere. Your wisdom, guidance, and support is greatly appreciated. — Anne Kocsis

To my eighth-grade daughter Alexis and all the other middle school students in my life. No one has taught me better than you. — M.E. Griffith

Table of Contents

Chapter 2: Choosing the Right Work Environment 45

Chapter 3: Seeking Employment as an Educator   69

Chapter 4: Making a Living as an Educator   89

Chapter 5:
Teaching Relationships and Your Go-To Crew   105

Chapter 6:
Creating a Classroom Conducive to Learning   125

Chapter 9:
The Core of Teaching — Lesson Plans   177

Chapter 10: Making the Grade   199

Chapter 11: Classroom Management 101 — Rules and Discipline   227

Chapter 13: Handling the Unexpected   269

Chapter 14: Politics and Education   289

Foreword

When I tell people what I do, they look at me as if I am nuts. It seems inconceivable to many people that I would voluntarily spend hours each day with 20 middle schoolers. After all, they are not cute anymore like elementary students, yet they are not as mature as high school students. And perhaps I am a bit crazy. Still, I would not trade my job for anything in the world.

I decided to teach middle school when I was in seventh grade, but I began my teaching career long before then. When I was five, I taught my 14-month-old sister to say "No," and shortly thereafter, I taught her to say "Get up, Mommy!" Neither lesson was endorsed by my mother. Later, I taught my four-year-old brother lengthy names of dinosaurs using one of a teacher's more important tools — enthusiasm — and I taught my sister how to count to ten in German as I accompanied her selling Girl Scout cookies door-to-door. However, I did not settle on education as a career until my seventh grade classmates kept coming to me for explanations and I realized I liked explaining things to them.

My path to my first year of teaching was fairly straightforward after that. In high school, I joined Future Teachers of America (FTA) and participated in opportunities to teach during Student-Teacher Switch Day. I also began teaching Sunday school halfway though high school, a job that gave me invaluable experience in lesson planning and controlling a classroom. Toward the end of high school and throughout college, I worked in the summers as a counselor for seventh and eighth grade boys at a summer camp, acquiring invaluable insight into the mind of the middle schooler. In college, I decided to double-major in history and education; in my sophomore year, I made up my mind to continue on for a master's degree in teaching. This meant that I stopped taking education courses so I would have enough for my fifth year, and thus, I began taking English and science courses. By the end of my graduate work, I had taken the requisite courses and Praxis II exams to be certified to teach middle school social studies, English, science, and math. I opted to have breadth in a certain age group rather than depth in a certain subject because I wanted to maximize my chances to be hired as a middle school teacher. Finally, after months of searching, I achieved my goal of becoming a middle school teacher.

I remember my first year of teaching middle school as if it were last year, which in fact it was. The first few weeks were extremely overwhelming. As helpful as the administration and various teachers in my school were, I wish that I had a book that walked me through the various pieces of the first year. Many things were new to me. Which supplies should I have on hand before school started? How do I organize the flood of papers from different sources? How do I make a good impression on the first day? And how do I deal with classroom management? *How to Be Successful in Your First Year of Teaching Middle School: Everything That You Need to Know That They Don't Teach You in School* is exactly the manual that I would have loved to have a year ago. It covers the entire process of becoming a teacher, from routes to teaching, to résumés and interviews, and then guides you through your first year of teaching. There are tips on a plethora of subjects, from the aforementioned questions that I had to the pros and cons of joining a union. Not only will first-year teachers benefit from this book but veterans will as well. One of the hallmarks of a good teacher is constantly seeking to improve one's practice, and this book will certainly further teachers in that goal.

As a teacher, there are several sayings that have been helpful to me. One is, "You are never fully dressed without a smile." Another is, "No one hits a homerun every time they are up to bat. The good players are the ones who keep trying." And then, there is a quotation from the comedian Sam Levenson, "You must learn from the mistakes of others. You can't possibly live long enough to make them all yourself." May the accumulated wisdom in this book help turn you into the best middle school teacher that you can be!

David Schwartz
Middle school social studies teacher
Bernard Zell Anshe Emet Day School
Chicago, Illinois

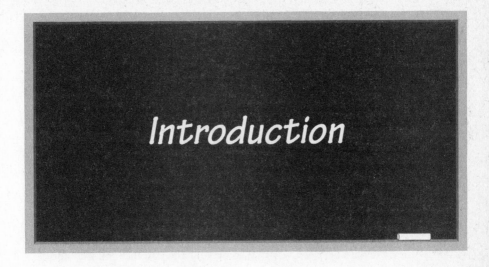

Introduction

"One looks back with appreciation to the brilliant teachers, but with gratitude to those who touched our human feelings. The curriculum is so much necessary raw material, but warmth is the vital element for the growing plant and for the soul of the child."

— *Carl Jung (Swiss founder of analytical psychiatry, 1875 to 1961)*

Middle school serves as a transition between elementary school and high school. In most cases, it includes grades six through eight. On average, the students are between the ages of 11 to 14, a time typically associated with raging hormones and puberty. This transition period between childhood and burgeoning adulthood creates added complications when teaching children of these ages.

These students come in all shapes and sizes but share some very distinct characteristics. Middle school students face numerous physical and emotional changes as they move from childhood dependence into a more independent young adult stage of life. As adolescents develop, their experiences and perceptions can become colored by their emotions. The following is a list of common middle school student traits frequently recognized by veteran middle school teachers across the country:

- They are plagued with self-doubt.
- They are rarely satisfied with their appearance.

- They face confusing changes to their bodies, such as changing voices, developing curves, growing hair on their bodies, and the onset of acne.

- They have insatiable appetites.

- They have frequent, often inexplicable mood swings.

- They laugh loudly and frequently.

- They are reduced to tears very easily.

- They tend to view events in terms of extremes.

- They exhibit strong opinions about the social issues that are important to them.

- They vacillate between wanting to be silly and carefree children and wanting to be taken seriously as young adults.

- They believe that life is not fair and that adults do not understand.

- They have a sudden need for privacy.

- They are embarrassed by their parents and other family members.

- They care deeply for their friends, yet habitually gossip behind their friends' backs.

- They require multiple opinions from others before making a decision.

- They spend hours using social networking technology on the computer and their cell phones.

- They have fleeting attention spans.

- They want to be taken seriously and given the chance to be independent.

USING THIS BOOK

Educating students during their most impressionable age encompasses much more than a few textbooks, cute bulletin boards, and some dry-erase markers. Successfully constructing an effective — yet comfortable — learning environment amid today's state standards, inclusion classes, and federal mandates is truly a notable accomplishment. Fortunately, we also teach in a digital age, which simplifies many tasks our predecessors found grueling.

Read this book and then keep it close as a reference throughout your first year. The field of education is fast-paced and busy. This book will assist you by bridging the gap between what you learned in school and what you will be expected to face each day as a middle school teacher. It will help you:

- Facilitate lasting, positive relationships with administrators, fellow faculty, and district and support staff.

- Create a well-organized, well-behaved, comfortable, "safe zone" classroom while adhering to district, state, and school expectations.

- Analyze pacing and curriculum guidelines and implement your state's standards into the units you will use in your classroom year after year.

- Define and provide ideas and offer samples and templates for academic teams, interdisciplinary units, and departmental planning.

- Employ strategies for creating a technologically savvy classroom that keeps students engaged with your lessons — instead of their MP3 players, gaming consoles, and multifunction cell phones.

- Facilitate the creation of positive partnerships with parents and show you how to turn even the most difficult parent into your most valuable ally.

- Understand the rationale behind federal programs such as English for Speakers of Other Languages (ESOL), the No Child Left Behind Act of 2001, and various special education laws.

- Ensure your students meet yearly progress goals as dictated by mandated testing while maintaining an effective, fun, and creative learning environment.

- Use numerous resources such as websites that offer free teacher instructional ideas, podcasts, and templates for lesson plans.

In the pages that follow, you will find information on the various routes to becoming a teacher, from a four-year education degree to the mid-career guest teacher path, and everything in between. It includes advice on student teaching, substitute teaching, writing your résumé, and preparing for the job interview. Additionally, information is provided to help you determine where you want to seek employment.

Once you have a job, there will be a host of other challenges to face. Teaching is a very rewarding profession, but it can also be very stressful, especially for a new teacher. Teaching middle school is particularly overwhelming. In addition to the pressures of a new job, new middle school teachers need to work with students going through puberty, as well as all the ensuing hormones surrounding that time period. Included are many comments from middle school students to help you understand their perception of their teachers, school, and education.

Many experienced teachers were interviewed to fill this book with the answers to the most commonly asked questions, along with tips and suggestions on handling a wide array of challenges facing middle school teachers today. Hopefully, this is just the first step in a long, successful, and very rewarding career.

CHAPTER 1:

Joining the World of Middle School Educators

According to a June 2009 U.S. Census Bureau press release, 2.9 million teachers are employed in elementary and middle schools in the United States. That might seem like a huge number, but good middle school teachers are always needed.

In 1794, a group in New York City known as the Society of Associated Teachers established the first recognized teacher requirements. City officials organized the association to create uniform teacher qualifications in the city. Eleven years later, a group called the Free School Society was the first to secure public funds to pay for teacher courses. It was not until 1885, however, that a college preparatory course was developed at Brown University. Now, more than a century later, all teachers must undergo some form of training in order to become certified and licensed to teach. There are many different ways to receive the necessary training, but ultimately, all full-time secondary teachers in the United States are expected to have the following:

- Bachelor's degree
- Student teaching experience
- Teacher certification
- Teacher's license

These are the basic requirements, but there are exceptions. For example, if you are seeking employment in a private school, you still need a bachelor's degree, but you do not need a license. Public schools have more government regulations regarding teaching requirements than private institutions; therefore, if you have fulfilled the requirements above, you will have more job opportunities from which to choose.

According to the U.S. Census Bureau, the United States employed approximately 6.5 million teachers from elementary school to university in 2005. There are some areas of the country experiencing a surplus of teachers in the market, while others still have difficulty filling teacher positions. Additionally, attrition is a major concern in this industry. According to the National Commission on Teaching and America's Future (NCTAF), over 30 percent quit within five years. In other words, there is always a need for new, enthusiastic teachers. Just as there are numerous types of teachers, there are multiple ways to get to this point. If you know you want to be a teacher, and have not yet received the necessary training, here are some of the ways to accomplish your goal:

- Traditional route
- Professional Development School (PDS)
- Part-time traditional route
- Internet degree option
- Fast-track programs
- Continuing education
- Guest teacher program
- Temporary certification

If you did not go to a four-year college to obtain a degree in education, you can still become a middle school teacher. Continue reading to understand the specifics involved in entering the profession by one of the following alternate routes.

THE TRADITIONAL ROUTE

The traditional route to becoming a middle school teacher requires attending a four-year college, majoring in education, and obtaining a bachelor's degree. Many younger teachers start out this way. By attending college immediately after high school and majoring in education, you will be able to take all of the courses you need. If you know from the start that you want to teach in a middle school, you will need to major in the subject you wish to teach. Each school has its own list of core accreditation requirements, but most expect aspiring teachers to take technology courses to keep up with the changing trends. These programs include student teaching and preparing for certification and licensure exams and are accredited by the National Council for Accreditation of Teacher Education (NCATE) and the Teacher Education Accreditation Council (TEAC).

The benefits of NCATE accreditation

Founded in 1954, the NCATE was set up to better prepare teachers and administrators. It was the collaboration of several other teaching organizations. It replaced the American Association of Colleges for Teacher Education (AACTE) as the primary source for accreditation. In conjunction with the AACTE, the National Association of State Directors of Teacher Education and Certification (NASDTEC), the National Education Association (NEA), the Council of Chief State School Officers (CCSSO), and the National School Boards Association (NSBA) all provided input for the standards set by the NCATE. The organization seeks to provide the best foundation for teachers so that they can provide quality education to all students. Many schools look for this accreditation on teacher's résumés. According to the NCATE website (**www.ncate.org**), teachers attending NCATE accredited schools benefit from the following:

- Having a thorough knowledge of subject matter
- Being equipped with effective teaching strategies
- Obtaining feedback on their practice teaching that assists them in adapting their instruction plans
- Learning to comprehend and communicate with students from different backgrounds
- Gaining the support and guidance of master teachers
- Acquiring the ability to integrate modern technology into their plans for instruction

If you decide to go the traditional route, consider attending a university that has been sanctioned by the NCATE. Professionals in the education field have reviewed these schools. In addition, the programs maintain higher standards for students recommended for certification and licensure. These universities offer courses on the most current teaching trends. This is a benefit when you are first looking for a job and do not have a lot of experience on your résumé. NCATE accreditation might also make it easier to get a job in another state. Each state has its own licensure requirements, but many states have agreements with NCATE-accredited schools that simplify the licensing process. To determine whether a school is accredited, visit the NCATE website (**www.ncate.org**), and click on the heading titled "public." On this page, click on the heading for "current and future teachers" on the left-hand side of the page. You will be directed to a page that contains a link to a list of accredited universities.

PROFESSIONAL DEVELOPMENT SCHOOLS (PDS)

Another option for individuals who have already earned a bachelor's degree is a professional development school (PDS) program, now offered in many states. These programs exist through partnerships between universities and specific schools. The one-year programs expedite the process by merging theory with practice. They allow students to experience a full year of teaching, with guidance and supervision. Individuals interested in these programs must apply through the university partnering with the secondary school. Think of it as an on-the-job training program. Professional development schools combine academics with practical experience. These institutions are formed between education degree programs and school systems serving preschool through twelfth grade. The concept was developed to help new teachers focus more on schools and classroom activities. The goal is to better prepare new teachers for the actual classroom by improving the student teaching experience. Because the PDS concept primarily concentrates on the classroom experience, it is sometimes criticized for not being as current on the constantly changing issues of education reform. Professional development schools are increasing in number each year. The AACTE currently maintains a database of over 1,000 of these types of schools.

PART-TIME TRADITIONAL ROUTE

Even if you have not recently graduated high school, you can still follow the traditional route. Many colleges offer night classes for individuals who are working their way through school. Consider taking one or two courses at a time until you obtain your education degree. If you already have a bachelor's degree in another field, particularly if it is in the subject you wish to teach, you are almost there. To teach in a public school, you might only need a limited number of additional credits in education in addition to a certain number of student teaching hours to receive certification. Other job opportunities might also be available outside the public school system. Some private schools do not require an education degree from their teachers, providing they have bachelor's degrees in a relevant subject matter.

If you decide to pursue the part-time traditional route, research your options. Look at the school district websites where you would like to work. Check the job postings to find out what the requirements are. If the information is not posted online, call the district office. When you know what you need to teach in the school of your choice, you can begin researching programs in your area that will help you complete your degree and the other necessary requirements.

INTERNET DEGREE OPTION

Online classes are available in virtually any subject. You can complete your education degree, take courses that enable you to specialize in a specific subject area, or simply further your education through online school. Once you determine what you want to teach, you can research what kind of classes you need in order to accomplish your goal. In searching for online teaching programs, you will find numerous schools offering teacher certification programs through online classes. Start by visiting a website such as EarnMyDegree.com (**www.earnmydegree.com**). It posts links to a multitude of schools organized by area of interest, making it easier to find a program to fit your needs.

These programs can be an effective alternative to attending school in a college classroom setting. Some colleges and universities offer full online bachelor's programs or online courses as part of a degree program. Online learning opportunities are ideal for budding teachers who live in rural areas, are already employed in another field full time, or may be interested in teaching via the virtual schools now available to homebound middle schoolers. Be sure the online school you choose is accredited and not a scam. Research it before you begin your courses. Education Online (**www.educationonline.com**) can provide you with information about scam degrees as well as what to look for in your search for an online university.

FAST-TRACK PROGRAMS

Many individuals are deciding to become teachers as a second career. The idea of switching careers can be intimidating, particularly if it involves many more years of studying to acquire additional degrees. Now, fast-track programs enable individuals with bachelor's degrees to enroll in short-term programs to become certified to teach in as little as one year. The thought process is that these individuals have other career and life experiences to bring to the job. One organization that helps place these mid-career individuals into teaching jobs is the New York Teaching Fellows. They have assisted more than 9,000 career-changing individuals with securing teaching jobs in the city.

Because there is a shortage of certain types of teachers in some areas of the country, accelerated teaching programs were developed to fill specific needs. For example, in June 2009, Governor Ed Rendell of Pennsylvania set up a fast-track program to address the shortage in qualified secondary math and science teachers. The state program allows mid-career professionals with a bachelor's degree to complete a four-month teacher-training course instead of the traditional four-year education degree program. A variety of fast-track alternative teacher training courses are available in the United States. Other programs include, but are not limited, to the following:

- **Troops to Teachers**: Individuals retired from the various branches of service are eligible to begin second careers as teachers in public schools.

- **Teach for America:** Recent college graduates attend summer sessions sponsored through private, corporate, and government donations. Subsequently, they commit to teaching in rural and low-income urban areas for at least two years.

- **The New Teacher Project** (TNTP): This is a national non-profit organization that recruits, trains, and prepares select individuals to teach in shortage-area subjects and high-needs schools. Their goal is to improve the achievement level of high-needs students.

CONTINUING EDUCATION

Many private schools will accept teachers without education certification as long as they have a bachelor's degree in the subject they are teaching. Additionally, if there is an immediate need for a teacher in a specific subject, a school might allow you to teach while you are finishing your education degree. For example, if there is a need for a Chinese language instructor, a qualified individual might be hired while they are working to complete his or her degree. For special circumstances such as these, the school board must approve hiring the employee.

GUEST TEACHER PROGRAM

There is a huge need for middle school substitute teachers. There are two- to three-day programs available that provide expedited training to quickly increase the pool of available substitute teachers. In Pennsylvania, the Intermediate Unit offers this program and trains individuals who can substitute in 27 different school districts. The Intermediate Unit is an educational servicing agency that provides alternative education. The program is a good way to get into the school district. You can make money, build your credentials, and decide if you want to become a full-time teacher. It is also a great, highly flexible alternative if you only want to work part-time. If you decide you want to become a full-time middle school teacher, you can complete your credentials and become certified. If you do not enjoy teaching at this level, you have saved yourself time and money. Not everyone is cut out to be a middle school teacher. Check with the school district in your area regarding their policies for hiring substitute middle school teachers.

TEMPORARY CERTIFICATION

Most states have temporary certification programs as an alternative to traditional teaching routes. According to the National Center for Education Information, during the 2007 to 2008 school year, more than 62,000 people became teachers through alternative certification processes. These opportunities allow people with non-education degrees to take education courses and licensing exams to meet state requirements. Participants who complete the courses continue to teach in the classroom while they work toward full certification. For example, qualified applicants who obtain a middle school teaching position in Florida have three years to gather the credits they need to complete their certification and earn passing scores on the Florida Comprehensive Teaching Exam and a specific subject area exam. Once these tasks are accomplished, you can apply for a professional educator's certificate.

The certification department in the district where you are seeking employment can help you understand the state requirements for temporary certification. Make a personal appointment with the department and bring your college transcripts with you so you can find out whether you have the qualifications for temporary certification. You also will learn what subject area you can teach in and the courses you will need to take. Prospective educators who are excited about their subjects and eager to teach middle school are a commodity, and the state and districts will be happy to give you the information you need to achieve your goal. The certification professional usually will give you a form that explains which credits you need.

MIDDLE SCHOOL CRITICAL SHORTAGE

When a majority of districts in a state struggle to fill specific subject areas with qualified teachers, especially special-needs areas, they set up critical teacher shortage (CTS) financial-aid programs. CTS subject areas often include middle school science and math. These programs are ideal for people who want to teach but do not know how they will be able to afford the cost of tuition. CTS programs offer tuition reimbursement, student loan forgiveness, and in some areas, full tuition based on a contract to teach for a certain number of years. This avenue for financing your education is well worth investigating. Check your state education department's website or call the department to see which subject areas have teacher shortages. For example, below are some of the subject areas and specialties that appeared on a critical shortage list from New Hampshire's Department of Education for the 2007 to 2008 school term:

- Biology
- Chemistry
- Computer technology education
- Earth/space sciences
- English for speakers of other languages (ESOL)
- Family and consumer sciences
- Foreign languages
- Guidance counselor
- Library media specialists
- Mathematics
- Music education
- Physical sciences
- Physics
- Psychologist
- Reading specialists
- Special education
- Speech language specialist

- Technology education

At a four-year university, you will gain plenty of exposure to your subject area and enjoy an internship working side-by-side with a veteran teacher in your field. Furthermore, if your initial degree is focused on education, the courses for this degree already include the current federally mandated requirements such as ESOL endorsement (teaching English as a second language).

On the other hand, teachers who have taken the fast track or who have entered into education from a different field must complete these requirements during their first three years of teaching or face losing their certification.

CERTIFICATION AND LICENSURE

Regardless of the path you take to become a teacher, you will need to fulfill certain other requirements before seeking employment in this field. In order to be eligible to teach in the public school system, you must first be certified. Because every state has different certification and licensure requirements, you should research the licensing regulations in the area where you wish to teach prior to seeking employment. The type of certification required varies from state to state. It also depends on the age level and subject you plan to teach. Check with the state board of education to gather the specific requirements for your state. Information on who to contact is available online. The U.S. Department of Education in the Education Resources Organization Directory (EROD) also provides information on specific certification requirements on its website (**www2.ed.gov/erod**). Look for the box titled "simple search" and type in "state education agency." You will be directed to a list of all of the boards of education, listed alphabetically by state. Each state name features a Web link, a URL link, and an e-mail address for a contact person for each organization. State-specific certification details are also available at the Certification Map website (**http://certificationmap.com**). Log on and click on the state in which you wish to seek employment.

To save a lot of time and start working as a teacher much sooner, determine the school district you want to work in and research their specific certification requirements. All districts are listed on The U.S. Department of Education's website (**www.ed.gov**). The National Center for Education Statistics website (**http://nces.ed.gov**) includes information about each district in the country. Hover the cursor over the "School, College, & Library Search" tab at the top and click "Search for Public School Districts." You will find the district name and contact information for all districts in that state.

Each state board of education agency has its own licensure advisory committee, and each state has its own specific regulations. For example, Pennsylvania requires at least a 3.0 GPA in your major to apply for a secondary school license. In some states, such as Massachusetts and New York, a master's degree is required for licensure. Other states may require a master's degree for professional development or administrative positions of principal or higher. The following requirements, however, are standard licensure requirements in the United States:

- Bachelor's degree
- Completion of approved teacher training program
- Completion of a supervised student teaching program
- A passing grade on The Praxis Series™ test

The Praxis Series, created by the Educational Testing Service™ (ETS), is a series of assessments that most states use to certify teachers and provide them with the necessary license to teach. There are two different tests in the series that you may need to take for the jobs you are seeking:

- **Praxis ISM**: This test measures basic knowledge and skills, such as reading, writing, and math. Basic knowledge of these subject areas is required for entry into most teacher education programs.

- **Praxis IISM**: This test assesses specific subject matter knowledge. Because middle school teachers teach specific subjects, they would benefit from taking the Praxis II. It is a requirement for teacher licensure in 39 out of the 50 United States.

Like any other test, being prepared provides the best chance for success. The ETS has study aids and practice tests available at their website (**www.ets.org/praxis**).

The degree, student teaching observations, and test scores are all evaluated for licensure. The criteria varies by state, but licenses are granted in the following categories:

- Early childhood (preschool through third grade)
- Elementary (first through sixth grade, but may include up to eighth grade in some states)
- Middle school (fifth through eighth grades)
- Secondary school — by subject matter (seventh through 12th grades)
- Special subject — such as art and music (kindergarten through 12th grade)

BEFORE YOU CAN TEACH

Find out the laws regarding working with children in your area. In order to work with children in any capacity, either as a paid employee or as a volunteer, you must undergo certain background checks. If you have not already done so, the school will require you to acquire a number of clearances before you can start working. Check with individual school districts and employers to determine their specific requirements. You will incur a cost for each application. Ask to see whether the organization reimburses for the cost. Some do, but most do not. The following is a basic list of the types of clearances required by schools:

- State criminal background check
- Federal criminal background check, including fingerprinting
- Child abuse clearance

The information is checked against state police and FBI databases. The program searches for past criminal activity and any history of child abuse. The current system evolved from a series of government actions, including the National Child Protection Act of 1993 (NCPA), the Violent Crime Control Act of 1994, and the Volunteers for Children Act (part of the Crime Identification Act of 1998). Federal laws mandate these background checks.

Additionally, schools require proof of a recent tuberculosis (TB) test with negative results. Many colleges also recommend that students entering into their student teaching internship obtain professional liability insurance. Some universities make it mandatory for students to purchase it before they are allowed to enter into their student teaching. Student teaching liability insurance provisions offer protection in civil legal matters such as negligence, libel, grading disputes, and student injury. Because the student teachers are not paid, they are considered volunteers; therefore, the school they are teaching at does not cover them with their insurance. Student teachers are eligible to apply for insurance at a student rate. Information explaining how to apply for this insurance appears in all student teacher handbooks.

ACQUIRING TEACHING EXPERIENCE

As you apply for jobs, you will be asked about your teaching experience. Most new teachers immediately think of their student teaching internship. If you plan to teach in the public school system, student teaching is a critical endeavor, as it is a requirement for licensure. Given its importance, you need to make the most of the experience right from the beginning. In addition to student teaching, individuals can acquire teaching experience by substitute teaching, mentoring, or coaching.

Student teaching

A student teacher is a student at a college or university working toward the completion of his or her education degree. The student-teacher internship is completed during the final semester of study. Depending on the university, student teachers may be required to gain field experience in multiple settings, such as urban and suburban schools. Most student teachers must also teach in two different classrooms and be observed or supervised by two separate teachers, known as cooperating or "co-op" teachers.

"When I did my student teaching, the great advice my cooperating teacher gave me that has proven to be correct, was 'You must expect great things out of students. Sometimes you may only get mediocre, but you sometimes get great; but if you expect mediocre, you will get nothing.'"

— Donna Benson, veteran teacher,
Cumberland Valley, Pennsylvania

Every college has its own approach for handling the student teaching portion of the curriculum. Despite a few simple variations, they are all relatively similar. Each college has its own student-teaching handbook. The handbooks might also contain school- or state-specific information, such as forms for certification and licensure.

Despite variations, the student-teaching handbooks usually address the following:

- Defined terms of the student-teaching assignment
- Goals for the student teacher
- Performance evaluation items
- Responsibilities and expectations

The student-teaching assignments vary. Students planning to teach in a secondary school environment may be observed by multiple supervisors. There will be a student teacher supervisor who reviews the following domains:

- Planning and preparation
- Classroom environment
- Instructional delivery
- Overall professionalism

Additionally, student-teaching assignments will include some form of subject-specific observation. This evaluation consists of the following areas of assessment:

- Grasp of the subject

- Instructional delivery
- Evaluation of lesson plans

"When you go to observe a teacher, do not focus solely on the lesson and how it is implemented. Instead, place your focus on how they control the classroom environment. When the bell rings, are students seated or all over the place? Does the teacher just call on students randomly, expecting an answer, or do they call on volunteers? How does the teacher refocus students who are not paying attention? Pay attention to these subtleties of classroom management, because it is these minor details that need to be in place before you worry about creating effective lessons."

— Mike Lutz, world cultures teacher,
Cumberland Valley, Pennsylvania

Depending on the program, you might also need to submit a video of yourself in the classroom and written reports on assigned topics related to the student teaching semester. In addition to understanding what academic requirements you need to fulfill for certification from the college, you should spend some time determining what the school expects from you while you are teaching there.

CASE STUDY: PREPARING FOR STUDENT TEACHING

Harold Bricker
Supervisor of Student Teachers
Penn State University – Harrisburg
Campus
Middletown, PA
butchbricker@comcast.net

Harold "Butch" Bricker is currently the supervisor of student teaching at Penn State — Harrisburg. He holds a bachelor's and master's degree in social sciences. He has worked in the field of education for 40 years. Prior to working with student teachers at Penn State — Harrisburg, he taught social studies at Camp Hill and Cumberland Valley High Schools. He also served as an assistant principal, principal, director of secondary education, and assistant superintendent at Cumberland Valley High School. He offers a list of tips for anyone preparing for their student teacher internship:

- **Have clearances ready.** Before student teaching begins, make sure you have a TB test and all your clearances in order so you meet the requirements to student teach.

- **Contact cooperating teacher.** As soon as you receive your student-teaching assignment, contact your cooperating teacher to see when you can meet with them. Arrange a meeting at his or her convenience to discuss your teaching assignment.

- **Understand the assignment.** Familiarize yourself with the lessons you will be teaching. Request a copy of the textbook and other materials that might help you prepare.

- **Make a good first impression.** When you meet, it is extremely important that you make a good first impression. Dress professionally. If you have piercings, take them out. If you have tattoos, keep them covered. Be very polite, enthusiastic, and always respectful.

- **Ask questions.** Ask meaningful questions to help you understand what you will be doing, but do not ask needless questions or try to dominate conversations.

- **Learn about the school.** As soon as you receive your teaching assignment, visit the school district's website. Learn as much about the school and community as possible.

- **Know who is in charge.** Learn the names of key figures in the administration.

- **Know the school policies**. If the student handbook is online, read it thoroughly. If not, ask for a copy.

- **Use your handbook.** Become familiar with your college student-teaching handbook and all the requirements associated with student teaching. If you get an early start on all of the above, you will feel more prepared and comfortable as you begin your assignment.

- **Work when the teacher works**. Plan to be at school the same hours as your cooperating teacher.

- **Do not miss work.** Do not be absent unless you are very ill.

- **Student teaching is your priority this semester.** If you have a part-time job, you may want to consider not working during student teaching. A teacher's day can be challenging and exhausting. Additionally, you will need a large amount of time in the evenings to prepare your lessons. This is the beginning of a great opportunity to see what teaching is really like.

- **Make the most out of the experience.** Work hard, ask for feedback on a regular basis from your co-op and college supervisor, and have fun.

- **Have realistic expectations.** Understand that you will have some good days and some bad days.

- **Reevaluate and decide.** When your student teaching assignment is over, you will know whether this is the right profession for you.

Substitute teaching

Some individuals are lucky enough to be offered a job while they are doing their student teaching in their last semester of college. Most people, however, have to spend time looking for a job after they graduate or at another point in their life. This is a good time to accrue other teaching experience until you get a full-time job. One of the best ways to do this is through substitute teaching. Whether you went to school to become a teacher and do not have a job yet, or you are thinking about entering the profession as a second career, substitute teaching is a great way to get experience in the field.

A substitute teacher is one who stands in for the regular teacher when he or she is unable to be in the classroom for the day or even part of a day. Each district maintains a substitute list, which lists individuals that may be called upon to fill in for regular teachers — either for scheduled absences or short-notice emergency reasons. Although each school district has its own regulations for substitute teachers, most schools do not require substitute teachers to have a degree in education. Check with your school district to see what the qualifications are for getting on the substitute list at the local middle schools.

To get on the district's sub list, you will typically need at least the following:

- Résumé or curriculum vitae
- Copy of teaching certificate and licensure (where required)
- Completed application
- Necessary clearance documentation

After you submit your application to a public school district office, the school board will review it. In private or other school types, it may only need to be reviewed by a principal or other administrator. Once you receive approval, you are placed on a list and a substitute coordinator can call you at any time.

CASE STUDY: CALLING ALL SUBSTITUTES

Vicky Weidner
Human resources coordinator
Cumberland Valley School District
6746 Carlisle Pike
Mechanicsburg, Pennsylvania 17050-1796
www.cvschools.org

Cumberland Valley School District uses several types of substitutes: professionals, nurses, support staff, guest teachers, and retirees. Professional substitutes must have a teaching certificate and nurse substitutes must have a nursing certificate. Guest teachers must have a college degree, but not a teaching certificate.

In order to become a substitute teacher in the district, individuals must acquire an information packet from the district office or online at the Cumberland Valley School District website (**www.cvschools.org**). In addition to filling out the packet, applicants must submit a résumé, pass a TB test, and have all the necessary clearances required for working with children in Pennsylvania. Note that all clearances must be less than one year old to be considered applicable. These include:

- Act 34 Clearance (Pennsylvania Criminal Background Check)
- Act 151 Clearance (Child Abuse Clearance)
- Act 114 Clearance (FBI Fingerprinting Criminal Background Check)

All of the district's substitutes must be board-approved; however, once the necessary paperwork is completed, the district can place substitutes on the call list pending Board approval. Cumberland Valley uses the state-mandated guidelines for Pennsylvania professional substitutes, based on the Public School Employees Retirement System (PSERS) guidelines. Substitutes must be called in the following order:

- Professional substitutes
- Guest teachers
- Retirees

In other words, if an absence is scheduled, the district must first attempt to fill the position with a professional certified substitute. If none are available, the spot may be filled with a guest teacher substitute. Lastly, if neither are available, a retiree may be used. According to Pennsylvania state law, retired teachers may not be called unless all other options are exhausted first. Violations to this policy may affect retirement pension plans. Exceptions to this rule only apply in cases of emergency, such as last-minute call-offs.

Cumberland Valley School District uses an automated system called Aesop to notify substitutes of vacancies. Employees enter their absences into Aesop. A substitute can then log on to Aesop and view available jobs, choosing the positions in which they are interested. If the position is not filled within the two days prior to the absence, Aesop will phone all available substitutes. The fill rate with Aesop is much higher than the district's previous use of a substitute coordinator because Aesop allows substitutes to be pro-active and responsible for their own schedules. Aesop follows the PSERS guidelines, offering positions to substitutes in the appropriate manner as explained above.

In the last ten years, there has been a shortage of teachers and substitute teachers. To compensate, many states created programs to prepare individuals to work in the classroom. These courses are called "guest teacher programs," designed for individuals who do not have education degrees, but wish to work in the teaching profession on a part-time basis. Most schools require substitutes to have an undergraduate bachelor's degree and at least some training to prepare them for the classroom. If you did not go to college specifically to become a teacher, but are thinking of entering the profession, this is an excellent opportunity to see whether you would like to work in a secondary school and whether it is a good match for you.

Each state has its own requirements for becoming a substitute teacher. One source for your state's requirements is the Become a Substitute Teacher website (**www.teacher-world.com/substitute-teacher.html**). By substituting, you gain experience and build relationships, which might help you if jobs open up in that school in the future. If not, you will at least increase your pool of references.

There are many opportunities for teaching besides those already discussed. If you are not currently employed full-time in the field, there are multiple ways to gain experience and build your résumé. For example:

- Acting as a teacher's assistant or aide
- Tutoring
- Providing lessons
- Coaching
- Mentoring
- Volunteering in a youth-centered activity, such as a church youth group

CASE STUDY: GAINING EXPERIENCE IN SUPPORT STAFF POSITIONS

Deb Jones
Support staff substitute
Chambersburg Area School District
Chambersburg, Pennsylvania

Deb Jones is a permanent substitute for Chambersburg Area School District. For medical reasons, she chose the flexibility of substituting over a permanent position. By agreeing to substitute in support staff positions, she increased the amount of job assignments available to her. She believes she has benefited greatly by gaining experience in a number of different positions in multiple schools.

Substituting in staff support positions offers many different types of experiences that can be useful in the teaching profession. It also offers you a new perspective on the other jobs in the school and, ultimately, provides you with a better understanding and appreciation for everyone's part in getting things to run smoothly.

I have substituted for secretaries, personal aides, classroom aides, and lunchroom aides. I have enjoyed the variety and the chance to see many different schools in the district as well as working with children at all grade levels. There are positions available on a daily basis, so I am able to work any day that school is in session.

When I am called for a job, I may only be given the title and place I need to be. More specific instructions are provided when I get to the school in question. By being open to the possibilities, I am constantly gaining new job skills and gathering additional experience. Each position brings new challenges and a feeling of accomplishment. I have been lucky enough to substitute in a multitude of positions in the district, learning something new from each endeavor.

As a personal aide, I work one-on-one helping individual students who need a little more direction and attention. I help keep them on task and assist them with getting homework completed. Working with the students makes me feel important, needed, and gives me a sense of accomplishment after each day. The students respond well to the one-on-one attention.

As a classroom aide, I work in a specific classroom all day helping the teacher with a variety of items such as bulletin boards, copying, laminating, sorting, grading, and getting projects ready for the students.

I have also substituted for office personnel. As a secretary, I have used interpersonal skills to answer calls from parents. I have had to employ excellent organizational skills while filing, copying, and aiding teachers with numerous tasks that need to be done every day.

I have even worked as a cafeteria aide, teaching me how to keep order and discipline in a large group of children. I love my job, and I believe it is important and valuable. If I were to give advice to anyone planning on working in a school environment, I would say this:

- You need to love children and want to make a difference.
- Never take anyone for granted.
- Pay attention to the tasks being done by others.
  Everyone matters.
- Love what you do.

CHAPTER 2:
Choosing the Right Work Environment

There are many factors you need to take into account before choosing an environment to work in. Here are some points to consider:

- What area of the country do you want to work in?
- How far are you willing to travel to go to work each day?
- Is income a predominant deciding factor?
- Do you prefer an urban, suburban, or rural setting?
- Do you prefer to teach to a small group or a larger class?
- Would you prefer teaching in a public school, a private school, or another alternative, such as a charter school?
- How important is working in an environment with endless resources and the most current technological advances?

It is important to be honest with yourself as you answer these questions. Many people act impulsively when they take their first job, settling for whatever is offered to them. Resist the temptation to take just any job. Better yet, be sure to apply only to schools you feel will be a good match. For example, if you grew up in the city and thrive in a fast-paced environment, a rural setting may not be the right choice for you. The following sections offer information on various types of middle school environments.

AREA OF THE COUNTRY

Many variables affect a teacher's working environment. First, you need to determine the area in which you would prefer to work. There are three generalized types of school districts. They are:

- **Urban:** The U.S. Census Bureau defines an urban area as one that has a population density of at least 1,000 people per square mile.

- **Suburban:** In the United States, suburban areas are characterized by small plots of land, single-family homes, and a higher standard of living. Suburban areas have a prevalence of usually detached single-family homes. Urban and suburban areas contain 70 percent of all individuals living the United States.

- **Rural:** The Census Bureau found that rural areas comprise 98 percent of the land in the United States even though they have the lowest population density. An area can be considered rural with a population density between one and 999 people per square mile.

SIZE OF SCHOOL

In addition to the type of residential area, you need to consider whether you have a preference on school size. In the United States, there is a tremendous variable considering school size. Would you prefer a small school community to a large environment, or perhaps something in between?

TYPE OF SCHOOL

Another important decision is considering the type of school in which you plan to work. There are many choices, including:

- **Public:** A U.S. school that does not require tuition from the students. It is funded by taxes and run by a school board.

- **Private (for profit):** Privately established schools that are run without government assistance and are supported by endowment and tuition. For-profit institutions are businesses that charge more and make money in the process.

- **Charter schools:** Experimental schools created and organized by teachers and parents and community leaders. They are run like businesses and operate independently of other schools. They receive public money but are free from many of the public school regulations. In exchange for the funds, they have some degree of accountability for producing certain results, set forth in each school's charter. According the US Charter Schools website (**www.uscharterschools.org**), charters are granted by sponsoring states or local school boards and generally last three to five years. The charters establish academic and fiscal goals that must be met during that time.

- **Private, parochial, or other non-profit:** Schools open to a select number of individuals who fit certain criteria and/or pay tuition. Religious schools fall into this category.

Area of the country and how it affects education

There are numerous job opportunities for teachers all over the world. This book, however, concentrates on careers in the United States. That being said, the United States is huge. According to the last census estimates, there were more than 73 million children between the ages of five to 17 living in 50 different states, in countless different environments. Furthermore, the way the United States handles education and funding is constantly changing. There are still children in this country who are not getting a good education. Under the No Child Left Behind (NCLB) Act, state testing requirements are in place to help identify schools that are under-performing. Schools that fall in this spectrum have three years to make adjustments and improve student scores. If a school is unable to comply, the government may come in and make massive changes. These changes include dismissing administrators and teachers, and in some cases, disbanding the school entirely. It is important for you to understand how your school fares in respect to meeting the state requirements, because it could ultimately affect your job. If the school fails to meet its goals, it might be eligible for grant money to help make the necessary improvements, but these improvements might include the elimination of current staff.

On Dec. 3, 2009, U.S. Secretary of Education Arne Duncan announced plans for allocating $3.5 billion to low-performing schools that meet the requirements of the Title I School Improvement grant project. The grant money is available to school districts that apply, meet the criteria, and are willing to adhere to one of the following four transformation models:

1. **Turnaround model:** In the turnaround model, the school needs to be willing to agree to major changes. First, the district must be willing to replace the existing principal. Additionally, the staff must undergo a major overhaul, with no more than 50 percent of the former staff retaining their positions. The new principal must be granted a certain amount of flexibility as it pertains to staffing, time allocation, and budgeting in the approach to improve the school and the student outcomes.

2. **Restart model:** In the restart model, the school must consent to close and reopen in a different form, such as a charter school operator, a charter management organization, or an education management organization. To be eligible, the school must submit to an arduous review process.

3. **School closure:** In some cases, the school must be permanently closed. In these instances, the students from the school in question are disbanded and re-enrolled in another school in the same area that has better student performance.

4. **Transformation model:** In the transformation model, schools must implement specific strategies. According to the U.S. Department of Education, the changes must include all of the following:
    *   Replace the principal

- Take initiative in improving school leader and teacher effectiveness
- Be willing to institute comprehensive instructional reforms
- Increase amount of learning time
- Create community-oriented schools
- Provide operational flexibility and sustained support

Student performance is not the only factor to consider when looking at schools. There are a number of environmental issues to consider as well. Schools are classified in many ways. To simplify the categories, school types are broken down into three primary groupings: Urban, suburban, and rural schools. This does not mean that every school in this country falls directly into one of these categories, but it may help you determine a general region you prefer working and living in. Some of the general pros and cons of each type of school are listed below.

Urban schools

What should you expect if you take a job in an urban or inner-city middle school? Let's look at the pros and cons.

Pros:

- They offer potentially higher salaries.
- Some schools in these areas will entice new teachers by offering signing bonuses or paying off student loans.
- The student body and staff are culturally diverse.
- The need for good teachers in these areas is important.
- Teaching in these schools provides a challenge and an increased sense of accomplishment when your students achieve.
- Assistance is available from special programs such as the Center for Urban School Partnerships at Texas A&M University (**http://tlac.tamu.edu**). The CUSP center researches and offers support to projects on collaborative learning in urban education environments. One of these CUSP initiatives offers mentoring from veteran teachers

through professional development for urban teaching. The University of Alabama's Urban Teacher Enhancement Program (UTEP) also offers urban school recruitment, tuition support, and mentoring for new teachers, among other resources. Visit the website at **www.ed.uab.edu/utep.**

Cons:

- There is a lack of funding stemming from impoverished areas, resulting in a shortage of resources, outdated textbooks and other materials, potentially creating problems with the curriculum.

- Classrooms are often overcrowded and facilities may be rundown.

- Students experience significant problems outside of school.

- There is high student turnover and an increased dropout rate.

- Apathetic students create an overall lower achievement level.

- The potential for insecurity, fear, fatigue, and stress are greater for new teachers, particularly if they are unfamiliar with the environment.

Suburban schools

What should you expect if you take a job in a suburban middle school? Let's look at the pros and cons.

Pros:

- Average to above average income areas result in greater taxes and increased funds.

- Increased funding provides for better supplies, materials, and field trips.

- Better overall resources are less likely to be outdated.

- Suburban schools experience a lower dropout rate.

- They enjoy a greater overall achievement rate, which some studies suggest is directly proportionate to the income levels of the surrounding area.

- Schools offer increased security to combat challenges.

Cons:

- Increased family income may cause entitlement and apathy among students.
- Student body and staff may be less culturally diverse, depending on the area.
- The environment is not as significantly challenging.
- More desirable neighborhoods create greater competition for jobs.
- A larger pool of applicants might lead to lower salaries and benefits.

Rural schools

What should you expect if you take a job in a rural middle school? Let's look at the pros and cons.

Pros:

- Rural schools generally have smaller class sizes.
- There is less competition for jobs because of a less dense population.
- Rural areas offer a slower lifestyle pace for those who prefer it.
- The environment is potentially safer.
- Programs such as the Rural Education Achievement Program (REAP) offer supplemental income and resources.

Cons:

- Limited district funds translate into decreased curriculum offerings.
- The student body and staff may feature less cultural diversity, depending on the area.
- Poverty is usually an issue.
- Distance between locations is generally farther, equating to a potentially farther commute.
- Resources and materials may be outdated, and they may lack program options and the technology for educational purposes.

- Higher dropout rates when individuals begin working in the family business.

- Students experience confusion and despair in areas where farmland is being sold and developed.

- Students exhibit lower self-esteem and lower achievement rates.

- Schools offer lower salaries and fewer available jobs.

- Teachers take on increased responsibilities.

The issue of size

How does the size of a school affect its teachers? Does it have a general impact on salaries and curriculum? Thoughts concerning school size continue to change. In the 1950s, studies suggested the need for larger schools. The belief was that schools with enrollments larger than 1,000 students created greater competition. Since then, school size has been debated several times. At any given time, there have been arguments producing data on either side. Here are some of the prevailing thoughts on both sides of the debate. The bottom line is that you should choose the environment in which you feel most comfortable.

Large schools (1,000 or more students)

The size of the student body affects the environment. The following are some pros and cons of working in a large middle school.

Pros:

- A larger pool of students creates greater competition and higher achievement rates.

- Large schools offer increased course offerings.

- Large schools might have more resources, depending on the location of the school and its budget.

- More people mean more chances for students to find a niche and develop friendships with others like them, creating less isolation issues for teachers.

- A larger student body usually translates to greater diversity.

Cons:

- Larger schools may mean less money spent per student.
- There is less opportunity for direct teacher-student interaction.

Looking for a job is a numbers game. Once you decide what type of environment you want to work in, start researching jobs in that area. Information pertaining to school type and student teacher ratio is available online. Certain websites provide this information to assist parents looking for the right school for their children. Teachers can also use the following sites to find detailed information about schools in the United States:

- Great Schools (**www.greatschools.org**)
- Local Schools Directory (**www.localschooldirectory.com**)

If you prefer a larger school district, the following are the top ten largest school districts in the United States. This information was compiled in 2009 and appeared on the Local School Directory website (**www.localschooldirectory.com**). Under the "National Statistics" section, you can find information on districts nationwide.

1. Los Angeles Unified School District
2. City of Chicago School District 299
3. Dade County School District (Miami)
4. Clark School District (Las Vegas)
5. Houston Independent School District
6. Broward County School District (Ft. Lauderdale, Florida)
7. Hawaii Department of Education School District
8. Philadelphia City School District
9. Hillsborough County School District (Tampa)
10. Detroit City School District

Smaller schools (500 or less total students)

Some individuals prefer working in a smaller environment with fewer students. The following are some pros and cons of working in a smaller middle school.

Pros:

- Class sizes are usually smaller. Some private schools have middle school classes with less than ten students.
- Smaller schools typically have lower student-teacher ratios.
- Teachers become more familiar with students' individual circumstances.
- Family involvement might be increased, depending on school type.
- There is potential for increased earnings, depending on school type.

Cons:

- Because of the smaller size, everyone tends to know everything about everyone else.
- You may be paid less, depending on school type. Teachers at small parochial schools tend to make the least amount of money.
- Student population is less diverse.
- There is less potential for competition.
- Fringe students experience greater isolation.

The debate continues on the advantages and disadvantages of school size. Current documentation tends to favor small schools, in respect to student success. However, they have the highest turnover rate amongst faculty.

The smallest schools in the country tend to be private institutions. If you want to work with fewer students, you may want to research these types of schools. There are different types of private schools as well. There are schools that make a profit and may pay more, and there are non-profit private schools, such as parochial and other religious institutions.

Different types of schools offer different environments

Public schools

Public schools are the most prevalent form of education in the United States. According to information posted on the U.S. Department of State's embassy website (**www.usembassy.gov**), in July of 2009, approximately 90 percent of all school-aged students in the United States attended public schools. These institutions are those that do not require students to pay tuition. The government funds the schools with income derived primarily from local property taxes. Decisions concerning finances, curriculum, policy issues, and teachers are made by a locally elected group of individuals known as a school board. Each school district, an area designated by the state, has its own school board. For more information on the public schools in your area, refer to the following Public School Review website (**www.publicschoolreview.com**).

The following are some pros and cons concerning public schools.

Pros:

- Student body is more diverse.
- There is a greater earning potential.
- Government funding may allow for better resources, depending on the school location.
- Public schools might offer additional programs in the arts.
- Assistance is provided for special-needs students.

Cons:

- Government mandates may hinder teachers' freedom in curriculum.
- Depending on the school location, funding may result in less resources.
- There is a direct correlation between socio-economic factors and student achievement.
- There is a greater likelihood for disruptive students to pose challenges.

- Public schools place significant emphasis on state testing.

Charter schools

The first charter school started in St. Paul, Minnesota in 1992. Since then, they have become increasingly popular. A charter school is a specific type of public school that operates without many of the regulations affecting traditional public schools. These alternative schools still must provide 180 days of instruction and must take part in state testing, but are exempt from numerous other government mandated school policies, as stated in the state's charter laws. For example, according to their charter, the following are a few items Pennsylvania Charter schools are exempt from:

- Driver education course standards
- 25-pupil class size limit
- Requirements to maintain grades kindergarten through twelve
- Latchkey operating requirements

These schools have a document, or charter, that serves as a performance contract. It explains the school's directives, including the charter school's mission statement as well as information concerning the programs and proposed student outcomes. Additional specifics spell out the methods of assessment. Most charter schools are granted their status for approximately three to five years. At the conclusion of the charter, the school must provide documentation on the results to its sponsor, which is generally the school board. At that time, it may apply to renew its charter. The documentation pertains to a statement of accountability agreed upon at the time of the original charter. Each charter creates goals unique to the individual school pertaining to student achievement and operational functions. The charter also contains mission statements and concise measurable goals.

For example, according to the New York State Education Department, the Data-driven Differentiated Instruction and Learning Project (D3IL) is a partnership of ten separate New York City charter schools. The project began in 2007 under the direction of the Partnership for Innovation in Compensation for Charter Schools

(PICCS). The website (**www.nysed.gov**) lists the goals of Williamsburg Charter High School as part of the D3IL partnership. The goals are:

1. Increase the leadership skills of participating building administrators to create professional learning communities of teachers that work to increase data literacy among all staff.

2. Design and implement school- and grade-level collaboration strategies that emphasize shared norms and values, ongoing data-driven dialogue and collaborative inquiry, with sufficient time and structure for collaboration.

3. Increase the type, amount, and frequency of data used by the entire school community as part of the ongoing system for continuous improvement to enhance instructional practice and increase student learning.

4. Improve instructional skills of teachers as measured by the alignment of learning goals, instruction, and assessments, the utilization of research and best practices, and supplemental programs and interventions to prevent failure.

5. Create a culture that supports internal responsibility rather than external accountability and focuses on opportunities for all.

6. Add to teachers' professional belief systems that all children are capable of high levels of achievement.

For a charter school to be able to stay open and renew their charter, they must be able to prove with documented measurable statistics that they have met each of the goals stated in the charter.

According to the US Charter Schools website (**www.uscharterschools.org**), these schools work well because, although they receive some public funding, they are independent from government intervention. Instead, they have an increased accountability to the charter's sponsor. They must be accountable fiscally and academically to the charter sponsor, the community that funds them, the students, and the parents who choose to send their children there. According to the Center for Education Reform (**www.edreform.com**), as of November 2009, more than 1.5 million students were currently enrolled in charter schools in the United States.

President Obama is currently focused on improving the school system in the United States. A recent report from the Alliance for Excellent Education (**www.all4ed.org**) stated that currently only 69 percent of high school students in the United States graduate with a regular diploma in four years. Given these statistics, the trend in the near future may be an increase in the number of charter schools.

The following are some pros and cons for teaching in charter schools.

Pros:

- Exemption from government regulations provides more freedom.
- Teachers enjoy increased earning potential, depending on the school. (Note: A new charter school in New York offered a salary of $125,000 in order to obtain the best teachers.)
- Charter schools have lower student-teacher ratios and smaller class sizes.
- The environment is safer.
- They create a greater chance for one-on-one instruction to meet individual needs.
- Charter schools demand higher academic standards.
- They offer increased availability of quality educational resources.
- Teacher freedom allows more creativity.
- Parents are more involved in their children's education.
- Teachers have the potential to earn higher wages.

Cons:

- Schools operate as businesses, and may be affected by economic fluctuations, resulting in decreased job stability.
- Teachers may face more challenges in accountability.
- Student performance is difficult to measure and enforce.
- A small population means less chance for diversity and socialization.
- Schools offer less support for special needs.

CASE STUDY: CHARTER SCHOOLS – A GREAT OPTION FOR STUDENTS AND TEACHERS

Betsy Rogers
Parent of students at Pennsylvania
Cyber Charter School
Midland, Pennsylvania

Betsy Rogers lives in the Cumberland Valley School District, but needed to explore other options for her children. She currently has two children enrolled in the Pennsylvania Cyber Charter School full time: one in middle school and one in high school.

My oldest son, Sam, had been diagnosed with a language arts learning disability very early in his school career. Although he received learning support in elementary school, he still was behind in his skills. Additionally, he was diagnosed as having Asperger's syndrome. This made school even more challenging. In fourth and fifth grades, his learning support teachers were amazing, and we felt like he turned the corner academically. Unfortunately, he was still really struggling socially. Sixth grade was a nightmare.

A friend told us about Cyber School. Being a state charter school, this is open to anyone living in the state. There is no charge. The state sends the portion of the funds allotted to educate your child to the school district you live in. When you sign up for a charter school, the school district then sends 80 percent of that money to the charter school. That covers all the expenses. Because they can house teachers in commercial settings, the expense is less than the multiple expensive buildings school districts must maintain, not to mention all the extracurricular activities, equipment, and extraneous staff (food service staff, librarians, aides, etc). Some teachers teach from home. The school Sam attends is based in Midland (near Pittsburgh, Pennsylvania), but there are multiple support centers all over the state.

We were assigned an instructional supervisor (IS). This is the designated liaison. They help you choose classes and work with you to handle questions and problems. They call us on a regular basis to check that all is well. Sam was required to take an online test to determine what level he was at. Each student takes this test in the fall and again in the winter to make sure they are progressing as they should.

We had the choice of self-paced classes (do-it-yourself) or real-time instruction (virtual classroom with a state-certified, real teacher). The computer, printer, books, and supplies all came in the mail. We had a teleconference call to set up Sam's individualized education plan (IEP). All seemed well. The classes started. It is kind of like being in a chat room with a PowerPoint presentation. You can talk and communicate via emoticons.

There is a list of people in your class. The teacher has the capability to place you in breakout rooms, which are small group projects. Teachers also have the ability to do what is called an "over the shoulder" to see if you are having difficulty getting onto a website or need assistance opening a document. They run a series of slides for objectives, content, and homework to teach whatever the lesson for the day is. This gives teachers the capability to give each student what they need and help the students work at their own pace.

Students can work faster or slower depending on their capabilities. This eliminates many teacher frustrations because they do not need to teach everyone at the same pace as they do in traditional class environments. The students are held accountable, and the teachers request specific emoticons at regular intervals.

The books my children use are from high-quality companies currently being used in the Cumberland Valley school district. They have class every Monday, Wednesday, and Friday at a designated time. Because the classes are only three days a week, they are a bit longer. Tuesday and Thursdays are set aside for homework, projects, tests and quizzes, essays, enrichment videos, or reading ahead for the next class. Tutoring is also available, with each teacher holding specific office hours.

In reference to other specifics, the PA Cyber Charter School reimburses for Internet connection on a quarterly basis. The students are still required to sit for Pennsylvania System of School Assessment tests, just like everyone else. Instead of taking them at school, Sam goes to a local hotel and takes the tests on a condensed schedule. PA Cyber made the Adequate Yearly Progress (AYP) assessment last year. The teachers are all state certified and are state employees because the school is state chartered.

Private schools

In the United States, private schools are independent entities not funded and therefore not directly run by the government. As a result, these schools are able to select and retain students of their choice. Most private schools are funded entirely, or at least partially, by student tuition. There are several categories of private schools:

1. **Preparatory ("prep") schools:** Prep schools prepare students for college and can be either boarding schools or day schools. They are unique in their ability to charge increased tuitions in order to make a profit. In return, they maintain higher standards and offer the best facilities and materials, better teachers, and lower student-to-teacher ratios. Many of these schools are privately owned and operated. Since the majority of private schools do not accept public funding, they are not bound by federal and state mandates. In other words, they are not affected by the No Child Left Behind laws, and therefore teachers are not forced to "teach to the test."

The following are a few aspects to consider regarding teaching at a prep school.

Pros:

- Boarding schools provide teacher housing, offsetting cost-of-living expenses.
- Private schools offer higher potential for increased earnings than their parochial counterparts.
- Class sizes are smaller and have lower student-teacher ratios.
- Higher family incomes may result in better resources for the school.
- Studies have shown a potential for greater academic competition and higher achievement rates at many of these schools.
- School uniforms decrease dress code problems.
- Teachers do not need to plan lesson plans around mandated tests.

Cons:

- Potential for less diversity, particularly in the socio-economic category.

- Possibility of entitlement issues among parents and students.

2. **Military academies:** A military school places value on tradition, discipline, and honor. The schools have traditional school subjects, but also encourage physical and military training. Unlike military schools in some other countries, most United States military schools are privately owned and operated. They have never received public funds. During the early 1800s, the Continental Congress debated developing these types of schools, but decided against it. They agreed only to provide funds for a military college instead. As a result, the United States Military Academy at West Point was developed. West Point opened in 1802 during Thomas Jefferson's presidency. At this time, military schools were very popular in the United States. Some of them are still in operation today. For example, St. John's Military School in Kansas was founded in 1887 and was awarded the Parents' Top Choice Private School Award in 2009.

The following are some pros and cons of working at a military academy.

Pros:

- Military schools have long-standing traditions.
- They have excellent academics.
- Schools offer military training for those individuals who plan on careers as military officers.
- Salary is higher than in public schools.
- Teamwork and leadership are paramount.
- Moral code instills a sense of honor and ethics.
- Discipline is enforced.
- Uniforms eliminate dress code issues.

Cons:

- Many military schools are known for being private reform schools for troubled teenagers.
- They require military training.
- They are not for those who thrive on creativity and open expression.

3. **Religious schools:** Another subcategory of private schools includes those that are religiously affiliated. Many of these schools, such as Catholic schools, include religious education as part of the curriculum. Other religious schools are merely labeled to denote the beliefs of the school's founders. There are multiple denominations providing specific schools in the United States. According to the Council for American Private Education (CAPE), 11 percent of all students in kindergarten through twelfth grade were registered to attend private schools during the beginning of the 2009 school term. According to the National Center of Education Statistics (NCES), the chart below depicts a breakdown of religious private schools during the 2007–2008 school year.

DENOMINATION	% of Private School Students Enrolled
Catholic	42.5%
Nonsectarian	19.4%
Conservative Christian	15.2%
Baptist	5.5%
Jewish	4.7%
Lutheran	3.7%
Episcopal	2.1%
Seventh-day Adventist	1.1%
Calvinist	0.6%
Friends	0.4%

The majority of all private schools in the country are Catholic schools, at 42.5 percent. That is a decline from 20 years ago, when the number was close to 55 percent. The second greatest percentage of private schools listed is non-religious schools, at 19.4 percent. Because a majority of private and religious schools in the country are Catholic, specific information concerning those schools is included here.

According to the National Catholic Education Association, there were 7,248 Catholic schools operating in the U.S. during the 2008 to 2009 school term. Those schools include enrollments of more than two million students and have waiting lists for more than 2,000 students. These schools employ approximately 157,615 professional staff members — and of those, only four percent of that number are religious personnel.

Catholic schools in the U.S. are accredited by independent and/or state agencies. The schools are primarily supported through tuition payments but subsidize their expenses through the church and fund raising. There are scholarships and vouchers funded by the private sector and the government to allow admittance to those who are financially challenged.

Some Catholic schools have their own school board with the parish priest as a member of the board, while others are run by the diocese, with the bishop acting in the role of superintendent.

The number of Catholic schools has declined over the last decade. They are still favored, however, in many inner city areas. In fact, 42 percent of the Catholic schools in the U.S. today are located in urban areas. For more specific information concerning Catholic schools, refer to the National Catholic Education Association website (**www.ncea.org**).

The following is a list of pros and cons for working in a private, religion-based, school.

Pros:
- Catholic schools have a smaller environment, class size, and student-to-teacher ratio.
- Stricter rules provide more teacher control.

- There is greater potential for family involvement.
- Uniforms lessen dress code issues; teachers do not need to discipline students dressed inappropriately.
- Administrators and teachers have more control over the curriculum because mandated tests do not apply.
- The school can remove disruptive students.

Cons:

- Salaries are lower.
- In times of economic challenges, lower enrollment may force teacher layoffs or school closings.
- Catholic schools offer less chance of diversity, particularly by exposure to alternate religious views.
- Curriculum has course selections.
- There is a decreased chance of teachers receiving assistance for special needs students.
- Instructors have to teach religion as part of the curriculum (a negative if you do not fully embrace the views).

"Catholic schools can remove students when needed. Although public districts may also do so, Catholic schools have a different set of expectations. The tolerance level is low for students who do not want to be there and do not act appropriately. I spend very little time with "classroom management" because of the expectations that our school has regarding its learning environment."

— John Cominsky, Trinity High School, Shiremanstown, PA

4. **Special assistance schools:** In addition to the schools mentioned above, there are a number of schools in the United States devoted specifically to providing an education to students with special needs. Many students who need special attention are attending mainstream schools, but some parents feel that their children need a different type of environment

with teachers trained to work with individuals with special needs. These schools offer that assistance.

The following are some pros and cons for working in a special needs environment.

Pros:

- Special assistance schools have a small student-to-teacher ratio.
- The environment is tailored to special-needs kids and equipped with all necessary materials.
- A private school atmosphere means a high salary potential as opposed to a similar job at a public school.
- Less conflicts arise from interactions between individuals insensitive to special needs.

Cons:

- There is less diversity.
- The environment can be challenging.
- Usually, you must complete extra schooling or certification in order to work at these institutions. This may not be possible for some.

5. **Cyber schools:** Another type of school system called online education has emerged recently. Online schools, or cyber schools, provide an alternative to traditional forms of education. In many instances, traditional schooling is not working for some students. Cyber schools allow individuals the ability to obtain a home-schooled education from a teacher other than their parents, using a personal computer. All different types of schools, including public, charter, and private schools, offer this type of education.

Cyber education is still a relatively new concept. Some are funded by the state, while others are privately owned and operated. It is another opportunity to research when looking for teaching jobs.

Some individuals prefer teaching in cyber schools. The following are some pros and cons to teaching in this type of environment.

Pros:

- Virtual teaching jobs allow you flexibility in working wherever you want.
- Some opportunities offer flexibility in hours.
- They have small class sizes.
- Virtual education offers opportunities to teach different subjects, as well as the option to teach English as a second language to students in other countries.
- Depending on the program, you may not need an education degree.

Cons:

- It is not a traditional classroom environment.
- The pay is lower than jobs in most public schools.
- It may be frustrating for those who prefer a more hands-on approach to teaching.

"I currently teach geography to approximately 100 students enrolled in the Pennsylvania Cyber School. One of the biggest advantages is the ability to keep teaching without disruptions. This kind of environment makes classroom management relatively easy by eliminating most behavioral issues."

— James Van der Schaaff, social studies
teacher, Pennsylvania Cyber School

Before you begin the application process, take time to review the factors that are most important to you. Research sources online to find out which school districts meet your needs. Again, the National Center for Education Statistics website (**http://nces.ed.gov**) includes information about each district in the country. From there, you can determine the types of schools in each district. With modern technology, virtually all the information you need is available online. If you prefer looking through a book, *Patterson's American Education*, a reference book compiled and published by Educational Directories, lists facts pertaining to each school district in every state. The book is updated every October.

CHAPTER 3:
Seeking Employment as an Educator

Middle school teachers are often paradoxes: They are professional and knowledgeable but also whimsical enough to hold the attention of an adolescent at the peak of puberty. The person who can reflect these special gifts in his or her résumé, cover letter, and interview is the one who will land the job. Approach the application process professionally, but let your personality and passion for teaching shine through.

INTRODUCING YOURSELF

Most school districts now have online applications. Compile your résumé, use that information to fill out your district's online application, and then send your résumé with cover letters to the schools where you would like to work. Although you should apply for the open positions the district posts on its website or otherwise advertises, it cannot hurt to send a résumé and cover letter to your ideal school.

When you decide which type of school you want to work in, you can begin the application process. Research schools that interest you, and develop your résumé to highlight skills pertaining to the specific job you are seeking. Unless you are applying at the school where you did your student teaching, the application packet will be the school's first impression of you. For that reason, it is extremely important to get it right. There are five main parts to the written part of the application process. They are:

1. **Application.** A pre-printed form that must be filled out. Some states are working toward simplifying the application process. They belong to an organization known as the National School Applications Network (NSAN). Schools belonging to this group have general forms online that may be downloaded and completed as part of the application process. As of March 2010, the following states participate with the NSAN:

   - Connecticut
   - Iowa
   - Kentucky
   - Michigan
   - Missouri
   - New Mexico
   - Ohio
   - Pennsylvania
   - Texas

   If you are applying to a school in a state that does not participate, you may obtain applications at the school district office, online at the school district's website, or from the state board of education. Standard applications require the following:

   - Position desired
   - Name, address, e-mail address, phone number(s)
   - Certification information, including area of certification, issuing state, and date issued
   - Tenure status
   - Date available for employment
   - Education background
   - Work experience
   - Student or practice teaching information
   - References
   - Criminal activity questions

- Clearance or background check information
- Signature

In most cases, schools will require you to fill in the application even if you have a résumé or curriculum vitae attached. Some applications will also require you to write a personal statement or answer another essay question.

2. **Cover letter.** A letter that introduces yourself, explaining why you are seeking a certain position, and why you are the person most suited for the job. The cover letter should be placed on top of the other papers in the front of the application packet. The letter should include a strong statement that will make the reader want to look at your application more closely.

3. **Résumé or curriculum vitae.** The formal documentation depicting your education, skills, and experience. This document also needs to stand out from others by highlighting the most important facts about you and your experience. A curriculum vitae (CV) may be a little longer but is not much different from a résumé. Even if you fill out an application with all of the necessary information concerning your education and experience, you should submit a formal résumé or CV with your application packet. It is much more professional.

4. **Follow-up letter.** The first three items are submitted together as an application packet. After you have submitted the packet, it is appropriate to write a follow-up letter in a few days to a week. The follow-up reintroduces you and helps you stand out from the other applicants. It does not need to be long. It should consist of the following elements:

    - **Greeting:** Simply restate who you are.
    - **Reason:** Remind the school what position you are interested in.
    - **Attention grabber:** List one or two specific relevant accomplishments that make you perfect for the job.
    - **Request:** Request an interview. In other words: "I look forward to meeting with you to further discuss my qualifications."

- **Follow-up statement:** States that you expect to hear from them and will continue to follow-up if you do not. For example, "If I do not hear from you beforehand, I will follow-up with you in two weeks to set up a time to discuss my application."

5. **Thank-you letter.** After you have met with a member of the human resources department or have been interviewed, you should send a thank-you letter to the person you spoke with. This is another reminder of who you are. Sometimes, it is the follow-up letter or thank-you note that makes the determination between two similar candidates.

WRITING YOUR RÉSUMÉ

Résumés often determine who gets to the interview stage. No matter how much experience you have or how great a teacher you are, you need to present yourself well on paper. In the field of education, there are two ways to display this information: with a résumé or a CV. Regardless of which you choose, it is imperative that you make it look professional. Here are some tips for developing a professional document.

- **Use quality paper.** Use high-quality, 24-pound, watermarked paper. The extra cost of watermarked paper is worth the professionalism it reflects, and the added weight of the paper will ensure its sturdiness. Do not use anything with a bright color or a design on it. You want the words to stand out, not the paper.

- **Keep it simple.** It should be the neatly typed in a simple, easy-to-read font. Make it look professional. According to the A+ Résumés for Teachers website (**www.resumes-for-teachers.com**), the average résumé gets only a cursory glance of ten to 20 seconds. The site also suggests that the document should be easy to read with bullet points and lots of white space.

- **Proofread.** If you are applying for a middle-school teaching position, you should not have any typographical or grammatical errors on your résumé. If you do, it is highly unlikely you will get the job. Once you have proofread it, give it to someone else to review as well, perhaps another teacher or an editor.

- **Add headings.** Bold headings will make the document easier to read. Add headings to identify specific areas of your information. For example, a middle-school teacher's résumé may include the following headings.

    - **Objective:** This is a description of yourself and the job you desire, such as "Enthusiastic educator seeking secondary school teaching position in positive environment."

    - **Experience:** List your jobs and other teaching, training, and coaching experiences.

    - **Technical knowledge:** List skills that apply to the job, such as computer programs and knowledge of smart-boards.

    - **Education:** Include colleges, degrees, workshops, and special training.

    - **Certification:** Provide information regarding your teaching certificate and license.

    - **References upon request:** Include this phrase at the end of your résumé to indicate that you will provide the contact information for individuals who can provide character and work experience references for you.

- **Briefly describe education and employment experiences.** In addition to student teaching and substituting, do not forget to mention volunteer positions such as mentoring, tutoring, and coaching; any clubs or organizations you belong to; and any publications or projects you have worked on. Make sure they reflect the middle school employee position you are seeking. If you are young and fresh out of college with limited work experience, think about the skills you have used even in your part-time employment and include them in your job description. For example, working in a fast food restaurant might not be a teaching job, but it is relevant. It provided you with a chance to improve your interpersonal and communication skills.

- **References upon request.** Type up a copy of your references and contact information and take it with you to the interview. Compile pertinent information concerning your references and have it readily available when asked for. Of course, teaching references are optimal, but do not worry if this is your first professional employment search. Choose references who will tell a potential employer that you have a positive work ethic, which is a highly valued trait. Additionally, if you have worked on projects with your professors, ask them if they will provide you with a reference. Showing you are a hardworking student speaks volumes for the type of example you will set for your own students.

If you have no idea where to start, do some research online. There are numerous websites that offer templates for résumés and cover letters. The following three websites have particularly helpful examples. These websites are specifically designed for assisting teachers in creating résumés and cover letters:

- Résumés for Teachers (**www.resumes-for-teachers.com/teacher-resume-examples.htm**). This website is geared specifically to teachers. It has numerous helpful suggestions on creating résumés and cover letters for any teaching job and shows multiple examples. Additionally, the moderator, Candace Davies, provides contact information for anyone who has questions not already answered on the site.

- A to Z Teacher Stuff (**http://atozteacherstuff.com/pages/1876.shtml**). This website contains basic information on everything teachers need to know, including suggestions for effective résumés.

- Sample Résumés (**www.bestsampleresume.com/teachers-resumes.html**). This website has a couple of simple outline formats for prospective teachers to use as guidelines.

When creating your teacher's résumé, the following four areas are the most critical for showcasing who you are:

- **Identification:** All résumés should have your name in a large, bold, clear font on the top. Under that, you should include your address, home and cell phone numbers, and your e-mail address.

- **Career objective:** Include a statement about the type of job you are seeking and the type of environment you would prefer to work in.

- **Education and certification:** In addition to listing the schools you attended and the degrees you earned, you should provide any teaching certification you attained.

- **Teaching experience:** Be sure to highlight any actual teaching experience you may have. Include student teaching, substitute teaching, and any other related positions.

At the end of your document, you may add other pertinent information, such as professional development courses, special skills, achievements, and professional memberships. *Refer to Appendix A for a sample curriculum vitae.* In addition to a flawless résumé, be sure to include a strong, well-written cover letter.

DO NOT FORGET THE COVER LETTER

Cover letters should grab the employer's attention. Employers expect them, so always send a personalized cover letter with your résumé or curriculum vitae. Prospective employers can spot a generic cover letter a mile away and it is tiresome for them. Applying for a job with the right qualifications is only half the battle. First, you need them to review your qualifications and take the time to meet with you in person. A well-written cover letter helps you get to the next stage. The following are the most important points to consider:

- Limit your cover letter to one page.
- Address it to someone specific. Do the research and find out the name of the person doing the hiring. A letter addressed to "Dear Sir or Madam" is not very impressive.
- Briefly state the position you are interested in.

- Highlight just a few (not a huge list) of your strongest qualifications that make you perfect for the job.

- Mention something about the school that you like — a reason you may want to work there.

- State that you will follow up with a call, and mention when. For example, "I will follow up with you next week to set up a time to meet and go over my application in person."

- Close with "Sincerely," and your name typewritten, as well as your signature.

- Add the word "enclosures" at the bottom to indicate that your résumé is included in the packet.

For an example of a formal, generic cover letter, refer to Appendix A. Use the sample as a guideline and personalize it with information about yourself, following the advice in the bullets above.

YOUR APPLICATION

When you decide on a specific location, you can develop your résumé to highlight skills pertaining to the specific job you are seeking. In addition to compiling a résumé and cover letter, you will need to fill out job applications. These applications are available through the school district, online, or from the state board of education.

Before filling out applications and sending résumés, take time to review the factors that are most important to you. Research sources online to find out which school districts meet your needs. The National Center for Education Statistics website (**http://nces.ed.gov**) includes information about each district in the country. From there, you can determine the types of schools in each district.

CASE STUDY: GETTING THE JOB

Jake Miller
English teacher
Good Hope Middle School
Mechanicsburg, Pennsylvania

Jake Miller has a bachelor's degree in secondary education, history, and political science from Bloomsburg University. He also has a master's degree in educational leadership from Shippensburg University. He currently teaches eighth-grade English at Good Hope Middle School in Mechanicsburg, Pennsylvania. In this Case Study, Miller provides his thoughts on maximizing your chances for getting a job as a middle school teacher.

From day one to putting in overtime on day 200, I love every single minute of my job. For the past five years, I have looked forward to every school day as a challenge to be better than the previous one. These statements make me great at what I do. If a person truly loves his or her profession, he or she is on a path of predestined greatness. I have been in the profession for five years now and the following are some tips to help you in your first few years.

1. Max-out your student teaching. Make everything you do student-centered. You will see the glimmer in your students' eyes after they do a mock trial, not after a PowerPoint. Spend more time crafting your lessons rather than following a specific format for your lesson plans. Observe other successful teachers working in their classroom; too many student-teachers become absorbed in their own world. You are still a student, so go venture and learn!

2. Be sure to network. Every one of your college professors has connections in the education world. Ask your professor if he or she would be inclined to share a few who would find you a solid teaching candidate.

3. Stand out from the pack. No book or article can help you land a job, but I can help you get an interview. What does your résumé have that others do not? The following are some things you can do:

- Be an asset to your school. I have taught every subject because the district needed that and I was the only one certified and qualified to do so.

- Send a picture of yourself with students learning or spruce up your résumé in unconventional ways so it does not blend in with the rest.

- Clean up or delete your Facebook page. The Web is public domain, and interviewers are going to check you out before bringing you in for an interview.

- Hand-deliver your résumé to the secretary with a big smile. There is nothing more powerful than saying, "Hello, I'm here, and I want to come back!" You will find your résumé on the good pile.

4. During the interview, hit the following key points:

- Provide a copy of your materials for everyone at the interview. Six mini-portfolios will serve you better than a massive one.

- While they are perusing your materials, ask for everyone's name at the interview, and then write them down in a seating chart format.

- Bring the lesson you were most proud of as well as the one you were least proud of, and be prepared to discuss how you learned from both.

- Showcase some of your students' previous work — not just your top-notch students, but students who have had some major progression throughout the year.

- Cite specific methods you have used in the middle school setting to defray issues such as bullying, swearing, cheating, and other infractions of the typical tween.

- Be unorthodox. We hired a reading teacher at our school because she brought a beach ball to the interview and began the interview by using it as an icebreaker for us.

- Speak about how you have empowered students; be someone who maxes out the potential in *every* student.

- Bring your biggest heartwarming story. There are three students who are now history teachers, they claim, because of me. I am so proud of that!

- Mention how you handle discipline within your own classroom, not in the office.

- Discuss your experience with standardized testing. It's the elephant in the room — what do you bring to the table to make the school better?

- Indicate that you are a team player, and support with details.

- Show that you are going to teach everyday like it is your last, because you never know when it is going to be the one that changes a student's life.

5. While every principal wants an all-star teacher in their ranks, they do not want one who is a robot. Talk about what is special in your life other than teaching. Begin to make connections in your life to the people at the interview. Always ask, "What are you looking for in the perfect candidate for the position?" Then prove to them you are the perfect candidate.

6. Call the school where you interviewed and thank whomever was in charge of the interview, whether it was the principal or the department chair. Write an e-mail to the staff members who were at the interview. Hopefully, you wrote down their names. Just mention something that made you stand out during the interview ("Jake, the guy with the beach ball") and thank them for their time.

7. And finally: Don't get down on yourself if you do not receive your dream position. It is very competitive right now in the education world. Remain optimistic! Go forth and find more opportunities.

THE INTERVIEW PROCESS

If you have prepared an excellent application packet, you should hopefully be called for an interview. In order to obtain the job you want, you will first need to succeed in the interview. In order to do your best, prepare ahead of time. Research the school you apply to. Many of the interview questions may pertain to challenges specific to that school. Researching the school may also provide you with a list of questions to ask the interviewer. Displaying your knowledge of the school will impress the interviewer. In addition to knowing everything about the school, you need to prepare yourself. Be sure this is really what you want to do. If it is not, it will come across in your interview.

When preparing for your interview, keep in mind that the interview may take place with one person or multiple individuals. If this is the case, it will most likely be a principal, a superintendent, or human resources personnel. It is also possible that you will interview in front of a panel with as many as six people, consisting of the principal, the superintendent, and part of the school board.

In a middle school interview, you more than likely will meet with the principal, the assistant principals, and your department head. Most prospective faculty decisions are made in the school. In some districts, however, you may need to have an additional interview with human resources at the school board office. Do not feel discouraged if you need a second interview. It means the administration at the school likes you for this position and you have made it up another step on the ladder.

"I interviewed for 17 positions before I became a finalist in two of them. I was the runner-up for both positions and was unsuccessful in finding a job. Then, one day I received a call for a last-minute retirement to teach ninth grade American government. I went for the interview and they called me on my ride home to offer me the job!"

— Jake Miller, eighth grade teacher, Good Hope
Middle School, Mechanicsburg, Pennsylvania

Although most interviews follow a similar pattern, some aspects will be different at each one. Regardless, you will most likely enter the room where the interviewer(s) waits. At this point, shake hands and start to build some rapport. Usually the first question is, "Tell me about yourself." Eventually, the interviewer(s) will bring up the position and the district. You will be asked several questions to determine whether you are a good fit for the position. The following are a few sample questions to help you prepare for the interview:

- Why do you want to be a teacher?
- What are your strengths and weaknesses?
- Inclusion is important in our school. How would you develop lessons that would include special-needs students in your classroom?
- How would you circumvent negative attitudes in order to create a positive learning environment in your classroom?
- What would you do if you encountered bullying among the students in your classroom?
- What is your experience with technology in the classroom, and how would you use it in your lesson plans?
- Middle-school-aged children can be a challenge. Why do you want to teach at this level?
- Imagine the following scenario: An angry parent accompanying his child marches into your room questioning the child's placement in a certain class level. How would you handle the situation?
- What do you know about developmental levels of middle schoolers?
- You are asked to teach a sixth- and eighth-grade class in the same subject, explain the difference in class rules and expectations for each grade.
- Give an example of how you would encourage creativity in a specific lesson.
- In your opinion, what would constitute a successful lesson?
- How would you handle an irate phone call from a parent concerning your grading practices?

The best way to respond to interview questions is to be thorough and honest. To prepare, practice having a friend ask you potential interview questions. Take your time. It is better to think about your answer than to stutter or act visibly nervous. The job requires strong communication skills. How you respond is just as important as what you say.

Read over the list of questions again. Do you see how some require thought about the issues? A good example is, "What is your philosophy on teaching?" This question is important to the interviewer because he or she is looking to hear your views and beliefs about teaching.

Another question to give thought to is, "What are your strengths and weaknesses?" Even your weaknesses should be strengths. If your answer is that you have a tendency to create your lesson plans for the whole year before it even begins, the interviewer will not view this as a weakness. When interviewers inquire about your weaknesses, they do not expect what is usually perceived as weak, but rather a strength that can be somewhat bothersome or annoying to you personally. They certainly do not want to hear that you sometimes lose your temper or that you have a tendency to scream when students will not listen. These traits could reflect badly on the school and the district, and that is not what they want to see in you as a prospective teacher.

Some interviewers prefer to do a behavior-based interview. This type of interview asks questions about past behavior, skills, experiences, and knowledge. The idea is that the interviewer will learn about what your future performance might be by basing it on what your past performance was in a similar situation. Having specific examples of your skills in your portfolio is the best preparation for a behavior-based interview. Because you might not know what type of interview you will have, it is best to be prepared for anything. Questions you might face in a behavior-based interview include:

- Tell us of a time you had to deal with a student who was disrupting your class.
- Describe a team project you have done.

- Tell us about a difficult situation you were in, how you handled the situation, what the outcome was, what you learned from it, and what you would do differently if a similar situation occurred today.

A behavior-based interview is simply a way to learn about how you will handle your students, difficult situations that may arise, discipline, and disruptive behavior.

While you are being interviewed, you need to remember you are interviewing the school as well. Just as they want to be certain you are a good fit for them, you want to be certain this school is a good fit for you. You do not have to wait until the end of the interview to ask your questions; you will be able to tell the appropriate time to do so. It is acceptable to take an index card with a list of questions if you feel you need to. Here are some examples of what you may want to ask your interviewer(s):

- What administrative (or other) tasks are required outside of teaching hours?
- What is the teacher turnover rate at this school?
- What is the average class size at this school?
- Do all teachers participate in extracurricular activities?
- Is there a set curriculum?
- Do you have regular staff meetings?
- Can you tell me about the students who attend this school?
- Is there a support system or mentor program for new teachers?
- Are there in-service training opportunities for the teachers?
- How active are the parents in this school?
- What types of special education are used in your district?
- What is your vision for your school?
- How do your grade levels support one another?

Do not ask about pay, pensions, or sick days until you are offered the position. This is considered inappropriate and tells the interviewer(s) your priorities are not in order.

Once the interview is over, send a thank-you note by regular mail or e-mail. Keep it personal, and address the note to your interviewer by name. The following are a few generic lines that you can personalize with information relative to your interview:

> "It was great meeting with you, and I enjoyed our interview time together. I am highly interested in the position we discussed, so please do not hesitate to call me with any further questions or comments you may have. Thank you for considering me for this position."

You might wish to add a line about interesting information shared with you during the meeting to show you were there 100 percent; something unique you liked about the school; or perhaps an anecdote you shared with the principal or other key individuals during your interview time together. Send a thank-you note even if you think the interviewer may not get it before he or she calls you to follow up, for example, in the day or two after your interview. No matter what, thank-you notes are common professional courtesy and, even if you are hired, can only boost respect for your work ethic. In addition, if you are not hired for a specific position, there may be another opening you will want to interview for in the future. If you have sent a thank-you note, you have begun to establish a working relationship with your potential employer. This puts you ahead of others who are interviewing with this person for the first time.

Very seldom does anyone hire in a hurry. Do not be impatient or think the worst if you do not hear from any of your interviewer(s) right away; you will hear something in time. Please keep in mind that any teachers who are already under contract must be placed before administration is allowed to start new hires. There are no set rules for when a principal or superintendent will hire. Some will hire new teachers as soon as school is out for the summer, while others will wait until the day the new school year starts. Sometimes openings arise during the school year. Keep these thoughts in mind while you wait to hear from your interviewer(s), if you start to feel anxious, upset, or impatient, or if you received news the school you set your heart on has already hired. You will find a middle-school teaching job. Maybe the one you land will be a better-suited opportunity for you than the one you originally wanted.

CASE STUDY: INTERVIEWING TO BECOME A TEACHER

Cindi Rigsbee
Gravelly Hill Middle School
Efland, North Carolina
tchrc@aol.com

Cindi Rigsbee is currently a national board certified reading teacher at Gravelly Hill Middle School in Orange County, North Carolina. In the past, she also worked as a high school English teacher, dance studio operator, junior high dance and drama teacher, middle school language arts teacher, school district new-teacher coordinator, reading teacher, teacher trainer in a staff-development office, and a middle school language arts and social studies teacher. She was named the North Carolina Teacher of the Year in 2008 and was a finalist for National Teacher of the Year in 2009. In addition to teaching, she mentors new teachers, does speaking engagements, and writes a teaching blog. Recently, she completed a book on her passion for teaching, titled Finding Mrs. Warnecke: The Difference Teachers Make. *Through years of experience she has developed the opinion that some people are called to teach, while others probably should not be teaching at all.*

First of all, let me say that I was not one of those little girls who lined up her dolls in a row and pretended to teach them. I did not really see the point. We were in school all day; teaching did not seem that exciting to me at the time. Instead, I wanted to be a Dallas Cowboys Cheerleader when I grew up. That being said, I now know that I was born to be a teacher. It is what I am supposed to do, and I truly believe that I was called to teach. I also believe that not everyone has that calling.

For some reason, however, many men and women I have encountered over the years feel they are qualified to be teachers merely because they spent some time in a classroom as a child. Along those lines, I despise hearing the quote "Those who can, do. Those who can't, teach." Teaching is hard work. It takes patience and perseverance and years to perfect as a craft.

There are some individuals who come to teaching later in life. I did not make the decision myself until I was in my junior year of college. So, it is not about *when* you decide to become a teacher. It is about knowing that this is what you want to do more than anything and that you will do whatever it takes to make a difference to kids. Over the years, I have had the opportunity to sit in on some teacher hiring boards. It is always instantly apparent who wants to be there for the right reasons.

If you know beyond a doubt that you want to be a teacher and you are ready to apply for a teaching position, keep the following in mind.

- Dress as if it matters. Most teachers do not wear full suits and high heel dress shoes to work every day. By dressing that way for the interview, however, you show that you care enough to make an extra effort. It shows that the job matters to you. Subsequently, it shows the interviewer that you are more likely to make an effort with your students.

- Display a teacher's presence. When an individual walks into a classroom and everyone gets quiet just waiting to see what comes next, I call that a "teacher's presence." Each year before school starts, I am a little nervous myself. I have a sleepless night imagining a new group of students completely out of my control and hanging out the windows or lesson plans that are not complete and materials not gathered. When that first day starts, those nerves may be jangling in the back of my mind, but my students never know it. I take a deep breath, raise my energy level a few decibels to show my excitement, and head into the year.

- In conjunction with nerves, do not let them affect your speaking. If you come into an interview and cannot articulate your thoughts clearly and succinctly, you probably will not get the job. How can you be expected to face a classroom of potentially unruly students day after day if you cannot even communicate one-on-one in an interview? Public speaking is the most important part of the job. If you cannot speak to people, this is not the career for you.

- Display energy and enthusiasm. Interviewers are looking for individuals who are excited about the job. If you have energy and enthusiasm in the job interview, you are more likely to have that same energy and enthusiasm in the classroom. Again, teaching is hard work. You must have boundless energy to get the job done.

- Be prepared to showcase your work. The individuals who come to the interview with something besides their résumé and transcript always impress me. Think about what you have accomplished so far and prepare a portfolio to take with you. It can include awards you have earned, letters of recommendation, and examples of student work you accumulated during your time as a student teacher. It could even include photos of you interacting with the class. Put together a meaningful group of items that showcase who you are.

- Be passionate about the job and let your energy and enthusiasm show through.

BACKGROUND CHECKS

Once the interview process is over and you have landed a post in a middle school, you will have to go through a series of checks. In most districts this means a background check and drug test. This system has evolved from a series of government actions as well as laws regarding working with children, including the National Child Protection Act of 1993, the Violent Crime Control and Law Enforcement Act of 1994, and the Volunteers for Children Act (part of the Crime Identification Technology Act of 1998). For middle school teachers, these laws mean you will be required to submit to fingerprinting and background checks. You must fill out a series of applications, including a fingerprint test that checks you against police and FBI databases.

Specifically, these programs search for past criminal activity and any history of child abuse. Federal laws mandate these background checks, but check with individual school districts and employers to determine their specific requirements. If you contact the human resources department, they will have all the information you need and will explain anything you do not understand about the process in your district. You more than will likely incur a cost for your fingerprint application.

Be sure to check with the district you are applying with before getting any fingerprint or background checks on your own. You do not want to be responsible for paying fees twice.

CHAPTER 4:
Making a Living as an Educator

If you have been offered that job you were hoping for, hopefully you have made it far enough in your professional education and job-seeking journey to understand that while teaching has many benefits, money is not one of them. If you missed that piece of information, you may want to back out now and find a more lucrative career. Careers working with children and adolescents in the United States, from teaching to social work, are not particularly profitable. The effort and expertise expended by teachers unfortunately far outweigh the compensation received.

Educators might receive minimal pay, but that does not diminish the importance of the job. Teachers are responsible for educating all other professions and can be thanked for affecting the lives of the most significant leaders of our time — an accomplishment immeasurable by any standard. With that said, districts do offer many compensatory benefits, and teaching is a decent living, but does not afford a six-figure salary. The good news is that flexible hours and summers allow teachers to supplement their income through other avenues. This makes teaching a very attractive career for people whose hobbies, such as writing, art, and software design, may not provide a full-time living. Teachers historically have been able to retire quite comfortably on a stable income from the savings benefits offered to them through their districts.

PAY SCALES

Payroll may fall under different departments depending on the size of the district. It may be in accounting, human resources, risk management, or, in bigger districts, simply the payroll department. You will certainly want to be familiar with this particular department.

The payroll department has information on pay scales and salary schedules. Although statistics vary slightly in each state and district, the average teacher's starting salary is in the mid- $30,000s, according to TeacherPortal. In May 2008, the Bureau of Labor Statistics cited the median salary range of U.S. middle school teachers to be between $47,100 and $51,180.

TeacherPortal is a good reference point for an in-depth comparison of teachers' salaries from state to state. Visit TeacherPortal (**http://teacherportal.com**) and click on "Teacher Salaries" for comparisons of starting pay scales and average salaries. More revealing is TeacherPortal's "Comfort Score Index." This informative index ranks teacher salaries in any given state while considering the cost of living. At publication time, the top three contenders were Illinois, Delaware, and Georgia. This is important information for relocating job-seekers, as it shows you that gravitating toward higher-salaried states such as New Jersey or Connecticut is not necessarily where you will get the most for your dollar. TeacherPortal portrays a more accurate picture and shows where a teacher's salary will go the farthest.

Base salaries are negotiated through a union in most districts. The amount is tied to the number of years of service and, at times, the type of contract you are under. The following is an example of a salary scale in Palm Beach County, Florida. The "step" is the amount of years in service.

Teacher Salary Schedule - Bachelor Degree - FY09			
Salary	Step Annual / Professional Service Continuing Contract	Salary	Step Annual / Professional Service Continuing Contract
1	$36,822	14	$49,648
2	$36,924	15	$51,152
3	$37,485	16	$52,411
4	$38,260	17	$53,652
5	$38,403	18	$55,129
6	$39,423	19	$56,618
7	$40,379	20	$58,332
8	$41,310	21	$60,046
9	$42,508	22	$61,851
10	$43,554	23	$63,687
11	$44,870	24	$64,631
12	$46,647	25	$65,576
13	$48,190	26	$66,200
		Longevity Step	$71,245

Pay often varies for teachers on an annual contract and those working within the realm of a professional services contract. An annual contract means the district has the right to renew or not renew the teacher's contract at the end of each school year. A professional services contract, historically known as "tenure," means the teacher has an ongoing contract and does not need to renew each year. Many districts require you to work under an "annual contract" for three to five years before you fall under the "professional services contract." Barring any serious infractions on the teacher's part, the teacher can assume his or her job is safe from year to year after achieving a continuing contract status.

Furthermore, pay "steps" are somewhat more substantial for teachers who have acquired tenure. Note that Palm Beach County's pay raise, or "step," as shown in the chart from the first to second year is $102. From year three to four, the raise is $775. From year three to four is when a teacher initially achieves continuing contract status.

Pay schedules

Teachers are often given a choice whether to take their annual salaries over ten months (throughout the school year) or 12 months, which includes the summer. Salary schedules vary from district to district, but generally, an educator will be paid every two weeks or twice monthly. If you are self-disciplined and fiscally savvy, taking pay over a ten-month period is the wiser option. You can earn interest on the money you put into savings during the year.

However, during your first year teaching, it is highly recommended that you take your salary over 12 months. Summers are for vacations, professional development, and re-energizing for the upcoming year. It is not time to stress and scramble to pay bills or to live on a diet of peanut butter and jelly sandwiches.

Additional incentives

Because many districts have additional pay incentives, check to see what is offered in your area. The following are examples of common incentives:

- **Critical shortage areas:** Some teaching positions are more difficult for districts to fill than others. These are known as "critical shortage areas." They usually include science, math, special education, and English for speakers of other languages (ESOL). There are many benefits for teachers with the expertise and education to fill these positions. Compensation may range from hiring bonuses to student loan forgiveness programs.

- **Higher degrees and certifications:** Districts regularly offer supplementary compensation to teachers with additional credentials. This may include a master's degree in a specific subject area, an ESOL endorsement, or National Board Certification. Payment may be a one-time bonus or a salary increase.

- **Travel and lower-economic school incentives:** Lower-economic and rural areas are difficult to staff. To attract quality instructors, stipends are offered in addition to regular salary as compensation for time and travel. If this is an option for you, be sure to consider not only mileage and wear and tear on your car, but also whether, in your first year of teaching, you will be able to meet the many challenges faced by teachers of lower-economic students. These problems often include lower-level student performance and behavior. Sometimes these students simply do not have money in the home for necessary school supplies; sometimes behavioral issues are aggravated because of an absent parent or alcoholism.

- **Adequate yearly progress bonus:** Adequate yearly progress (AYP) is determined by statewide assessment testing in conjunction with the No Child Left Behind Act. Funding is offered to schools and/or districts that meet the goals set forth by AYP standards. How this money is spent is somewhat controversial and varies even from school to school, but it could mean a yearly bonus for you, ranging from a couple hundred dollars to more than $1,000.

- **Sick and personal days:** Teachers normally get a set amount of sick and personal days they can use during the year. Check with your district and find out whether you will lose these days if you do not take them. Often, you will have the option to carry over sick days from year to year. Save them in case you need them for important life events, such as maternity leave. If sick leave and personal days remain untouched when it is time for retirement, the school district will calculate the amount of time saved. Teachers then receive a lump-sum parting payment upon retiring. This can add up to quite a hefty amount, even if you save only a few sick or personal days each year.

As addressed earlier in this section, teaching does have some monetary rewards, but mostly your career will offer unlimited intrinsic compensation. You literally will be shaping the future of your community, your state, and your country. By the time you retire, you will have been responsible for the intellectual lives of thousands. In addition, if you are successful, you will never be forgotten.

Other factors that affect pay

Even if you find several schools matching your perfect job criteria, there may be other factors affecting your salary offer and subsequent raises. For example:

- **The economy.** Public school teacher's salaries come out of taxes. When the economy is weak, it affects the cost of living and teacher's salaries may remain stagnant.

- **Teacher's level of education.** There are many ways to attain teaching certification. In addition, there are different levels of degree and specialization. A new teacher with a master's degree in math or science will probably make more than a recent college graduate with a bachelor's degree in education.

- **Experience.** The amount of years spent teaching affects your starting salary and raises.

- **Subject matter.** This is strictly an issue of supply and demand. For example, there is currently a shortage of qualified upper-level math and science teachers in the United States; therefore, certified teachers with proficiency in those areas may start at higher salaries.

- **Benefits.** The amount offered in benefits packages may vary. If you are single, you will most likely accept the package as is. If you are married and your spouse has benefits, you may be able to save some money by avoiding an unnecessary income deduction.

- **Union fees.** Membership has its price, another income reduction. Union involvement is another factor. Traditionally, northern states have greater involvement than many of the southern states.

- **Continuing education.** Schools might require continuing education, or you might want to take classes to enhance your skill set. Some schools will pay for some or all of your continued education.

General opinion

According to a study conducted by Learning Point Associates and Public Agenda, teachers' views on compensation may depend on their own age and experience. For example, younger teachers have different expectations than their more experienced peers, and they appear to have an increased sense of social responsibility. Despite that, the vast majority seems to be in agreement on one item currently debated by the Department of Education (DOE): The DOE wants to compensate teachers based on student achievement. Most teachers agree that compensation should definitely not be tied to student performance because there are too many variables, such as student capability and socio-economic factors. Teacher views on compensation have changed over the past several decades. A majority of teachers agree however, that they should be compensated for their efforts, particularly when it comes to teaching hard-to-reach students.

WHAT YOU NEED TO KNOW ABOUT UNIONS

Soon after you accept a job as a teacher, you will be approached by a teacher's union representative and asked to join. The first contact will come in the form of an information packet once you start the job. Depending on the school, area of the country, and the union's presence in the district, the representative may attempt to contact you by phone or e-mail as well. He or she will continue to seek you out until you make a definitive decision. In order to be prepared, research the issue and make a decision ahead of time. There is viable information both in support of and against unions online. In addition to reading information on the Internet, discuss the issue with other teachers in your school district. Union participation varies from area to area. Some schools have close to 100 percent participation, while others have little or no participation.

What exactly are teachers' unions?

Teacher unions are paid membership groups for individuals in the education industry. Their purpose is to ensure quality working conditions and fair compensation for all teachers. The national union organizations have multiple local chapters in each state. Becoming part of a teachers' union is a personal choice, and it will probably depend on the union's activity level at the school in which you decide to work. There are many benefits to belonging to a teacher's union. For example, unions offer legal protection and good representation for collective bargaining. They are often tied to credit unions, which provide better interest rates than regular banks. They also assist with contract negotiations. In some areas, you must belong to the union to get an improved salary after contract negotiations. If you do not belong when a union assists in contract negotiations, you might be expected to pay a fee to attain the new salary. On the negative side, most unions have high membership dues. They are also very political entities, and some decisions might differ from your personal political views.

There are two main national teacher unions for public school teachers, and other unions, such as the National Association of Catholic School Teachers, represent specialized groups.

National Teacher Unions

There are different levels of teachers' unions. The three most prominent national organizations are:

- **National Education Association (NEA):** Founded in 1857, it has 3.2 million members and partnered with the AFT in 1966. The NEA is the largest professional organization and largest labor union in the United States. They represent public school teachers and support staff. Visit the website at **www.nea.org**.

- **American Federation of Teachers (AFT):** Founded in 1916, the AFT has more than 3,000 local affiliates nationwide, 43 state affiliates, and more than 1.4 million members. Visit the website at **www.aft.org**.

- **National Association of Catholic School Teachers (NACST):** This union was founded in 1978. Visit the website at **www.nacst.com**.

PAID VERSUS NON-PAID SCHOOL-RELATED ENDEAVORS

In order to supplement their incomes, many teachers take on additional responsibilities at the school when extra pay is offered. Many of these opportunities exist, but not all schools pay their teachers to assume these extra responsibilities, so you should inquire before agreeing to take anything else on. Additionally, as a new teacher, you may not make a large amount of money, but you may want to first consider the time allocation before taking on any additional responsibilities. The following are a few jobs that may potentially augment a teacher's salary:

- Coaching after-school athletics
- Advising after-school clubs
- Becoming a new teacher mentor
- Tutoring
- Administering and grading placement exams
- Teaching summer school or home-bound programs

"At our school, teachers run almost all of the clubs. I believe this is relatively common in most Catholic high schools. There is generally a very modest stipend provided to the teachers for their time and efforts. The compensation ranges from a few hundred to a couple thousand dollars, depending on the amount of time involved. In the past, we had many coaches in the building, but not so many now. Their stipends are very low. The head coaches are the highest paid at approximately $3,000 to $4,000 a year."

— John Cominsky, religion teacher,
Trinity High School

CASE STUDY: WHAT YOU NEED TO KNOW ABOUT SCHOOL DISTRICT HIERARCHIES

Richard Bradley
School board member
Mechanicsburg Area School District
Mechanicsburg, Pennsylvania
www.mbgsd.org

Richard Bradley is one of the nine members on the Mechanicsburg Area School Board. He is currently serving his first term on the board. Bradley's Case Study provides insight into a typical school district hierarchy and the resulting pay scales. He provides information pertaining to the factors that go into agreeing on a teacher's salary from the school board's perspective.

As in most industries, the higher the degree one holds, the higher the pay scale. Most people in the school district administrative positions, such as the superintendent, financial officer, and principal, have at least a master's degree, and in most cases, they also have a doctorate. It is not a job requirement for administrators to go beyond a master's degree, but in most cases, it is a requirement when applying for certain higher positions.

Teachers' salaries are based on a standard range for the school district and its surrounding area. Many factors go into setting the range. Information is gathered and judged against a broad spectrum of criteria implemented by the state. In Pennsylvania, teachers are covered under a union contract that establishes ranges for years of experience, degrees, and area of expertise. Salary increases are negotiated through a four-year contract. There are local divisions of national and state teacher unions representing each given school district. Because there are 501 school districts in Pennsylvania, there is a wide range of teacher salaries.

For school district administrators and support personnel, pay scales are based on a range consisting of a minimum and a maximum for each category of job being performed. Administrators are salaried employees, while most of the administrative support staffers, such as teacher's assistants, secretaries, building aides, food service workers, and custodians are paid on an hourly wage basis. Hourly employees are also each placed in specific wage earning ranges and paid accordingly.

The following is generally the order of pay. This example is relevant to our school district. Other districts may have additional positions not included in this list. As stated above, this is an example, but the pay can vary because of the ranges and is dependent on years of service, experience level, and degrees held by the individual.

SCHOOL DISTRICT SALARY HIERARCHY

- **Superintendent:** The chief school administrator oversees the district and has executive power and administration rights within the school district.

- **Chief fiscal officer:** The chief fiscal officer is essentially a treasurer of sorts for the school district. He or she handles the money that comes in from the federal and state tax bureaus. He or she must understand all of the current state and federal regulations.

- **Assistant superintendent:** The second in command to the superintendent has responsibilities in grant writing, staff development, curriculum design, assessment supervision, budget development, and technology.

- **Directors of student services:** A member of the superintendent's senior management team. Oversees the district's guidance program, nursing services, IEP and 504 coordination, home schooling, and student appeal processes, as well as supervises the school principals.

- **High school and middle school principals:** Principals are responsible for administering policies and procedures, developing school budgets, implementing school site programs, conferring with staff on curriculums, evaluating classroom instructors, and handling safety concerns.

- **Elementary school principals:** These officials oversee the day-to-day running of their schools. They also hire and evaluate teachers, prepare budgets, and develop academic programs.

- **Assistant principals at all levels:** Duties include assisting principals, administering school student personnel programs, counseling and disciplining students, supervising student activity programs, supervising guidance, maintaining student attendance, and overseeing student and substitute teachers.

- **Technology director:** This person oversees the district's technology department, including purchasing, maintenance, and repair of computer networks, video/audio equipment, and other systems.

- **School psychologists:** Psychologists are responsible for testing students who may qualify for special needs services, making recommendation on adaptations for students in the classroom, and working with guidance counselors and teachers to assist students.

- **Directors of athletics, facility, and food services:** These individuals are responsible for overseeing their respective departments and the individuals who work in them.

- **Teachers:** To reiterate, the teacher scale is broad and wide. The pay can range from the lowest level of the hierarchy all the way up to the assistant principal's level. It depends on education, years of experience, and the district. Each district has a different pay scale.

There is a separate pay structure and subsequent hierarchy for hourly employees as well. These are:

- Administrative assistants to the central district office
- Administrative assistants to the school
- Administrative aides
- Special education instructional aides
- Food service employees
- Custodial employees
- Teacher's aides

In addition to the positions listed above, most districts have a group of individuals set up as a governing board, known as the school board. This is a group of elected officials. In respect to the overall job title hierarchy and chain of command, the school board has final say on all decisions affecting the school district, including hiring and firing. For the most part, this is simply a formality, but it provides a means of checks and balances. It is an unpaid position. The overall decision-making hierarchy for most public school districts in order of highest to lowest authority is as follows:

- School board
- Superintendent
- Chief fiscal officer
- Assistant superintendent
- Directors of student services
- High school principals
- Middle school principals
- Elementary school principals
- Assistant principals at all levels
- Directors
- School psychologists and guidance staff
- Teachers
- Administrative staff
- Other support staff

SCHOOL DISTRICT DEPARTMENTS

Each district is unique in size and structure, but many will have similar departments serving particular needs. Although the titles, amount, and size of the district departments may differ, the following four departments are essential for teachers to explore.

Payroll

This department tracks payroll and schedules, disburses paychecks, and handles all accounts payable information related to employees.

Human resources

Although the actual interview and hiring is usually left to the administration of the school where you applied, the human resources department in most school districts will advertise positions and qualify prospective educators for positions. Many schools will interview only applicants whom human resources has approved. This includes passing background checks, fingerprinting, and in most districts, drug testing.

Human resources also often serves as the liaison between insurance companies and teachers and will provide information on benefits such as medical insurance, life insurance, disability options, and retirement savings plans. Undoubtedly, you will find a human resources specialist at your new-teacher orientation meetings.

Curriculum and development

By closely following the curriculum map, you can achieve an innovative classroom atmosphere that meets both district and school expectations. In general, the curriculum department often comprises several individuals headed by one person whom you will meet at your first academic-subject area meeting. The curriculum head takes information from the department heads of individual schools, such as suggestions on which texts the district should adopt or how to implement them, and brings it back to the school board for approval.

Certification

Middle school public educators must be certified to teach in the United States. Certification particulars vary from state to state, so it is imperative that each district has staffers who keep track of this information. This department is a district's "credential keeper." It obtains and verifies prospective employees' transcripts and certification examination status and does not stop monitoring accomplishments or requirements once you are hired.

Often, new teachers are given a period of time to complete mandated requirements. Some districts will allow you to teach while completing your final courses or while taking and awaiting state certification scores. The certification department also may monitor federally mandated requirements such as the English as a second language (ESL) endorsement, a current mandate for all teachers of students whose native language is not English. The rules and regulations might vary from state to state, and your certification department can provide you with exactly what is expected from your district.

As with many other fields, even after you have met all the requirements and obtained professional licensure, you will need to renew these certifications every five years. This means you must obtain a certain number of "points" for renewal. You can earn points by taking college classes related to your subject area — such as science, math, or geography — or professional education courses provided by the district, such as classroom management strategies that incorporate all subjects. Some districts combine points to make it easier and less time-consuming for teachers to keep their certification and knowledge up to date. For example, a teacher attending classes for the federally mandated ESL certification or endorsement also might use these points for recertification in his or her subject area, such as social studies.

Depending on the size of the district, one person might be considered the contact for certification, or there might be an entire department of several individuals with a supervisor. In larger districts such as New York City or Dade County, Florida, teachers might wish to befriend or find one specific contact in certification. A person who is familiar with your particular situation will not only keep you from having to explain information over and over again, but may save you the frustration of putting time into a class you did not need because someone gave you erroneous information. It happens, and it happens often. If you stay informed about your state's certification requirements and consult your certification contact regularly, you will be able to avoid any confusion.

SCHOOL BOARD AND MISSION STATEMENT

Each district's mission statement can be a relevant guide on which to base goals for you, your school, and your students. The mission statement starts with your board's vision and will undoubtedly define what your district expects from its teachers. This is an example of a mission statement from a school district in Morris County, New Jersey:

"The mission of the East Hanover School District is to prepare our young people to be positive, contributing members of society. Through a diversified curriculum which incorporates the expectation that all students achieve the New Jersey Core Curriculum Content Standards (NJCCCS) at all grade levels and a school environment that fosters self-esteem, independent thinking, and respect for individual differences, we provide our students with the skills and experiences necessary to assist them in achieving their fullest potential as unique individuals and to meet the challenges of life."

As you can see, East Hanover's primary expectation, and how you and your students' achievements will be measured, is clearly laid out: "…incorporates the expectation that all students achieve the New Jersey Core Curriculum Content Standards." Common-sense mission statements such as East Hanover's are utilized throughout the United States. New teachers who familiarize themselves with their school boards' missions will have a clear grasp of what their district expects from them.

CHAPTER 5:
Teaching Relationships and Your Go-To Crew

The early days of middle school might seem overwhelmingly filled with meetings, information, and a plethora of paperwork. However, during pre-planning — your first days at your new school before the students arrive — you will make your first impression. This is where you will meet the people you will be working with all year. This includes your principal, vice principal, guidance counselor, and other colleagues. You have joined the ranks of the extraordinary. After all, it takes a special person to work with an age group that most others quickly run screaming from and never look back.

Knowing where to go for guidance in your first year as an educator will make the seemingly infinite tasks of a middle school teacher remarkably more manageable. The middle school hierarchy is simple. You first responsibility is to the administration, including the superintendent and school board. On a daily basis, you will also answer to the principal and any assistant principals your school might have. Non-instructional personnel comprise your support staff. The faculty makes up all of the instructional positions in your middle school. By cultivating mutually advantageous relationships, you can establish a network that will continuously contribute to an effective classroom and lasting partnerships in education.

PRINCIPAL'S PRINCIPLES AND EXPECTATIONS

The principal is at the helm of every middle school's motley crew. He or she guides the ship through the rough waters of unhappy teachers, belligerent children, and enraged parents — even though at times the budget he or she juggles to keep the vessel afloat could not fix a leak on a sinking canoe. Sometimes the principal is pleasant to work for, and, understandably so, sometimes not. Regardless, if you couple the vision of your district with the vision of your principal and follow that lead, you can be confident that what you are doing is effective and on-task.

Your principal has developed an educational philosophy and set of standards based on experience. A principal taught classes for several years, worked as an assistant principal for another few years, and finally became a principal. Listen to what he or she has to say. Usually in the first school-year faculty meeting, if a principal feels strongly about a goal, treatment of students or fellow teachers, or any other issue, he or she will share it with the faculty as a whole. You will want to know what those principles are and be able to act accordingly. You cannot do so if you do not know.

Some principals have a more democratic system where decisions such as discipline, dress code, and curriculum planning are designated to teachers. This is very common in today's "single-school culture," in which shared education norms and rules are consistent throughout the school. Some principals feel it necessary to micromanage. It is important you know what course he or she wishes to travel so you can assist.

Know your administrators

Good teachers are the most important resource a principal has. Take the time to learn your school district hierarchy. Learn the names of your superintendent, school board, and other district leaders. Understand their responsibilities as educational leaders.

In order to have adequate support as a new teacher or even a veteran teacher, there must be a good relationship between the teacher and the administrator. It is critical that administrators support their teachers and ensure a positive learning environment in their schools. You want your administrator to have a moral purpose. He or she needs to understand the change process, listen to those who point out flaws in proposed changes, and adjust to those changes accordingly. A good administrator will continuously strive to develop and nurture relationships with his or her teachers, knowing the importance of those relationships. A good administrator will not buckle under the continuous demands of politics and people in the community but will remain focused on what should be the main goal: Student learning.

Unfortunately, you as a teacher do not have the ability to change your school principal. This is why it is crucial, if at all possible, to learn ahead of time about the principal of the school where you are interested in teaching. As a new, incoming teacher, it is important to look for an accessible, respectful, supportive, and caring principal.

The significance of the relationship between administrators and teachers has become apparent to educators and educational researchers alike over the years. After working for a number of schools, Kelly Graves, a specialist in organizational conflict resolutions, said it is obvious the most important asset a school can have for students to be successful is a principal and teachers who work together to achieve their common goal: A positive, comfortable learning environment in which students can succeed.

Assistant principals

Assistant principals are the backbone of a healthy middle school system. The number of assistant principals a school has depends on the number of teachers and students in a school; whether the area is rural, suburban, or urban; and the funding allotted by the school district. Assistant principals support the infrastructure necessary to sustain a successful learning environment and may be delegated to be in charge of buses, custodians, testing, and other various departments. They are the principal's eyes and ears.

In many schools throughout the country, they also act as immediate supervisors for faculty. In larger middle schools with more than 1,300 students, you may be assigned to one assistant principal who will monitor your progress as a new teacher throughout the year. In addition to being your first-year guide, your assistant principal will hand out discipline to students who do not respond to your classroom-management strategies.

Most importantly, an assistant principal may be your evaluator during your first year — this person may be the assistant principal assigned to your grade level or an assistant principal assigned to support new teachers. Find out who your administrator is and ask what he or she expects to see when visiting your classroom. Ask him or her to share with you the county-wide measurement system used to evaluate new teachers. These are checklists of clear-cut guidelines evaluators use to determine whether new teachers are meeting the minimum standards of good teaching. These will be useful to you. They have been put in place to ensure that a teacher facilitates student success in the classroom, and you can use them as a self-check system.

If you are required to have a professional-development plan — a form mandated by the district to show your goals as a teacher — see if you can work on it with your assistant principal because it is your first year. If your administrator seems open to taking the time to discuss such matters with you, do not hesitate to ask what kinds of things helped him or her in the first year of teaching. Thankfully, most administrators are willing to be of assistance. They were once new teachers themselves and should completely understand and welcome your willingness to learn and grow.

DEPARTMENT CHAIRS

Often, a veteran teacher well-versed in your school's policies and procedures will head the subject area you teach in. This is your department chair. Middle school department chairmen and chairwomen are in charge of various duties, primarily the care and tracking of textbooks and bringing information from the principal or district back to you at regularly scheduled department meetings. In some schools, they also might be in charge of the supplies for the teachers in your subject area.

Keep in mind, these individuals have teaching duties along with their departmental duties. They are incredibly busy during the first days of school accommodating other teachers and preparing their classrooms. They also receive an extra stipend for this position, however, so ask if you need something. Early in your classroom-preparation days, check that you have enough textbooks and a teacher edition for each one. This way, you can give yourself plenty of time to let your department head know you understand that he or she is busy and that you would like to go to the bookroom or supply room to get what you need at his or her convenience.

The number of teachers you will work with is subject to the size of your school. Faculty members are those who hold all the instructional positions. Staff members are those who hold all non-instructional positions. Early-year faculty meetings are great ways to find the countless winners in the game of education. New teachers will find, throughout their upcoming years as educators, that truly bad teachers are a minute minority. Most middle school teachers, regardless of their diverse personality traits and imperfections, love their classrooms and students in an appropriate manner. This is not a business you want to go to every day if you do not.

Therefore, even among the gossipers and whiners at the faculty meetings, you can always find a group of people who are incredibly effective with the students in their classrooms. Keeping principles above personalities allows you to enjoy the wit and wisdom of teaching experience. You never know whom you will learn from, even though some of your fellow teachers sharing this experience are not those you might invite over for a barbecue.

SPECIALISTS

Many special-needs students are able to attend mainstream school, but some still may need assistance. Therefore, you may be paired with a specialist to help you educate these special-needs children. This person might be a teacher's assistant with an associate's degree, or a Ph.D. expert in special education, such as the school psychologist or social worker. It may be someone who signs for a deaf student, a "shadow," or a teacher who specializes in working with students with physical disabilities. Regardless of their degrees or specializations, they will be there to help your student(s) succeed.

In your early days of school, seek out whomever you will be working with and what special needs a student might have. If you have a physically disabled student, perhaps he or she needs to sit at the desk closest to the door. Ask your principal whether he or she has the student's education plan, a document stating the accommodations that must be met for the student. For example, a desk with the chair attached may not be suitable for your student, and you will need to find one with a detached chair. Perhaps the specialist would appreciate a chair placed nearby so he or she can sit and work closely with the student. Not only will the specialist appreciate your forethought, it will save you from scrambling to provide appropriate accommodations for one student while 28 others look on.

CASE STUDY: THE IMPORTANCE OF LEARNING SUPPORT

Jen Mulhollen
Itinerant learning support teacher
Good Hope Middle School
Mechanicsburg, Pennsylvania

Jen Mulhollen is in her sixth year of teaching. She graduated from Shippensburg University with a bachelor's degree in education and a minor in psychology. She is also pursuing her master's degree. Currently, she works as an itinerant learning support teacher at Good Hope Middle School.

During the 21st century, groups such as the Early Childhood Research Institute on Inclusion (ECRII) have provided documentation on the benefits of inclusion. The term inclusion refers to including students with special needs in the regular classroom environment. In order to make these situations work, public school district employ itinerant learning support teachers. These teachers provide support for identified students and teachers through training, materials, and ongoing consultation.

The itinerant teacher's role varies from one district to another. The job generally includes identification, assessment, counseling, tutoring, and advocacy. Challenges abound for those in these positions. Job descriptions are not always clearly defined, and many itinerant programs in the United States are still in their infancy.

As a middle school special education teacher, I get the pleasure of working with many different types of students. I have some who want nothing to do with me and feel like they can do everything on their own, some who use me way too much and view me as a crutch, and yet others who want to do their very best but know their limitations and come for help when needed.

I teach itinerant learning support, which means that all of my students receive all of their academic instruction in the regular education setting and then come to me for extra support. I am there to offer support with things that they might not quite understand, adapt materials for my students, provide support in the classroom with staying on task and/or taking notes, and then my students will come to my room to take their tests, adapted or not adapted, in order to have a quiet testing room to lessen distractions.

I have anywhere from 20 to 50 students on my caseload, in the sixth to eighth grades, which means that I not only support them in their academics, but also provide a bridge between the parents and the school and also write each of their individual education plans (IEPs). Each student receives a plan for their personal education, which outlines their strengths as well as their academic needs.

They each have goals for the year as well as specially designed instruction, which includes necessary accommodations for the classroom. Each of the plans is unique to the student and there is at least one meeting per academic year with the student's parents to discuss their needs and develop this plan.

The best part of my job is when a student is really struggling in a certain area and all of a sudden "gets it"; it is the point where the light bulb is lit. It is so rewarding when you are able to experience this that it makes all the tough times worth it. There are tough times, especially when there are just so many students that need my attention at the same time and I have paperwork to do, but when I can see them succeed, it makes it all better. My job is so rewarding!

GUIDANCE

Middle school guidance counselors' responsibilities vary from district to district and school to school. They are required to have a master's degree in an accredited school guidance program and are paid the same scale as teachers with the same level of education. In a nutshell, they have the distinct challenges of acting as a confidant and consultant to an age group of individuals who are growing faster physically, emotionally, and hormonally than at any other time in their lives. Whereas high school guidance counselors act as career guides and elementary school guidance counselors facilitate support groups and classes, middle school counselors are mediators, brawl interventionists, and social workers.

The guidance department will support a classroom teacher in many ways. Among the most important of those roles is keeping teachers up to speed on students who may be facing challenges that affect their academics or classroom behavior. Guidance counselors can also act as liaisons in parent-teacher conferences. They are knowledgeable about the social and educational services that are offered for the children in your county and will often refer students in need. They can assist in presenting your concerns to parents, including a student's excessive absences, lack of homework completion, and signs of depression.

Guidance counselors must document all interactions with students and parents. Staying on top of your daily paperwork will help them. For example, if a student is missing more than the average number of school days and you are not keeping accurate attendance records, the task of contacting and investigating the issue becomes more time-consuming, as the counselor must seek out the information he or she should already have.

CASE STUDY: THE BENEFITS OF THE TEAM-TEACHING APPROACH

Karen Pomeroy
Sixth grade math teacher
Good Hope Middle School
Mechanicsburg, Pennsylvania
kpomeroy@cvschools.org

Karen Pomeroy began her teaching career in 1994 working with accelerated elementary math students. From 1998 to 2006, she taught middle school gifted students. For the last four years, she has taught math to sixth graders. She also serves as the Math Counts team coach for the school. Pomeroy has a master's degree in gifted education. Currently, she is part of the 6R team of teachers working with approximately 200 to 300 students each year. Her Case Study discusses the benefits of the team-teaching approach.

I am a math teacher on one of two sixth grade teams in my school. At Good Hope, a team typically consists of a teacher from each subject area, the guidance counselor, our principals, and any special education teachers or specialists with students on the team. We meet formally approximately once a week and informally almost daily. (Many of us have a common planning period or are able to stay in contact via e-mail.) In our district, sixth grade is the first year in middle school, and students often find the adjustment from elementary school to be a big one. Teams can help to make the transition easier. Below I list some of the benefits I have seen to a team approach at the middle school level.

A team approach helps us to understand the students' backgrounds and personalities; this allows us to make adjustments to our teaching to maximize the students' learning. Our guidance counselors, in particular, are able to share relevant information with the team. Each guidance counselor in our school stays with his or her group of students as they progress through the three years of middle school. Therefore, the counselor is able to provide information on what motivates or alienates particular students and about home or environmental factors that may be affecting their learning. Guidance counselors can also share relevant testing information or details about the students' educational history, such as that they have switched schools often and may have gaps in their understanding. Special education teachers give the team suggestions on how to help when their students are struggling, and gifted support teachers can assist in providing the children with additional challenges. If a student has established rapport with a particular team teacher, the teacher can advise the other teachers on effective ways to interact with the child.

A team approach also results in interventions that are quicker and more effective. If one teacher suspects a difficulty with speech or handwriting, she can confirm this with other team members and a referral can be made. When family or neighborhood situations are affecting a student's learning, the principal can make contacts with social workers or authorities who can help to resolve the situation. If a student begins to have academic difficulty in his or her classes, a team is more likely to notice the overall trend and intervene early. When there is a personality conflict or bullying situation between students, all members of the team can quickly be made aware of it so that it does not escalate.

Working with a team can be easier for parents because they can communicate with one teacher and ask that individual to share information with the group. Teaching teams also tend to have fairly uniform procedures, making it easier for parents to keep track of what is happening. For example, getting work for an educational trip is handled in a standard way on our team and so are parent-teacher conferences.

A teaching team provides additional manpower for special educational events. For example, each year our school hosts an event called Children of the World Day. The annual tradition is relevant to the sixth-grade geography curriculum. Students come dressed in costumes depicting some portion of their ancestry. The social studies teachers arrange for a day of special speakers, activities, foods, and dancing to expand the children's knowledge of the world. All members of the sixth grade teams contribute to making the day a memorable one for the students. Several other team-wide special events occur throughout the year. They help to create a feeling of family within the team and are something that the students eagerly anticipate.

Being on a team allows each person to use his or her gifts for the good of the group. One teacher may be called upon when a student needs warmth and encouragement, another when a student needs tough love, and another when a student needs assistance with organization. One teacher might be good with details while another is more global. Teachers comfortable with technology might have opportunities to help colleagues with less expertise. Being on a teaching team allows us to learn from each other and use our natural strengths to benefit the students.

A team approach makes cross-curricular connections easier. When we are meeting regularly, we are more knowledgeable about each others' curriculum. As a math teacher, I can make references to math portions of books the students are reading in language arts class. The reading teacher can share with me how he or she teaches highlighting and note-taking, and I can use this as I work with the students on word problems. The social studies teacher helps the students with fractions and ratios as he or she teaches scale of miles and use of an almanac. Cross-curricular connections help the students to see the relevance of the material they are learning.

Finally, being on a healthy team can help teachers to feel happier and better connected. This may not benefit the students directly, but it certainly benefits them indirectly. Having someone to print your substitute plans when you are sick, someone to laugh with, someone to listen on a rough day, and someone who remembers your birthday are all benefits to being on a healthy teaching team.

MEDIA SPECIALIST

What was once known as the "library" is now the "media center." It is not only filled with books, but also computers and other digital equipment. The media specialist is the gatekeeper to all of these valuable educational tools. Some teachers seem to forget it is still a library. The media center is for research, checking out books, and computer testing if terminals are not available in the teacher's classroom. It is not a student dumping ground. Teachers need to determine from the media specialist how many students are acceptable to send at one time.

If students have not already learned how to behave in a media center, they should learn now. It is a place for concentration, and students who concentrate should not be running around, goofing off, and talking loudly. Although elementary school is the time for students to learn what a "library" voice is, you might have to remind them in the early days of middle school, before they go to the media center either individually or as a class. If you feel your students need assistance in further understanding the media center and its function, most media specialists are happy to help.

Another bane of the media specialist is overdue and lost books. Some schools charge fines, and others will not allow students to participate in after-school activities and field trips without returning or replacing the lost item. Either way, be sure to reinforce these consequences with your students. Additionally, help prevent lost and overdue items by being sure your students get any overdue notices sent to your class and add planning time for students to go to the media center two or three at a time.

Keep in mind that teachers are responsible for students in their class, whether the students are physically in the classroom or not. It is important to be sure they are monitored at all times.

INFORMATION TECHNOLOGY ADVISOR

The amount of digital technology in your school is equal to the amount of funds your district is willing to put into it. Many middle schools provide computers and digital projectors for teachers. Some also have laptops for each child. Regardless, all schools today have technology of some sort, such as desktop computers for teachers, laptop carts for students, digital projectors, and so on. An information technology (IT) advisor is usually on hand to help you with everything from serious crashes to simple password losses. A middle school may have a full-time IT advisor or a part-time person who covers more than one school, or the advisor may be another teacher who has an added stipend and an extra planning period to get the job done.

Regardless, the IT advisor usually must be in more than one place at a time. Be sure to call the IT advisor only when absolutely necessary. There is nothing more maddening for a middle school IT advisor to have to take time out of his or her day to go to your classroom for a crashed computer, only to find it is not plugged in. If you are not familiar with the basics of computer hookups and the software you will be using, learn them.

SUPPORT STAFF

Without support staff, our schools would crumble. Take a look around your classroom. Someone made sure these tasks were accomplished:

- The room is clean.
- Your students have enough desks.
- You have keys to your classroom.
- Your W-2 form information is entered into the district payroll department's ledger.
- The front desk holds parents at bay so you can prepare your classroom before being stampeded with questions and concerns for their children's new teacher.
- You received the correct class rosters with your students on it.
- You received a copy of the faculty handbook.
- You are entered in the district's list of global e-mail addresses.

Teaching is not a solo gig. However, because the job is often quite challenging, we overlook the burdens of others and do not give the kind of recognition our support staff so often deserve. The individuals we work with outside of the classroom are often the power behind our success inside the classroom, and a simple hello, smile, or even a box of doughnuts goes a long way. At the very least, make your requests polite.

Front-office staff

On some days, the front counter is more aptly described as the front lines. The receptionists are answering the phones, while teachers are buzzing for attention on the intercom. Substitutes are waiting to see where they need to go next, while parents are impatiently glaring. In some middle schools, there is no school nurse, and the front-office clerks also have the responsibility of acting as emergency medical technicians.

They are often charged with getting work orders for repairs and other requests to the district and seeing that those requests are addressed in a timely fashion. Most districts move according to the "slow and steady wins the race" rule. As front-office staffers are often the go-between of the teacher and the district, in these matters they are often blasted from all corners.

Creating mutually positive feelings with the person at the front desk is relatively simple. As you learn to effectively manage your classroom, calling to the front office to have administrators remove unruly students will be particularly unusual. Therefore, if you do have a matter that needs to be addressed and it can wait, do not buzz the front office. Send an e-mail or note with a student so the office staff can address your concern when they have put out the fires and the embers are down to a slight glow.

A simple smile and a pleasant "good morning" when you enter your school each day will be more help than you think. As with all other individuals, thoughtful kindness, such as bringing a coffee cake for the secretarial staff, or a thank-you note for getting the district to fix your air conditioning before the next decade, will go a long way.

Bookkeeper

The bookkeeper in your middle school is your new best friend. The records of every cent you spend or receive will go through his or her office. Whether it be requesting classroom supplies or turning in collected field-trip funds, bookkeepers own the responsibility for keeping accurate records on school finances. He or she is in charge of accounts receivable, accounts payable, and possibly entering your payroll. The bookkeeper is the debt collector for bounced checks from parents and the accountant for all your school's organizations, clubs, and sport teams.

To make a bookkeeper's life a little easier, be sure that he or she has your accurate contact information and that all your forms are filled out correctly. Often bookkeepers will include their policy for submitting funds, such as monies collected, in the faculty handbook. Save he or she some time having to explain the school's bookkeeping procedures — and also save yourself some embarrassment after making a mistake — by reading the policies first.

Data entry/attendance clerk

Generally, schools hire a data entry clerk who also deals with the daily attendance recordkeeping. These clerks are in charge of keeping track of student information. Each day, they track student registration and attendance records and keep the district aware of where students are. One well-known gripe of data entry clerks is when teachers do no keep accurate attendance records. These records can be legal documents, and teachers are required to submit them accurately. Inaccurate records make life more difficult and time-consuming for the clerk and will mean having to answer to worried parents who are looking for children not accurately accounted for, as well as calls from the district inquiring as to why a student attended a class during the two weeks he or she was out with pneumonia. Make keeping attendance a priority and stay off the clerk's radar.

Custodians

Like other middle school departments, a head custodian usually leads the crew. Custodians are charged with everything from mowing the lawn to keeping the bathroom sanitary. They empty the garbage after school, clean the toilets, scrub graffiti off walls, and scrape gum off the bottoms of desks. Obviously, their tasks are not always pleasant. Custodians appreciate the people who make their lives a little easier. After each class, take a minute before the bell to make sure all materials are put away and books are off the floor. Keep an eye out for gum-chewing. You can bring a garbage can to the culprit and have them spit it out without missing a beat in your lesson. Watch who is sitting where and periodically check the desks for any graffiti. Greet your students by the door as they enter your room. Also, keep an eye on hallway etiquette. The floor is not the appropriate place to dump garbage. This will not only show your appreciation for the difficult job custodians do, but it is a teachable moment for your students: That it is considerate to act as if they are in the real world where no one wants to clean up after them.

School nurse

School nursing is unique as it combines nursing with academic concerns. According to the National Association of School Nurses (NASN), "school nurses facilitate normal development; promote health and safety; intervene with actual and potential health problems; provide case management services; and actively collaborate with others to build student and family capacity for adaptation, self-management, self-advocacy, and learning."

School nursing has changed dramatically over the last decade. More students with chronic conditions and disabilities are attending mainstream schools. Therefore, the understanding of conditions, warning signs, and medicine disbursement falls on the school nurse's shoulders. This is in addition to the traditional stomach bug and twisted ankles.

Despite changes in the nursing field overall, school nurses are still predominantly women. According to the NASN, the field is still almost 99 percent female. The nurse's job includes aspects of being a parent, a doctor, a counselor, and even a physical therapist. School nurses still perform vision and hearing tests and conduct height and weight assessments. In 2009, school nurses across the country were given the daunting task of screening and inoculating students and faculty against the swine flu. Additionally, the average school nurse has daily responsibilities in assisting students with diabetes, asthma, arthritis, attention-deficit hyperactivity disorder (ADHD), severe allergies, autism, and a host of physical disabilities. At any given time, she may need to assist someone with a catheter, respirator, insulin pump, or even feeding tube.

Given the additional responsibilities, the federal government recommends that each school have one nurse for every group of 750 typical healthy students. The sanction cites healthy students because certain diagnoses require schools to have additional nursing staff on hand. Unfortunately, there is a national nursing shortage. Therefore, despite the government proposal, the average school nurse in the United States is responsible for more than 1,100 students in two different buildings. At some schools in this country, secretaries and building aides are asked to cover for nurses when they are out of the building.

"Each school has a computer that provides information on students and pertinent health information, such as a diagnosis like asthma or diabetes. Additionally, there are notes in the office about certain students who frequent the nurse's office for other reasons. There is also information pertaining to kids who are "cutters," anorexic, or pregnant. This information is not on the computer file, but is kept in a secure location so the substitute nurses and aides know what is going on if they come in. Sometimes, the nurse's office is simply a refuge for students who feel overwhelmed. They want to talk about problems at home or just need a place to lie down for a little while. The nurse sometimes acts as a liaison between the student and the guardian.

In addition to standard emergency equipment, there are items to help disabled children take care of their issues, such as lifts in the bathroom. Most kids at this age are very independent and do not want help unless they absolutely need it. Each year there are a team of teachers and staff, who are trained to respond to student emergencies. Some of the personnel are EMTs trained in CPR and AED use. When a code blue is called all members of the team react quickly and professionally to come to a student's aid."

— Linda Weaver, substitute nurse,
central Pennsylvania school districts

Bus drivers

Guidance counselors are exposed to daytime drama, but bus drivers are exposed to extreme wrestling mania. Somehow, they have to safely transport a busload of clamoring, cacophonous students while preventing name-calling, paper-throwing, and the occasional scuffle. Because they are so separated from the daily school routine, they are thought of and thanked rarely. Some schools, such as North County Road Middle School in New York, make sure drivers get the thanks and recognition they deserve with Bus Driver Appreciation Day — a great way to say "What you do is important." Language-arts teachers can encourage students to write simple thank-you notes, poems, or cards. Students in family consumer sciences can bake cookies. You can put Bus Driver Appreciation Day in the school newsletter and have parents join in by sending their children with a thank-you note.

Little monetary thanks is given for the colossal job each middle school employee does. Therefore, it is important to remain grateful to each other. Brightening the days of any support staffer at a middle school brightens the atmosphere of the school itself.

CHAPTER 6:

Creating a Classroom Conducive to Learning

Your classroom is your own personal domain, and as long as you are in accordance with the district rules and regulations, you may decide how it looks and how it runs. Taking the extra time to create and organize a comfortable atmosphere for you and your students requires some effort on your part, especially when you are just starting out. Eventually, you will figure out what works best for you and each year it will take less effort if you remain organized.

By the time you have a few years of teaching experience, you room will begin to express your personality. One middle school teacher interviewed for this book has a room that was warm and inviting with twinkle lights around the bulletin boards, colored tablecloths, and big bean bag chairs in a designated reading area. Another teacher decorated his room in a sports theme, relating all of the information to math concepts. Find out what the guidelines are in your school and start planning.

Many new teachers are overwhelmed with where to start concerning their classrooms. This chapter provides you with the necessary information to help you get started. It includes:

- Advice on learning your way around
- A list of items you will need
- Tips on where to find school funds to pay for necessary items
- Suggestions for finding items when there is no money allocated
- How to organize the room and your school supplies

- Tips on filing and paperwork

GETTING AROUND

Learn your way around the school. Depending on the size of the school, this may be a simple task or it may be completely overwhelming. Check your new-hire packet to see if it includes a map of the school. If it does not, ask one of the secretaries if there is a map of the school, and if so, whether you can have one. Either way, there are a number of places you need to locate immediately. They are:

- Faculty parking
- Human resources
- Main office
- Principal and assistant principal office(s)
- Attendance office
- Your classroom
- Nearest faculty-sanctioned bathroom (Some schools have separate bathrooms for student and faculty — others do not.)
- Faculty lounge
- Cafeteria
- Nurse's office
- Guidance counselor's office

These are the areas you will use first and most frequently. After that, you should acclimate yourself with the rest of the school so you can find your way around and help students find a specific location.

CLASSROOM SUPPLIES

The amount of time you have to prepare will depend on the circumstances surrounding your hiring. If you have the luxury of getting ready over the summer months, you can take your time setting up your classroom and getting your supplies organized. If not, concentrate on the priorities. The school and the subject matter you teach affect your supply requirements, so make sure you have all of the supplies you need. To begin with:

- Determine what you need and make a list.
- Assess what you already have that you can work with.
- Determine your budget and/or school allocated funds.
- Determine school purchasing procedures.
- Place an order for supplies that must be acquired from a distance.
- Purchase, find, or request other supplies as needed.
- Plan where you will put everything.
- Organize supplies.

Before you invest in your own supplies, find out what the school will provide for you and for the students. The best place to start is in the office. The school secretaries generally run the school. They will be able to tell you virtually everything you need to know. They will also be able to advise you on what you are permitted to do in respect to ordering materials such as textbooks. Each school differs, depending on school type and budget. For example, many public schools provide a certain amount of supplies. Parochial schools, on the other hand, require students and teachers to provide all necessary supplies at their own expense.

The following is a basic list of items and supplies you may need to stock in your classroom. Depending on your school, the subject you teach, and what you have included in your lesson plans, you may need additional items:

- **Date planner.** You will need some kind of agenda book for school holidays, fire drills, appointments, meetings, and assignments.

- **Assorted writing instruments.** Everyone has their own preference for writing, be it pens or pencils. Whatever you use, make sure you have plenty of back-ups. Supplies tend to disappear as time goes by. In addition you own writing instruments, you may also need different colored pens for grading. If you use pencils, be sure to invest in extra erasers.

- **Pencil sharpener.** Your classroom may or may not be equipped with a sharpener for the students. Regardless, you may want to have your own in or on your desk.

- **Chalk and/or whiteboard markers and erasers.** Most schools have gone to whiteboards, either on the walls or on rollers. If so, it is nice to have a variety of colored markers for any diagrams or notes you may want to write during your lectures.

- **Scissors.** You will need these to cut out items for bulletin boards or for other class projects.

- **Scotch and masking tape.** Tape is necessary for securing items to the walls, or for putting together projects.

- **Pushpins.** Pushpins and thumbtacks will secure items to bulletin boards. Make sure to ask about the school's policy about putting items on the walls of your classroom. Some schools will let you put anything you want up on the walls, while others have rules about what can go up and how it is secured.

- **Stapler and staples.** Make sure you have plenty of extra staples. Not only will you use this frequently, but students will come in with papers that have not been secured and ask to use your stapler, so be prepared.

- **A ruler and/or a yardstick.** You might use these for lesson plans, projects, drawing lines on the whiteboard, or measuring where you want to put a poster on the wall.

- **Fasteners.** You might have a specific preference for paper clips, or you might want to have an assortment of fasteners, such as paper clips, binder clips, and paper rings.

- **File folders.** First, consider what you are going to file and where it will go. Do you have a filing cabinet? If so, you may need hanging folders as well or some other means of separating types of files.

- **Labels.** You will be more organized if you label everything. In addition to using them on your files, you can use labels for identifying your personal belongings, such as an extra bookcase or lamp you may have purchased on your own.

- **Paper.** Depending on the subject you teach and the types of lesson plans you have, you will probably need a variety of different types of paper. You may need some lined and some unlined paper. If you have a computer printer in your room, you may need printer paper. For projects and bulletin boards, you may need construction and/or poster paper.

- **Note cards.** Note cards come in different sizes and colors. Some are lined and some are unlined. Gather a variety to use for lectures, projects, and notes regarding students.

- **A hole-punch.** You may want two separate hole-punches: one three-hole-punch for papers that can be stored in a binder and a single, hand-held hole-punch for items that only require a circular ring.

- **Calculator.** If you are a math teacher, you may want an advanced calculator with multiple functions. If not, you will still need a basic calculator for grading.

- **Correction fluid.** You will need correction fluid or tape to go over any mistakes you might make.

- **Tissues.** You will want tissues for yourself and for students with colds. Many teachers ask students to donate boxes of tissues throughout the year. Some teachers even offer extra credit to students who bring them in.

- **Cleaning supplies.** You might want to keep some extra cleaning supplies on hand, particularly during cold and flu season. First check with the school sanitation engineers on school policy. Many schools are now turning to eco-friendly products and are banning certain cleaning agents.

- **First-aid kit.** You can always send people to the nurse, but depending on the size of the school and the distance between your classroom and the nurse's office, it might be a good idea to stock some simple items, such as small adhesive bandages, in your room. Your school will have a policy regarding major student injuries and illnesses. Having a few first-aid items in your room might help minimize class disruptions. Ask about the school policies and question other teachers on how they handle these situations. You might want to include some items for yourself as well, such as aspirin for the occasional headache.

STUDENT SUPPLIES AND COST-EFFICIENT LENDING

Middle school students will assure you and all the adults around them that they have gained complete independence and no longer need teacher or parental intervention. Yet they cannot remember to bring a pencil to class. Supply distribution services may not be in your job description, but not providing students with the supplies they need is counterproductive to the learning process and will create disruption in the classroom.

Pencils and paper

Teachers historically have used various interventions to guarantee that students remember to bring their supplies to class, and they have found that no matter what the intervention, students will forget, lose, chew on, crumple, and throw pencils and paper. It cannot be avoided, and therefore you will need an abundant supply. This does create an additional expense, but there are ways for you to keep students provided with materials without having to invest your own life savings.

One way to avoid unnecessary spending on supplies is to have students borrow instead of keep pencils and pens. In order to safeguard the return of borrowed items, have students surrender something of value. This may be a school identification card or an agenda book, which are mandatory in many schools. Some teachers even have students surrender one of their shoes — a smelly but effective way to have materials returned.

Another way to keep costs down is to send students home with a "wish list." When supply lists go out for students, teachers may request a box of pencils and pack of paper from each student, along with other supplies they may need in the classroom. Your syllabus also could have a list of supplies the students will need. You can include a separate list of "requested but not required" items.

"One of the most important things for me to establish right away is a comfortable classroom atmosphere. When students know that they are safe and that their opinions are appreciated, they will be more willing to take risks in discussions, therefore gaining more intellectual freedom. I suggest creating an atmosphere that is welcoming. I also have a corner with a sofa and chair so that students can come in and read comfortably. Use colors and keep it neat and organized. Students generally feel more comfortable when their surroundings are clean."

— Rachele Dominick, English teacher,
Cumberland Valley School District, Pennsylvania

ORGANIZING YOUR CLASSROOM

After you have obtained your supplies, you can start thinking about how you want to organize your classroom. You will most likely be given a set of keys to a room that is potentially messy. The following are some suggestions for approaching the task of getting it ready:

1. **Arrange the desks in the classroom first.** They take up the greatest amount of space. Doing this first makes setting up the rest of the room easier. When choosing a layout for the room, consider your teaching style, the subject matter, and the types of students you will be teaching. In a middle school environment, you will want to arrange the desks in such a way that you can see all of the students at all times. If you plan to do a lot of lecturing, you may decide to choose a U-shaped alignment. This provides you with the ability to see everyone and encourages better group discussions.

2. **Position your desk based on personal preference.** There are many schools of thought on the appropriate placement for the teacher's desk. Some teachers prefer to see the door from their desk, while others do not believe it is necessary as long as they can see all of their students. Try something out — if it does not work, then you can always move it. Many teachers seem to have success with positioning their desk in a corner that has a view of all the other desks. Another factor to consider is placing your desk and other items away from the door. This may eliminate potential theft and other problems.

3. **Determine the placement of any other furniture.** This includes filing cabinets, bookcases, and extra chairs. If you invest in or bring in your own furniture, be sure to label it so that it does not accidentally get removed from your classroom. When you place these items, consider where everyone will be sitting and where they will need to look. Try to prevent an arrangement that may block someone's view.

4. **Assess technology.** If you have computers, overhead projectors, SMART Boards, or other audio/visual equipment, check to make sure they are all working. If they are not, ask the appropriate staff member what you need to do to have them fixed or replaced. Be sure to do this immediately. If the technology and maintenance departments get numerous requests of this nature, it may take awhile for the repair to occur.

5. **Break out the cleaning supplies.** After the furniture is placed, wipe everything down before putting away your materials. Chances are you will not wipe it down again until next summer when you pack up for the year.

6. **Draw a floor plan.** Before putting everything in its place, draw a plan that details where everything will be kept. Make a copy of this and keep it in your desk drawer in case you forget where you put something. This is also helpful for substitute teachers who may not know where you keep your supplies.

7. **Organize your bookcases.** This will help you find books and supplies quickly and easily.

8. **Use slat files for items you need all the time.** Consider purchasing hanging or standing slat file systems to handle paperwork that you need to access quickly.

9. **Set up files and folders with tabs.** In addition to subject-specific files, you may want to organize your files by the month, season, or marking period.

10. **Address the walls and bulletin boards.** Consider the overall look and feel of the room. What subject do you teach? If you are an English literature teacher, you might want to cover your walls with pictures and quotes that pertain to the classics. If you are a science teacher, you might display items pertaining to the topics the students are learning.

11. **Add items as necessary.** Everything is overwhelming during your first year. As time goes on, you will think of other things you need or want to have. For instance, if you are a history teacher, you might want to add maps that pertain to the time period the class is studying. If you are a science teacher, you might need to update lab equipment as you change experiments. An English teacher might keep costumes or props to act out plays during certain lesson plans. When you walk by an experienced teacher's classroom and notice that it is full of books and other interesting items, remember they probably started out with blank walls and shelves just like you.

YOUR DESK: CLASSROOM HUB

Your desk is the Grand Central Station of your room. A flood of children, adults, and paperwork will visit your desk during the year. Arranging a system that creates clarity for all of these eliminates the abundance of stress you might experience if trying to find a particular form or lesson plan in a panic while keeping 30 middle school students on task.

Set up your desk long before the students arrive for the first day of school so you have workspace to prepare for them. With this in mind, your first priority in situating your desk will be strategically locating it so you can see all angles of the classroom and each student.

As enjoyable as they are to work with, middle school students are tricky. They might seem impatient, yet they often have the fortitude to wait until a teacher is not looking to make mischief without making a sound. This can include, but is not limited to: throwing paper, passing notes, and emitting spitballs through self-designed shooters. Ideally, you will circulate through your classroom, which will decrease the chances of horseplay.

Another consideration is accessibility to materials. Keeping staplers, tape, pencils, and paper stocked and refills close by is immeasurably helpful in allowing you to address your first priority during instructional periods: to facilitate learning by engaging students. Keep rubber bands and paper clips within your reach and out of students' reach. New teachers, especially those who were well-behaved during their middle school years, would be surprised how efficiently a middle school student can design dangerous toys with a simple rubber band and paper clip.

According to safety regulations set by the Occupational Safety and Health Administration (OSHA), teachers are required to keep a blood-borne pathogen kit within reach. The kit provides necessary supplies such as gloves, a mask, a gown, and other cleaning items for handling bodily fluids. You should be able to handle a student with a serious injury or even a simple nosebleed without the student having to wait while you search for your rubber gloves.

Hand sanitizer is a necessity, and you should use it often throughout the day. Even new teachers with the best immune systems will be exposed to influenza and the common cold on a daily basis. Surprising as it may be, some middle schools students are still learning appropriate hygiene skills. Hand sanitizer will help block contagious germs while allowing you to do your duty.

Personalizing your desk gives it character. You will want a cozy space where you are comfortable and want to spend some time. Your desk perhaps will include small mementos of where you are in your professional life, pictures of family and friends, and, as the years go by, gifts from grateful parents and students that remind you of the success you are having in your career. Just beware of glass or highly valuable desk items, especially if they are breakable. Students are around a teacher's desk on a daily basis, and the middle school years are some of the most awkward and klutzy. They will feel as badly as you do should something you care for accidentally break. Having a cozy space that is a reflection of you is important — just remember the age group you are instructing.

Another addition to your desk may be a podium or high desk at the front of the room. Often, teachers spend the first ten to 15 minutes of class explaining assignments and using visual aids at the board before students work independently or in groups. A podium or high desk gives you a place to put your materials without having to situate a desk directly in front of the whiteboard or chalkboard.

THOUGHTS ON STUDENT SEATING

You can set up student seating in many ways: rows, groups, and squares, for instance. There are many different ideas on desk arrangement and student seating. The issue is largely determined by three factors:

- Classroom layout
- School policy
- Personal choice

In your first few weeks of teaching, arrange student desks in rows before experimenting with grouping. Although working in groups and getting peer input is vital for most successful students, classroom management may be a bit more challenging when they are grouped together. Therefore, begin the year in rows and simply have students group their desks on the days they work on collaborative lessons. This will give you the opportunity to fine-tune your classroom-management skills before trying different desk arrangements that may create a ruckus.

When seating students, first be sure they can see you and the whiteboard from where they are sitting. Focus is a challenge faced by many middle school students.

They are easily distracted. If they cannot see what is going on, they most certainly will lose concentration on the lesson.

Before setting up student seating, contact your guidance counselor or specialist to check on any students who may need special accommodations. Some students might need to sit by the door, while others might have an education plan that suggests you should seat them in the front of the room for optimum success. If an individualized education plan (IEP) recommends a student sit in front of the class because of hearing, vision, or attention issues, the student needs to abide by that. In many cases, the student will sit in the correct location on his or her own. In others, they may not. If that occurs, first approach the student alone and suggest he or she move to another seat. If it becomes an issue, you can move everyone in the class and make it appear as your own personal whim.

You likely will rearrange seating several times throughout the year, but this will help you prepare to get through your first weeks getting to know your students and where they would best fit into the arrangement.

Design your classroom before beginning to move furniture around. Ask whether your district uses a seating chart software program such as eSembler, which is Web-based gradebook software. Laying out the room online or on paper first might make it easier in the end. For some subjects, such as teaching science in a lab, desk arrangement is irrelevant. If, however, you teach a subject that occurs in a traditional classroom with moveable desks, you may want to consider how you want them arranged. If your school does not have a specific policy on desk arrangement, you may move them in a formation that is conducive to your teaching style. Some factors to consider include:

- Do you plan to do a lot of lecturing?
- Do you want students to converse freely and debate topics being discussed?
- Do you plan to do a lot of work with students working in pairs or in groups?
- Will everyone need to see a chalkboard, whiteboard, or overhead projection screen?

- Does the class require interaction with other materials as in art, family consumer sciences, computer, or technology education?

The best advice is to consider your lesson plan and start out with something that makes sense. Once you have students in your room, you will quickly be able to determine what works and what does not. Most school desks are relatively lightweight and easy to push around. If you need assistance, ask the maintenance staff to help.

TECHNOLOGY

Depending on the financial situation of the school, you might or might not have technological equipment in your classroom. In some affluent areas, every class is wireless and each teacher has his or her own laptop computer. In other schools, it may still be a struggle to find an overhead projector to borrow for presentations. If you work in a district that is technologically advanced, you may need to organize your classroom around the placement of equipment, chords, and wires. Make sure everything is placed safely. Chords that run through areas where someone could trip over them are a safety hazard.

Some schools keep equipment on moveable carts in a media room. The items are signed in and out by the teachers as they need them. Overhead projectors, SMART Boards, electrical carts, and other similar types of equipment may be at your disposal. If your classroom does not contain a screen, you may need to borrow one from the media center. It may be free-standing or hanging. A media specialist or custodian can assist you if it needs to be hung from the ceiling. Whiteboards might seem as effective as screens, but this is not always the case. Using a whiteboard as a screen prevents you from writing on the board during or even before a presentation. The slightest marks can distort projection, whether from digital equipment or an overhead projector.

There are different types of projectors available depending on your school's budget. Many schools are trending toward new advanced projection systems that provide a wide variety of visual options. If your school does not have that type of system available, it will most likely have overhead projectors. These small boxes use underlighting to project the image of the transparency placed on it up on the wall or screen. They are portable and easy to use, making them a favorite with many teachers.

Often, educational transparencies for overheads will come with your text, and they are easy to use. If you have access to the overhead but cannot find transparencies, you can order blank ones and create your own or call your textbook vendor, who can provide you with the ones that go with the textbook. Additionally, you can copy printed pages onto overhead transparencies — saving your students from an overabundance of paper and you from copying yet another lesson on the board. Most teachers utilize all three options for variety.

If you are not technologically savvy and need to use equipment for a lesson plan, be sure to ask a media specialist to assist you.

THOSE FOUR WALLS

After you have set up your room and put away your supplies, decide what to do with the surrounding walls. In some cases, you might not have a lot of options — every school is different.

The following are a few potential scenarios you might encounter:

- Portable classrooms or trailers have cloth-covered walls requiring pushpins for anything that hangs on the walls.
- Older schools have walls with textured surfaces, making it difficult to hang anything at all.
- Newly painted walls might have a district policy preventing you from putting anything on them.
- A room may contain chalkboards or whiteboards on every wall, leaving little space for anything else.
- You might have a single designated tack strip for all decorations to preserve the walls.

Before you decorate your classroom, you must first understand the school policy for putting anything up in the room. After that, you must figure what you want to do with the space you have. A lot depends on the subject you teach and your own personal style. Start with what you have available to you. Do any of your lesson plans or materials come with free posters or other items you can display? After that, what other inexpensive items can you use to depict something about your class? Here are a few options to consider:

- Posters
- Student artwork or written work
- Postcards
- Magazine photos or words
- Newspaper articles
- Quotes
- Motivational sayings
- Blank newsprint that students can write or draw on

For a new teacher, the best place to find no-cost supplies is in your own school. Many times, the media center will have rolls of paper that you can use as a board cover. Veteran teachers collect supplies over the years that sit in the closet gathering dust, and in some districts, there are teacher stores where a note from the principal is all you need in order to shop.

Veteran teacher treasures

You do not need to spend additional funds out of your limited first-year salaries when supplies are often simply a couple of classrooms down the hall.

New teachers can share their need for supplies at the department meeting. Veteran teachers' supply closets are often treasure chests full of surplus, and most veterans are more than willing to assist you, not to mention clean out the mess. You might find bulletin-board borders, art supplies, and maybe even some unopened packages of construction paper for your students' use later on.

Word walls

Left behind are the bulletin boards that change with the seasons. Many middle school teachers create bulletin boards, often called "word walls," that reflect what students are learning in the classroom. In fact, school administrators often require word walls in all content-area teachers' classrooms.

Word walls are made up of vocabulary words relating to the subject taught. For example, a sixth-grade language arts teacher introducing literary terms to students may include words such as *protagonist, antagonist, plot,* and *theme.* A seventh-grade math teacher might use concepts such as *probability, theoretical probability,* and *experimental probability.* Bulletin boards covered with roll paper from the media center and finished with a nice border are perfect for word walls. Words can be cut out, printed with an attractive font or word art, cut with scissors closely around the word, and backed with construction paper, or simply stenciled. The method you use depends on how long the word wall will stay up and what materials are available to you.

Students' handiwork

Creative student assignments are an excellent way to bring your classroom to life. For example, science projects are often quite decorative, math teachers might choose to display origami, and language arts teachers may have students create vocabulary pictures. Displaying student work encourages self-confidence and classroom ownership.

Teacher stores

One of the best-kept secrets in education is the district teacher store. Generally, districts have a warehouse with everything from used teacher furniture to construction paper. All sorts of materials and supplies may be available to make your classroom cozy yet efficient. Check with your department chair and see whether your district has a place like this. Most districts simply require that teachers have a note from their principal in order to gain access and shop for whatever is needed. Although there may be a limit to what you can take, you should be able to pick up at least the basic supplies, such as staplers, pens, pencils, construction paper, and maybe even bulletin-board borders. If your department chair is unsure, your bookkeeper will know how you can gain access to the warehouse or teacher store.

Whiteboards

In many schools, whiteboards have taken the place of chalkboards, and rightfully so. Teachers used to go home with hands, hair, clothes, and lungs covered in chalkboard dust. Now you just need to be careful about leaning on the board so as not to end up with clothes covered in dry-erase marker. Some companies have even developed markers that smell pleasant.

Train your students to have their eyes go to the whiteboard for the day's instruction. You can colorfully split your whiteboard into sections with half-inch electrical tape purchased at a hardware store. Include a small section for your daily agenda, essential questions or objectives for the day or week, materials needed, and homework.

Posting classroom rules

Once you have decided on classroom rules, post them where they are obvious to all who enter. For the first weeks of school, you may need to refer to those rules on several occasions, reminding your students of your expectations. Leave them there for the year lest they forget.

This is an easy way to cover sections of the wall. Make signs or posters pronouncing the rules or policies that are most important. They could also be simple hints such as "do not forget your homework" or "do not interrupt while someone else is speaking."

Think outside the box

Basic bulletin boards and items that hang on the walls are a great place to start, but what else can you do? How can you grab your students' attention as soon as they walk in the room? Think outside of the box. Some teachers display items pertaining to favorite sports teams or places to which they have traveled. Some teachers add a comfortable chair for reading or a podium for presentations. What about other decorations and props? You will spend a lot of time in this room. As long as you are permitted to do so, you might as well make it comfortable and inviting.

BUDGET CUTS REQUIRE TEACHERS TO GET CREATIVE

"East Bridgewater school officials say budget cuts will hurt education." "Town citizens raise concerns over school budget cuts." "Fort Mill school district considering major budget cuts." These are only a few of the actual headlines concerning school budget issues plaguing everyone during the economic slowdown of 2010. The cuts have been affecting teachers for a long time. The problem has become so intense that many states have entitled, or are considering entitling teachers, to a tax deduction for purchasing classroom supplies. Regardless, this ongoing problem is getting worse and teachers are forced to find a way to deal with it.

Budget cuts are a real concern, and are affecting school supplies. Before you panic, however, check all of your available resources. There is actually more money available for teaching supplies than most people realize. First, talk to the principal. Some school districts allocate a specific stipend of money per teacher for supplies. After that, check with the school's Parent Teacher Association (PTA) or Parent Teacher Organization (PTO). Many PTAs and PTOs are more than happy to help new teachers get the supplies they need, providing they have the money to give. More often than not, if they do not have the money, they will hold fundraisers to raise the money.

Due to budget cuts, it has become more common and necessary for teachers to revert to finding their own materials for activities. There are many places to look other than the ones previously mentioned. Parents might be willing to donate items when asked. It depends on the school district and the cost of the items you are requesting. Keep in mind the economy has hit everyone hard. Along those lines, do not expect parents or students to purchase expensive or unnecessary items for classroom projects.

Look over your lesson plans and activities to make a list of the supplies you will need for each activity. While you are making your supply list for each activity, write the date for when the activity is scheduled to take place beside it. Consider the supplies you will need for the first six or eight weeks and begin looking for them before school starts.

Another option is to send letters to the parents of your students and ask if they could start saving or looking for certain materials you will use. This is a particularly common practice in Catholic schools. Some teachers also offer bonus points to students who bring in items for the classroom at designated times. Before doing this, however, be sure this is an authorized practice at your school.

Plan to obtain what you need for the first few months of activities on your own. Between the PTO or the PTA, the supply room, and your allotted money from the district, you should have a decent start at obtaining what you need for the beginning of the year. You might also find useful supplies in unusual locations. For example, if you need costumes or props to act out plays, you may be able to locate them at thrift shops or garage sales for very little money. If you need cardboard boxes or packaging materials for science experiments, you may be able to find a store that can give you the items for free.

This is a perfect time to think outside the box. Enlist your middle school students to be creative as well. Encourage them to use only recycled materials found around the house for class projects. Have brainstorming sessions during class to come up with ideas for finding free or inexpensive items for a specific lesson plan. This is a great lesson to teach. Incorporate budget constraints into your lesson plan. Living on a budget is a very practical topic, one that not all teens are learning at home.

Talk to the students about reusing and repurposing items. Discuss places to find useful inexpensive items that can be used for multiple purposes. Look for items that are on sale, damaged, or have been discontinued. The following is a list of potential places to consider visiting when you are seeking inexpensive supplies:

- **Garage sales**: Look for used clothing and props for plays, copies of books, bookcases, filing cabinets, assorted organizational items, and office supplies.

- **Thrift shops** (such as Goodwill or the Salvation Army): Sift through used clothing and props for plays and used furniture, such as bookcases and filing cabinets.

- **Local newspapers:** Search classified section ads for used items for the classroom, including furniture, props, and office equipment. Newspapers are also good for storage, cleaning, and decorating bulletin boards.

- **Discount stores:** Inexpensive art supplies are great for projects and bulletin boards, furniture, and school supplies.

- **Home improvement stores:** Discounted items can be used to build projects or items needed in the classroom, such as bookcases and items for family consumer science and tech ed classes.

- **Craft/sewing stores:** Discounted items can be used to create class projects and artwork for bulletin boards.

- **Local industries:** Local companies may be willing to donate older model computers and other technological items; other local business items may be donated for special projects. Call around and be specific in your requests.

- **Grocery and liquor stores:** Sturdy boxes and crates make for handy storage or class projects.

- **Doctors' and dentists' offices:** Ask any place with a waiting room containing magazines and newspapers to save old copies for your class for cutting out pictures and words for projects and bulletin boards.

Use your imagination everywhere you go. Keep potential activities in the back of your mind everywhere you go. If you plan to include dramatic readings in your lesson plans, you could put together a trunk of old clothes and props from thrift stores and garage sales.

Local newspapers are usually willing to give away the ends of the paper rolls because they are useless for printing. This paper is great for creating murals for history lessons. Grocery stores and local industries will be thankful to have you pick up empty boxes rather than pay someone to take them away. Printing stores and industries also have stacks of papers that are printed on one side, but can be flipped to use the other side. When you use recycled materials, you can incorporate lessons about the environment and recycling.

The possibilities of what your students can create from the materials you will gather are endless. Starting out as a new teacher, gathering the supplies you need seems like an arduous task. As you continue year after year, however, you will continue to accumulate supplies, easing the burden in the future.

STORAGE

At this point, the room should be clean and arranged the way you want it. Now you need to figure out where to store textbooks, learning aids, and other school supplies. Every school is different, and rooms even differ within a school. First, determine what you have to work with. Next, check with the secretaries and custodians to see whether there are any extra shelves, tables, bookcases, or other storage units in the building. Finally, after exhausting those options, you may need to consider bringing in something from home or purchasing something inexpensive that you can use. The following is a general list of areas you will have available for storage:

- Your desk
- Bookshelves
- Tables
- Windowsills

- Filing cabinets
- Storage boxes or crates

Hopefully, you will inherit a room that already has bookshelves. You will need shelving for textbooks and supplementary materials that need to be easily accessible to students. You will also need shelving for your own books, binders, and other supplies. If you are lucky, your classroom will already be set up with what you need. Newer schools may have convenient built-in shelving and cabinets.

Some schools have discretionary funds to purchase classroom furniture. If that is the case with your school, your bookkeeper may check with you to see what you need. Peruse your room and make sure you have plenty of shelving. If not, and if your school makes the offer, take advantage of those discretionary funds. Teachers can never have too many shelves or cupboards. If you do not need them later and they are in your way, you can always have them sent to a storage closet.

Ideally, schools should provide each student with a book to take home and the teacher with a classroom set of the same text. That is not always the case, however. As you will soon discover, it is best to determine what is available and then determine how to best use those resources.

CHAPTER 7:
Handling Paperwork

Teaching requires organizing mounds of information, from education plans to lesson plans to worksheets. This plethora of paperwork can turn into a confusing load if not properly organized. Learn what you need at your fingertips and decide ahead of time what would best fit your organization style. For example, the day's lesson plans should be readily available, but most teachers need not crowd their desks with an entire unit.

When organizing your classroom, allocate sufficient space for paperwork. Some districts are trying to use less paper. In those districts, you may be allocated a computer for your classroom and have access to network software for lesson plans, seating charts, attendance sheets, and grading all in one. They may even have a program for digital textbook and equipment tracking. Regardless, it is still important to keep a hard copy of those records. The types of records and the amount of paperwork you keep depend on three things:

- School district requirements
- Subject matter specifics
- Personal choice

The teaching profession requires a large degree of paperwork in general. As a new teacher, this can be one of the most overwhelming areas. Here are some suggestions for keeping everything organized.

BINDERS

Binders allow for easy access for items that require filing, are not frequently viewed, and take up a lot of space. Use a three hole-punch for these files and store them in binders. A few examples of these items are:

- Attendance records
- Individualized student education plans
- Parent contact information
- Examples of student work
- Grade records for class, per semester
- Completed lesson plans

For easiest use, organize them in a logical sequence and keep the same system for all of your binders. If you have different systems, it may become confusing and difficult to locate items when you need them. The following are some suggestions for organizing your binders:

- **Priority:** Arrange papers from front to back, with the most important items in the front.

- **Date:** Assemble documents from front to back, with the newest items in the front.

- **Sequential:** Organize items alphabetically or numerically, depending on the item.

- **Class:** In some middle schools, you might teach multiple classes of individuals. In order to keep each class's paperwork separate, consider assigning each class a color.

Binders are relatively easy to store. Be sure to label them properly, so you can find what you need when you need it. Store the binders in a location that corresponds to the information contained within and how often you need to access it. For example:

- Desktop

- Desk drawer
- Bookshelves
- Tabletops
- Windowsills
- Filing cabinets

FILING

Paperwork that does not take up as much space and does not contain student-specific information is best maintained in a filing system. Files should be labeled with easy-to-read tabs. Multiple files that are similar in nature may be grouped together. For example, you may have one hanging file containing many singular files, each containing a stack of lesson plan worksheets. There are multiple ways to store files as well. You may be lucky enough to inherit some items from your predecessor. Some items may be available from a school supply closet and you may have to purchase a few items as well. The following are a few of the filing systems you could use:

- **Filing cabinets:** Preferably lockable, these are good for storing confidential files and personal belongings, such as a purse.

- **Hanging files:** These organizers come in many sizes, shapes, and colors. Some hang over a door, hung on a hook or suspended by magnet. Check the school policy before hammering anything into a wall. If something does need to be adhered to a wall surface, contact custodial services for assistance.

- **Slat files:** These sit atop of a desk, bookcase, filing cabinet, or windowsill and are good for items you need to access frequently.

- **Wire racks:** These are similar to free-standing wire racks that can sit on top of a desk or table.

Student-Oriented Paperwork

As a teacher, you will be deluged in paperwork from time to time. In order to stay organized, set up a filing system at the beginning of the year. Determine all the paperwork you will be responsible for, and label your files accordingly. The following sections describe some of the paperwork you might encounter.

Student records

As a teacher, you are responsible for keeping records on the students in your class. If there is a question about an issue concerning a student, you need to be able to produce documentation. For that reason, most school districts recommend keeping these records for three years after the students complete your class before shredding them. The following are a few examples of the information you need to document and file:

- Student attendance
- Parent/guardian contact information
- Record of conferences and other parent/guardian meetings
- Record of meetings or discussions with students
- Documentation on any disciplinary actions, such as interventions, warnings, detentions, or referrals
- Interim grade reports
- Anything requiring a parent or student signature
- Copies of certain pieces of graded work, either exemplary or items of concern
- Individualized lesson plans

Attendance

Schools require attendance records from homeroom period to determine who is present at the beginning of the day. Depending on the system at your school, the record may be a handwritten form that is hand-carried to the attendance office or it could be a computer-generated acknowledgement sent via inter-office mail from your classroom computer. The school maintains these records. You will want to keep you own attendance records of the students in each of your classes. This will be important if someone misses an assignment or a test. The expectation in most middle schools is that students should be responsible for getting notes, finding out the assignment, and speaking with the teacher about making up a test. The easiest place to maintain this information is in your grade book, either paper or electronic.

Student and parent contact information

The main office also maintains student and parent contact information. It is helpful to have this information available at a moment's notice. There are multiple ways to gather this information. Some schools have the information embedded in the software, and it may be attached to the student roster. Some schools maintain paper copies of student directories. If your school does not have either of these, you can collect the information yourself. You can request it from the office, or you can ask the students to fill out a form the first day of school.

Behavioral intervention

Another important student record to keep is a behavioral-intervention file. It is important to document issues involving student behavior. Your school might have a suggested format. This information is intended for your protection. If anyone questions your behavior or interactions with a student or guardian, you will be able to produce your notes on how you handled the situation. For most classes, you will simply need a log to record when you have called parents for positive or negative behavior issues and to track when you have assigned a detention or written a referral. Keep copies of detentions and referrals together in a file folder in case you need to provide proof at a later time. You should also keep information regarding contact with parents and guardians, especially anything that requires a signature.

Individualized lesson plans

A student requiring any form of classroom modification will have an individualized education plan (IEP). An IEP is a document required for any student requiring modified special education. Special education is education that needs to be modified for individuals who have different specific needs, such as handicapped or gifted students.

The IEP modifications can be simple, such as stating that a student focuses better when he or she sits in the front row. The modifications might be more complicated, recommending multiple modifications for a student with specific disabilities. Either way, you will need to refer to the information when setting up your classroom and again for each lesson plan. This information is confidential and must be stored accordingly. Students are identified if they meet certain state and federal requirements. *For more information on IEPs and special needs students, refer to the section on special needs students in Chapter 12.*

TEACHER-CENTRIC PAPERWORK

The following sections describe paperwork and other responsibilities you will encounter as a teacher.

Class syllabus and assignment calendar

One of the first things you will do as a new teacher is plan the material you will teach for the year. You will start with an overall topic goal, such as American history or English literature and then break it down into a series of subtopics you plan to cover. The overview of these lesson plans is your syllabus, or what you hope to accomplish for the year. In conjunction with the lesson plans, you will determine the class assignments. These dates make up the assignment calendar. The paperwork for these items can be kept in a binder, a file, or online. Some technologically advanced schools place all of this information online. If you work in one of these schools, you may be encouraged to develop your own Web page. If you put the syllabus, calendar, and homework information online, it is beneficial for students and parents who have access to computers. When a student misses class, he or she can check the information online. Many districts are headed in this direction, but there are still many more that do not have these capabilities yet. If you work in one of these districts, you will need to type or write out your plans, photocopy them, and keep copies in your files.

Lesson plans

As a new teacher, all of your lesson plans will be new. As you try things, you will discover that some of them work better than others. You will want to make notations as you go along. Keep successful lesson plans for future classes. In addition to the lesson plan form, you will have worksheets, visual aids, and tests to save as well. You can store these in a binder, a file, or on your computer. If you do keep information on your personal or a school computer, be sure to download a copy to a portable USB drive for safekeeping. Regardless of how you want to store these units or lesson plans, decide what you are going to use and prepare that storage system before you even write your first unit. You can modify your system throughout the year, but you will find your first weeks of school a whirlwind of activities, paperwork, and learning. The more organized you are beforehand, the better.

Professional employment files

In addition to student data and lesson plan information, you will have professional items you need to keep on file. Some of the items you might want to store in this area include:

- Professional development information
- Notes pertaining to meetings and in-service workshops
- Union documentation
- Copies of inter-office memos
- Employee contract information
- Copies of any documentation you wrote

- Documentation concerning extracurricular activities you advise
- Certification paperwork
- Continuing education documentation

Keep anything that might be beneficial when it is time for your annual performance review as a teacher. You will want background information on everything that shows you are not only doing your job, but anything that depicts that you are going above and beyond.

When first setting up your classroom, keep in mind that most districts regularly provide network software that helps teachers organize their lesson plans, seating charts, and grading all in one. They might even have a program for digital textbook and equipment tracking. However, it is still important to keep a hard copy of those records. First, when planning your day or writing your agenda on the board, it is easier when you have your plan in front of you. During your first year, you will be observed on several occasions. Demonstrate professionalism by handing the administrator doing your observation a copy of your plans along with any aids you may have given your students, so he or she might also be engaged in that period's activity. Furthermore, if you are absent, your substitute teacher will need your lesson plan, a seating chart, and a gradebook when covering your class. Finally, even with hard copies of your work, make sure you back up all your important information on a jump drive. You do not want to lose all the hard work you put into planning and tracking your classroom.

CHAPTER 8:

Getting Through the First Day of School

The first day of your first solo teaching experience is both exciting and terrifying. To minimize nervousness, be as organized and prepared as possible. A week in advance, make a list of things to go over to ensure the first day goes smoothly. Write down everything you need to attend to *prior* to the first day. For example:

- **Double-check your roster.** Make sure there have not been any last-minute changes. You need to ensure you have enough textbooks and other materials for everyone in your class. Of course, if there is a last-minute change, do not panic. You can always take care of it later — it is just easier to start out with all of the simple things taken care of.

- **Speaking of supplies, check the IEPs.** Some students will require special or additional supplies in accordance with their individualized education plans (IEP). If an IEP is already in place for a student, you will have the information prior to the start of the year. For example, a student who has physical limitations, health issues, or memory problems might need an extra set of books to keep at home. Make sure you have ordered or otherwise acquired everything you will need. In some instances, you might determine that a student needs an IEP during the course of the semester. If this happens, the school psychologist and guidance counselor will include you in discussions concerning the needs of the student in question.

- **Check all furnishings.** During the process of finalizing the setup of your room, confirm that you have the correct amount of desks and chairs that are all in good condition. The last thing you need is to have someone sit on a broken chair and fall down on your first day.

- **Verify condition of classroom equipment.** Make sure everything is in working condition and that you know how to use it. Confirm any media equipment you will need for the first few weeks.

- **Review important paperwork.** During the first week of school, you and your students will handle a lot of paperwork. Make sure you have what you need and that you know what you are supposed to do with it. What is sent to the office? What gets sent home with students? What should you keep copies of in your files? Make a checklist to prevent something critical from falling through the cracks.

- **Create a welcome packet.** Write a letter introducing yourself. Include your name, educational background, some of your interests, and your contact information, such as your school e-mail address. If you have a school website, mention that as well. Do not give out personal information, such as your home phone number and e-mail addresses, or social networking information, such as your Facebook® page. Revealing personal information can create problems later if your students see you more as a friend than an authority figure.

- **Plan an introduction.** You are new to the school. Most of the students are not, but some of them might be. Plan to introduce yourself to the class and have them introduce themselves to you and each other. This helps establish a positive and friendly learning environment.

- **Include a contact sheet.** Have students fill out a form providing you with contact information concerning them and their parents or guardians. Include e-mail address, cell phone numbers, and a preferred method and time to contact the person.

- **Prepare a syllabus.** Write out a brief introduction of the class and what you plan to accomplish for the year. In addition to unit concepts, the syllabus should include a list of reference materials. For instance, if you teach a literature class, some students may wish to borrow items from the library to begin reading them. The syllabus should mention fun items, such as field trips, and major papers or projects that require more work. Not all students work at the same pace. You will encounter many students who will wait until the last minute, but there will be plenty of others who prefer to plan and organize their workload in advance.

- **Lay down the law now.** With the packet, inform students of your expectations. Include what you expect if they will miss your class and what your classroom rules are. Spell out the consequences now. For example, "If work is not completed, your grade drops X number of points" or "Three rule infractions will earn you a detention." Whatever you decide, tell them now, and stick to it. If you start out too relaxed in this area, they will take advantage of you early on.

- **Review lesson plan.** Look over your first lesson plan. What does it involve for the first week? Do you have everything you need? Practice speaking in front of a mirror. It may seem awkward, but it will help you see what you look like while you are lecturing.

Everything is set up and ready to go. You have checked, double-checked, and triple-checked all of your lists. You are positive that you have not forgotten anything. You might develop a case of the first-day jitters — but relax. Most teachers admit to having this feeling every year before they go to bed before the first day of school. Join the club. It is very normal. If you truly have checked everything and feel prepared, try to expend some of that nervous energy by going for a walk or taking a relaxing bath. Do something for yourself and then try to get a good night's sleep.

The first days of middle school will be the most significant in terms of your students' perception of you and will determine the atmosphere of your classroom for the rest of the year. Be prepared with professionalism. Middle school students can sniff out a phony a mile away. Good teaching includes knowing your topic, knowing where to find answers, and most of all, being a model of integrity. If you do not know something, do not pretend you do. Be yourself and be prepared. Make sure you are organized with your syllabus and relevant handouts, as well as with your ideas about classroom management and how you will present them to your students. Be in control and have activities to use in order to create a comfortable and safe learning environment where students do not have to be concerned about being bullied.

This does not mean things have to go perfectly. Many new teachers are afraid to be themselves in front of students for fear of losing control or ending up with students who do not like them. Being honest and forthright will be well appreciated by adolescents and will earn you respect. Students will not be impressed if you try to act their age, nor are you likely to create a synergetic classroom with everyone working toward a common goal if you are stoic and unapproachable. If there is one thing a veteran middle school teacher who still loves the job will tell you, it is to be yourself. You cannot love a job if you have to turn into someone you, or anyone else, does not like.

You will absolutely need to know your subject well, but adolescents are at the age when they have realized neither their parents nor the adults around them are the all-knowing, omnipotent people they believed them to be when they were toddlers. If a student asks you a question that you cannot answer the first day of school, simply say you are not sure but will find the information they seek. Then, follow up. Use this honest approach throughout the school year. Not only will it bring you much respect if your students see you are candid and direct, but you are teaching them one does not have to pretend to know everything. This method also encourages questions.

As you begin your new position as a middle school teacher, remember, do not doubt yourself; you have what it takes. You made it through hours of sometimes death-defying boredom in your own classes, a semester or more of student teaching, and/or years in the workforce. Do not let first-day jitters steer your thinking down the path of self-doubt. You know what a good teacher is, and you are in control.

"My advice is to establish the tone of the class from the first day — that way the students won't take advantage of you. Other than that, learn to be flexible. Your schedule can change at the drop of a hat and you will need to be able to go with the flow."

— Laura Cleveland, veteran teacher,
Steelton-Highspire School District

FIRST DAY PLANS

It is here — the day you have been waiting for. What do you have planned? Some of the first day's agenda will be dictated by the school. Ask the secretaries and other teachers what to expect so that you can plan accordingly. Ultimately, much of the first day will involve paperwork and introductions. By the third time you have been through it, you will realize it is not as bad as you had feared. Just in case, have a plan to make things go smoothly. There is nothing worse than finishing your entire day's plan in 15 minutes and having to improvise the rest of the day. The following are a few ideas for fillers if you find yourself with extra time on your hands:

1. Have important paperwork and a welcome packet sitting on each desk as the students walk in. As they file into the classroom, they can start reviewing it or filling it out.

2. Have paper items lined up in piles on a table in the room. Some teachers prefer this. It takes a little more time as the students pick up the paperwork they need, allowing you to observe the students as they come into your room. How do they interact with each other? What kind of personalities will you have in this class?

3. Have paperwork organized and ready to go in one pile to be passed out. You can do this as the students enter the room, while asking them their names to get a head start on identifying them.

4. Have paperwork ready and do nothing until everyone is in the class and seated. At this time, you can pass it out as you are talking. Moving helps

calm some people. Another option is to have one of the students pass out papers as you are talking, taking some of the attention away from you. The option you choose depends on your comfort level. As the day goes on, you might decide to try different options to see which works best.

5. After everyone has their paperwork, go over what they need to do with it. What should be filled out? When does it need to be completed? To whom do they submit it when they are finished? If it comes back to you, make sure you have designated inboxes so you do not mix papers from different classes.

Your first-day survival kit

No matter how organized you are, the day will be fast-paced, crazy, and exhausting. Plan accordingly. The following are a few items that may help you ease you through the first day:

- **Bottle of water.** Talking all day can make your mouth dry. Many teachers start the day with a large mug of coffee, but caffeine can make you dehydrated if you do not replenish the fluids. Keep a couple of water bottles in your room in case you cannot get to a water fountain.

- **Throat lozenges.** Again, talking all day can make your mouth dry and might even give you a sore throat. Have some lozenges with you for emergencies.

- **Extra tissues.** It is a good idea to have extra tissues in case you end up with multiple people suffering from colds or allergies. In that case, one box of tissues can disappear quickly.

- **Piece of fruit, granola bar, or easy-to-eat item.** This is in case you cannot get out of your room all day or find yourself starving long before lunch. A loud, gurgling stomach can be embarrassing.

- Small sewing kit and safety pins. These are for minor wardrobe issues, such as a rip or tear that might occur from snagging an item of clothing on something in the classroom.

- **Extra shirt.** This is in case you spill something on yourself.

- **Hand sanitizer and hand cream.** If you are washing your hands and sanitizing all day, you might prevent germs, but you will also end up with dry, irritated hands.

- **Breath spray and deodorant.** As a teacher, you will work long hours and be in close contact with many people throughout the day. Be prepared with these items so you do not have to deal with embarrassing odors.

It is better to be over-prepared rather than find yourself wishing you had something you needed in an emergency. If you do not have space in the classroom, consider keeping small items in your desk and keeping a box of other emergency items in your car. If you will not have a car at school or close by, find out whether there are other areas to store items, such as a faculty lounge or locker.

FIRST IMPRESSIONS

You probably already understand the importance of first impressions. This is doubly important when you meet your new middle school students. You might have a doctorate degree, but if your students walk into a classroom to find a young teacher slouching with feet up on the desk or displaying unusual body piercings, you will not be remembered as the teacher with interesting lesson plans and a comfortable learning environment. The following are some tips for meeting your students that first day:

- **Greet your students at the door.** Get into the habit of greeting your students at the door. As you get to know their names, you will begin to use them, but on your first day, simply shake hands and introduce yourself as they enter. It is not always easy, and you will sometimes have to drop what you are doing between classes to get to the door, but starting this habit from the first day of school makes you approachable. It is a way for your students to see you as a human being and not as someone they cannot relate to. It also says to your students, "I value you enough to stop what I am doing and say hello."

- **Adhere to your school's dress code.** Your school will most likely have a student dress code. You will immediately lose reverence as the adult and leader in your classroom if your boxer shorts are hanging out of the top of your droopy, three-sizes-too-big pants or if your middle school students are eye level with your revealing cleavage. This is a matter of self-respect and respect for your students. Additionally, avoid wearing styles that students are reprimanded for, such as tongue or eyebrow piercings, backless shoes, and ripped jeans. Dress comfortably enough to move around a classroom and engage your students, but keep your clothing appropriate and professional. Remember you are an adult and a role model. In other words, do not dress like your students.

- **Do not overwhelm your students with new scents.** If you use perfume or cologne, keep it subtle. Primarily, if you teach a core subject such as math or language arts, you will probably have more than 100 students. Some of them might be allergic to the cologne you are wearing. It is also a good idea to keep extra deodorant and breath mints in your desk in case you find yourself in need. Students will hone in on your weak points and never let you forget them.

- **Have your first-aid information and kits ready.** Be prepared for even the smallest emergencies from your first day forward. Make sure you have checked with the school or district nurse and are aware of any student allergies and the EpiPen procedures. An EpiPen is used for extreme allergic reactions potentially causing blockages in airways. No school will allow you to administer even the most common medications, such as stomach aids or aspirin, so you are limited on what you can have in your first-aid kit, but it is still important. Bandages are especially necessary for your middle school classroom and will help your students avoid several unnecessary trips to the office. You also might want to buy a jumbo-size pump bottle of hand sanitizer for both you and your students to use.

Using hand sanitizer after contact with students who have colds or other illnesses will likely prevent you from having to use a sick day and can keep your students from having to be absent. Be especially cautious if it is your first year working around children, who are more likely to be germ carriers than adults.

- **Blood-borne pathogen kit.** Your principal has probably informed you about and supplied you with a blood-borne pathogen kit. If not, you can become familiar with the U.S. Department of Labor's Occupational Safety and Health Administration's regulations regarding blood-borne pathogens at **www.osha.gov**. All teachers are required to follow these common-sense guidelines. In a nutshell, they mean that "all human blood and certain human body fluids are treated as if known to be infectious for HIV, HBV, and other blood-borne pathogens." Your kit should be easily within reach so that you can quickly help a student with a serious injury or even a simple scrape.

- **Answer all questions honestly.** Do not miss a beat if a student, especially a sixth-grader who is also new to the school, has a question you cannot answer. Students dislike know-it-alls just like adults do, and it is better to provide accurate information rather than make something up to prove your worth. Let your students know from the first day of school that whether it is an academic topic, school policy, or cafeteria issue, if you do not have an answer, you will help them find one. Then follow up. Your honesty and action is their first introduction to your integrity.

- **Smile.** There is an age-old teacher adage that says, "Never smile the first week of school." Hogwash. Teachers who seem overly stoic and unapproachable often will be the same teachers whose nerves students love to trample on. They end up being the same teachers with record referral writing. Do not worry. You have established expectations for your classroom, you will be prepared with your syllabus, and you will use your leadership skills while getting respect from your students. Think about the teachers you most respected and loved. More than likely, on the top of the list are those with a sense of humor and whose smile you can remember.

- **Do not pretend to be perfect.** You are not perfect, and you will make mistakes. As long as they are mistakes and not careless oversights, they are human nature. Pretending otherwise will do two things: Lead students to believe mistakes are bad and alienate them from trusting your integrity. Additionally, you will create unnecessary stress for yourself. Instead, relax and do your best. Use your leadership skills to teach students how to rectify mistakes. And a sense of humor never hurts. Be open to listening to students. Let them know they are welcome to come to you before or after class with questions about miscalculated grades or simple misunderstandings.

Time for introductions

The easiest thing to do is talk about yourself and the class. Give the class an idea of what to expect during the course of the year. If you tend to get nervous or tongue-tied, read the information off the sheets in your welcome packet until you get comfortable.

Have the students introduce themselves, or to make it more interesting, write a list of questions on the board and pair people up that are not seated next to each other. Have them interview one another and present their findings to you and the rest of the class. In addition to stating the person's name, have each person ask probing questions, such as, "If you could hang out with one famous person for the day, who would it be, and why?" The answers will tell you a lot about the individuals in your class. Plus, it is a great icebreaker for everyone.

Icebreakers

Fit your introduction activities into your first few days of classes, depending on the time allotted in your curriculum map. Some curriculum maps, which determine what the district expects you to cover, do not leave room for too many introductory days. Even if they do not, obviously you want to use your class time wisely and engage your students in educational activities from the first bell to the last. However, activities such as learning rules, getting to know each other, and reviewing your syllabus are highly important for a good classroom foundation. Education World (**www.educationworld.com**), a website with tons of free lesson plans and activities, states that ice breakers "can reveal who the class leaders might be, what skills and special abilities students possess, and how well students might work together."

There are numerous types of icebreakers. One of the easiest educational middle school icebreaker ideas involves students introducing each other. At the beginning of the class, ask students to come up with five questions they would ask if they were interviewing a celebrity. Some examples of potential questions might include:

- What is your happiest moment?
- Who inspires you?
- What do you consider to be your greatest achievement to date?
- What is one interesting fact about you that people do not know?

Other time-fillers

The following are tips for ways to fill extra time you might have during your daily lesson:

- Find out how much the students know about the subject you are teaching. Ask questions and see who can answer them.

- Discuss current events that pertain to your subject matter.

- Have everyone pull out a blank piece of paper and write down one question they have about you or the class and fold them. Put them in a jar or other container and shake them up. Pull out questions at random to answer until the bell rings.

- Design an information-gathering scavenger hunt for them to use amongst themselves. Make sure to have enough questions to keep them busy and tell them they cannot use anyone more than once. For example, ask them to find one person in the class for each category. The following are a few suggestions:

- Find one person in the class who did not eat breakfast this morning.
- Find one person who had a birthday this summer.
- Find one person who saw a movie this summer.
- Find one person who left town this summer.
- Find one person who speaks another language.
- Find one person who plays a sport.
- Find one person who plays a musical instrument.
- Find one person who read an unassigned book this summer.

Tricks to memorize names

Being able to remember names correctly is an asset in any business, and teaching is no exception. It might not seem like much to teachers, but incorrectly pronouncing or spelling a student's name can cause resentment. Memorizing your students' names is one of the most important tasks that you will have to master as a teacher. Being able to call your students by name is the first step in getting to know them, creating a relationship with them, and gaining their respect, which helps you maintain control of your classroom. If you cannot memorize your students' names, they will view you as an insensitive and uncaring adult.

"Always try to call a student by his or her name. Get to know the names as soon as possible. This is a good idea for the other people you interact with as well. This is one of those tips from Dale Carnegie's book, *How to Win Friends and Influence People*. That book is my Bible; I have read it ten times. It is the best. I would recommend the book to anyone and everyone."

— Kathy Heisler, special interest teacher,
Cumberland Valley

One way to begin learning your students' names and their proper spelling is to review their records. While you look over the folder of each student, write his or her first and last name, and then jot down notes beside each name such as color of the student's hair or something funny he or she said. This will help you remember specifics about each student and, therefore, help you remember their names.

There are a number of other tips for helping you to remember your students' names. The following are a few suggestions:

- Make a seating chart and have students sit in assigned seats for several weeks until you can associate names with faces.

- When you read forms from your students, mentally picture each face with the information you are reading.

- Associate words or phrases with names as you get to know the students.

- Walk around the room while students are working, checking the roll with each pupil.

- On the first day of school, have each student say his or her name and repeat it to learn the correct pronunciation.

- Repeat student names each time you talk to them. This will help cement it in your memory.

- Note pronunciation remarks on your roster and mark notes about characteristics for each student.

- If you forget a student's name, admit it, and then ask for help. When the student says his or her name, repeat it, write it down, and say it again.

Watching your students interact with one another is a great way to get to know them. Helping them get to know one another is another way to learn about your students and also helps them learn to value one another.

CASE STUDY: GETTING TO KNOW YOUR STUDENTS

Sandy Baughman
Seventh grade English teacher
Good Hope Middle School
Mechanicsburg, Pennsylvania

Sandy Baughman has taught at both the elementary and middle school level in the Cumberland Valley school district. She has 15 years of teaching experience. She has a bachelor's degree in elementary education and a master's degree in reading. She acquired both degrees from Shippensburg University.

No matter how many years you have been teaching, the first day of school will always be filled with apprehension for the student and the teacher. While the student is nervous about who is going to be in their classes and what their teachers will be like this year, the teacher is thinking about possible behavior problems, individual student needs and all of the IEPs that need to be followed to the smallest detail. The first day of the school year sets the tone for the classroom environment. Respect for the teacher and for students is an essential part of a healthy learning environment. First impressions have never been so important. As a middle school teacher, it is imperative that you create an environment that is controlled, yet not stifling. It also needs to be inviting and relaxed. If you want the kids in your class to be successful, they need to feel accepted and comfortable enough to take risks. This first day is extremely important. Students will leave your class with an impression. Do you want them to be scared and anxious or interested and curious? It is up to you to make that first impression. The passion you have for your class needs to be evident to your students.

Expectations need to be high from day one. It is important, however, to not have unrealistic expectations. They range in age from 11 to 14 years old. Some of the students are very young and would still benefit from an elementary setting, while others are socially and emotionally ready for more responsibility. If you are teaching sixth grade, it is important to remember that these children are coming from an environment in which they possibly remained in one class all day long. It is important to consider all of the changes that these students are suddenly facing.

On the first day, it is important to take some time to get to know your students a little bit and let them know what you expect from them while they are in your classroom. First, go over the rules of your classroom. Do not overload them the first day. They are seeing at least five other teachers that day. Keep it light. You can tell them more as the year progresses. You also want to learn a little something about them. You do not want to pry into their personal life, but it is nice to know a little something about each of the kids. I will share some of the silly, fun, and somewhat informative games that I have played throughout the years.

The toilet paper game. Pass around a roll of toilet paper. You can start one roll at the opposite end of the room to speed up this process. Have the students take some toilet paper and pass it to the next person. Do not tell them how much to take. After everyone has torn off some paper, tell them that now they must count their squares. For each square they take, they must share something about themselves with the class.

The string game. This is the same idea as the toilet paper game. Pass a skein of yarn around the room and have each student cut a random length of string. When all have a piece of string, share with them that when it is their turn, they must wrap the string around their finger and talk about themselves for the amount of time it takes to wrap all of their string around a finger. If they stop talking, they need to stop wrapping.

Question ball. For this game, you will need to prepare a beach ball ahead of time. Divide the ball into many sections with a permanent marker. In each section write a question. Have the kids sit on top of their desks and gently pass the ball around the room to their classmates. When a student catches the ball he or she answers the question that is touching their left thumb. The game continues until all students have had a turn. Repeat as long as time allows.

Three truths and a lie. Have each child write down three statements about themselves. Three of the facts need to be true and one of them should be a lie. Have the students take turns reading their statements. The class then guesses which statement is a lie. The kids really enjoy this activity.

As the students are talking, think about what they are saying and try to make a connection with their names. At the end of the period, attempt to identify each student by using his or her first name. Continue to take five minutes of every day at the end of class to go over names. In the evening read over names and attempt to picture the student. You will be surprised at how many names you remember in two to three days.

INTRODUCING YOUR BEHAVIORAL EXPECTATIONS

Aside from introducing yourself, make your expectations of student behavior the first order of business. This way, students can participate in beginning-of-the-year activities and you have control of your classroom from day one. Display and point out the classroom-management rules. The school handbook usually has a page the student and parent must sign to indicate they have read and understood the policies and procedures. Some schools will have an assembly that explains the rules. This will include everything from the dress code to gum-chewing to the consequences of possessing a weapon on campus. The handbook of rules and policies is often distributed with early-year paperwork the first day of school. In the Lake County, Florida school district, each student gets a copy of the handbook. Eustis Middle School opted to introduce the students to the rules and regulations through technology. The school administration created a video with different segments that show the principal or one of the three assistant principals explaining school policy. It is shown the first few days of homeroom. Additionally, if a new student comes to school in the middle of the year, that student can view the video and have a clear understanding of policy and discipline at Eustis.

You can simply point out and verbally review expectations. It is often more memorable, however, to use activities to demonstrate the reason behind classroom guidelines. Help make the classroom a more comfortable learning environment for students by introducing your expectations and requesting their input. The following are some suggestions:

1. **Be seated, quiet, and ready to work when the bell rings.** After introducing yourself and handing out the syllabus for your class, have students copy the day's agenda and objectives, which you have written

on the board for them. Be prepared to offer pencil and paper, as some students will come to class unprepared. Have students write down your agenda, such as making a list of the papers you will be handing out for parent signatures. Each day, students should also copy activities and the daily objective written on the board in their planner or notebook as soon as they enter the class.

2. **Keep your hands and feet to yourselves.** A fun way to send your students a clear message about this issue is to use the analogy "stay in your hula-hoop." Create a visual by doing this exercise with your class on the first day of school when you are teaching your expectations. Use hula-hoops to demonstrate the approximate personal desk space a student can expect. You can pick them up for under $20 in most toy and department stores, or you can order them online. Demonstrate "staying in your hula-hoop" by placing two of the plastic rings next to each other. Have two students volunteer to stand in the middle of each hula-hoop. That is his or her personal space. The students may not reach outside of that space, throw anything outside of that space or touch anyone who is outside of that space. The message will be clear, and all you will have to say for your warning is "stay in your hula-hoop."

3. **Raise your hand and wait to be called on before speaking.** You will want to establish this procedure whether the students are working in rows, groups, or centers. If you or a fellow student is talking, students need to raise their hands and wait to be called on before they can speak. Hopefully, your classroom will be an interactive one, and there are times when students will be working cooperatively with others and conversation is necessary and encouraged. During instructions, whole-class discussions, or other quiet classroom times, however, students need to respectfully let others speak. Students understand and will be willing to share why this rule is an important one. They know chaos will ensue and no one will be able to hear everyone else if all students talk at once. You also might want to explain that this rule applies to college and graduate classrooms, too.

This is not a matter of children being on their best behavior, but a matter of common courtesy.

4. **Democratically established classroom expectations.** Have a discussion with your classes on what students believe are important expectations in a classroom where they learn. Ask what they believe should be expected of students their age. Tally the results, list them on the board or a large piece of paper, and have the students choose the two they feel are most important. Add them to your three original expectations. You have just facilitated the decision-making process with your students and given them ownership in their own classroom management.

FIRST-DAY PAPERWORK

You will need to track the plethora of paperwork that accompanies students home during their first days of school. This will include district-required documents such as Internet permission forms, emergency contact information, and the signed portion of your classroom syllabus. Keep paperwork in order by creating a file for each type of document. Keep them in the file until they have all been returned before sending them to the appropriate party, such as the media center or front office. Save any extra copies of forms for students who may enter your class at a later date. Also, be sure to track what has been returned by using a checklist. *There is a sample checklist in Appendix B of this book.*

YOUR SYLLABUS

A syllabus is not only your way of sharing classroom protocol and academics with your students, but for many teachers, it will be your first introduction to the adults in their lives. Let it be a professional reflection of you. Remember, this is middle school. Do not hesitate to share the excitement you have for your first year of teaching. The syllabus needs to be professional but reflect your personality. Students may be receiving several syllabi, and you do not want to frustrate them by making yours wordy and confusing. Include a paragraph or two to introduce yourself, and make it user-friendly with lots of white space and perhaps some graphics. Use bullets and lists and keep your font readable and at 12-point size. If the syllabus is difficult to understand, crowded, and verbose, it will not be read by your students. Keep in mind that middle school parents also will be reading several syllabi — probably six, one for each period — so the more reader-friendly, the better. Clear your syllabus with an administrator to make sure you have met all the requirements expected by your school and are not including any information the administration would prefer to leave out. The following are the items you will want to include:

- Head your syllabus with your name, position, and contact information. In the first paragraph, let parents know that this is how you can be contacted and that you will return e-mails or phone calls within 24 hours.

- List the name, authors, and publishers of any texts and/or workbooks you will be using during the year. If students are assigned their own text for the year, as opposed to using one of a class set, make sure parents have the information about fines should the book be lost or destroyed.

- Include a basic skeleton outline and/or samples of what you will be studying during the school year. You may want to include the district's curriculum map or a link to a website where it can be found, unless your administrators advise otherwise.

- Grading scales can vary from teacher to teacher. Some use points while others use percentages, so include it in your syllabus.

- Include your list of expectations — at least the three you established as important to your classroom — and the consequences for not following rules.

- Include a list of supplies and keep it minimal. Students are often responsible for their own supplies, such as paper, pencils and/or pens, notebooks, and folders. Be careful, however, and check with your administrator. You might be required to include a disclaimer letting parents know that students cannot be fined or denied a public education if they do not purchase supplies.

- Finally, be sure to include a signature line stating that both the student and parent have read and understood the syllabus in its entirety. Make that section detachable so parents can keep the syllabus to refer to during the school year.

During the first few days of school, review the syllabus with your students and leave plenty of time for a question-and-answer period. Offer students extra credit if they bring back the signed portion the day after it has been distributed. Keep extra copies for students who join your classroom later in the year. Be ready for this. It is common in suburban and urban areas in today's transient society to get new students on a regular basis. Ask your fellow teachers whether this is a common occurrence at your school. If it is, keep easily accessible copies of documents that help your new students fit right in.

Your syllabus might be the first contact a parent has with you. Use it not only to relay your expectations, but to inform parents what their children will need to be successful in your classroom during the school year. *Refer to Appendix C for a sample syllabus that includes all of the above and foreshadows the excitement the teacher feels about the upcoming school year.*

"One of the biggest challenges I had was learning how to deal with students who needed to get caught up on the material. There were several situations during my first year of teaching where I needed to help students who were new, on vacation, or out sick catch up on over a week's worth of material. My advice to other new teachers is to have students identify homework partners who can help them with notes and assignments that they may have missed."

— Mike Lutz, world cultures teacher,
Cumberland Valley school district

SEATING CHARTS

Teachers have different opinions on setting up seating charts for the first day of school. Some teachers believe it is the only way to avoid chaos. Other teachers let students sit where they want on the first day so that they can better observe their behavior. For example, by allowing them to sit where they want, you may be able to gain valuable insight about your students from day one. For example:

- Do they sit with their friends?

- Who are their friends?

- Are they talkative or withdrawn?

- Do they gravitate to the front of the room or head for the back?

- Do they appear engaged or distracted?

On the other hand, providing a seating chart for students their first day in your classroom can create order and help you get to know their names. It depends on your individual teaching style and your ability to remember names and faces. Furthermore, establishing and keeping updated seating charts will make it easier for anyone covering your classes during meetings or absences.

If you want to create a seating chart for the first day and have no idea where to start, you can ask the guidance counselor for assistance or you can simply arrange everyone alphabetically until you get to know your students better.

Some schools have computer technology such as eSembler that will create a seating chart for you. *Refer to Appendix D for an example of a seating chart arranged by eSembler.* Find out if your school uses eSembler or a similar computerized seating chart before creating one manually.

If you plan to follow a seating chart on the first day of school, label each desk with a name tag so the students can easily find their desks. Have them use these name tags for the first week or so until you are comfortable with all of the names and faces in each of your classes. Once you get to know your students, you will have a better idea of where to seat them in order to provide the best educational experience.

CHAPTER 9:
The Core of Teaching — Lesson Plans

You have prepared the room and made it through the first day of school. Now, it is time to get into the essence of teaching: the lesson plan. Lesson planning is important for all teachers, but it is particularly important for first-year teachers. This task will take an inordinate amount of time your first year. Accept that now and you will save yourself a lot of frustration. Find time in your daily schedule to create, review, and revise lesson plans. Make textbooks, a computer, and all of your other resources available while you are working on the plans.

The good news is once you find certain lesson plans that work, they can be reused with only a little tweaking in subsequent years. It is worth the effort you will spend. As the proverb goes, "If you fail to plan, you plan to fail."

INTERDISCIPLINARY UNITS

A favorite and effective strategy of student-centered planning among proponents of single-school culture is interdisciplinary units. These are themed units taught in more than one subject and can encompass anything from two teachers covering two different academic areas to one themed unit covering all academic disciplines. These units are particularly effective. Interdisciplinary units assist students in making connections in the vital relationships between subjects. For example, note the following image. It is taken from a middle school student's "Periodic Table of Elements Family Album." During this lesson, students can learn the use of "personification" in poetry and prose and how to apply it in their own writing. In science, they learn the periodic table of elements.

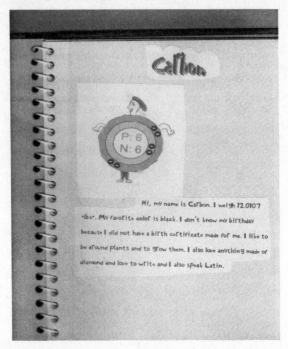

"My advice is to be creative and put yourself in the mindset of the student. These individuals are surrounded with images from TV, movies, the Internet, music, and video games. If the subject you teach is not exciting, think to yourself, "How would I most enjoy learning about this?" You need to think outside the box when working in this environment or you will lose the students to the distractions they have within their home. Along those lines, I like the following quote from Plato: 'Do not train children to learning by force or harshness, but direct them to it by what amuses their minds, so that you may be better able to discover with accuracy the peculiar bent of the genius of each.'"

—Jim VanderSchaaff, social studies
teacher, Pennsylvania Cyber School

ENGAGING UNITS

Creating units that will engage and educate your students is an exciting experience for new teachers. In the beginning, you might find it a little time-consuming. Luckily, there is a plethora of experience and resources at your fingertips. Follow the simple rules of teaching and the guidance you will find in this chapter, which includes the following basics:

1. Find plans that will encourage your students to live up to their potential.

2. Be sure to know how to read your district's pacing and curriculum guides.

3. Know your state's standards and/or benchmarks.

4. Vary your lesson structure between centers, small and whole groups, and individual tasks throughout the week.

"One of the things I like best about teaching middle school students is their responsiveness. They are the perfect age for teaching. They are old enough to really understand things, and they can be quite intelligent and forthcoming. They are also still young enough to not be jaded. My best advice for new middle school teachers is to engage your students and celebrate them. When they feel that you are genuinely interested in them, they will really respond."

— Nancie Menapace, English teacher,
Good Hope Middle School

How you plan will also depend on the structure of your school. For example, if your school is incorporating single-school culture, you will have academic teams in which teachers with the same grade level and subject plan together. Some schools utilize interdisciplinary planning in which lessons are coordinated across the academic subject areas.

Although you might encounter unusual elective subjects such as agriculture in certain areas of the country, the basics are the same everywhere: math, reading/language arts/English, science, social studies, physical education, art, and music.

CHOOSING A FORMAT

Creating lesson plans is one of the most important aspects of your job as a teacher. When you are hired, ask whether your school has a specific lesson plan format it wants you to use. If it does, use it. If the school has a standard, there is a reason. Embrace it no matter what you were taught in school. Some school districts have individuals hired to help teachers with lesson plans. In Pennsylvania, school districts use the learning-focused strategies (LFS) model.

Dr. Max Thompson founded the Learning-Focused company in Boone, North Carolina. His idea was to develop an improved mechanism for lesson planning that would maximize teacher efforts and increase student achievement levels. The strategies work with lesson planning from kindergarten through 12th grade. The strategy is currently used in more than 2,000 schools.

According to the Learning-Focused website (**www.learningfocused.com**), the model is based on five primary areas: planning, curriculum, instruction, assessment, and school organization. The Learning-Focused schools model has provided state-of-the-art professional development and innovative instructional resources, products, and technology to more than 2,000 schools, districts, and educational agencies across the nation.

At Cumberland Valley High School, they employ two individuals as instructional coaches. It is their responsibility to assist teachers with the LFS lesson plan-related issues, such as:

- Questions concerning instructional strategies
- Expanding teachers' use of a variety of resources
- Model the end results you wish to see from your students
- Provide follow-up on professional development
- Research best practices in education

- Meet one-on-one with teachers to reflect and provide feedback
- Assist teachers in using data to drive instructional decisions at the classroom and school level
- Support the mentoring program
- Design professional development workshops

If your school district does not use a specific program or format for lesson plans, there are numerous Internet sites that provide examples. The following are a few free websites to visit to get ideas:

- Teachers.net (**http://teachers.net/lessons**): This website includes over 4,000 free lesson plans. You can browse the plans by grade level and subject matter.

- Teacher Planet (**www.teacherplanet.com**): In addition to a variety of lesson plans for each grade and subject matter, this site includes templates, guidelines, and advice for finding other lesson information online.

- Lesson Planet (**www.lessonplanet.com**): Lesson Planet allows you to set up an account to access more than 225,000 pre-qualified lesson plans and accompanying materials that have been reviewed by professionals in the field.

- Teacher Vision (**www.teachervision.fen.com**): This website provides ideas and examples for lesson plans and graphic organizers. It also includes worksheets that may be printed off. The information is provided by grade, subject area, and theme.

CASE STUDY: THE IMPORTANCE OF APPROPRIATE LESSON PLANNING

Cheryl Gruver
Instructional coach
Cumberland Valley School District
6746 Carlisle Pike
Mechanicsburg, Pennsylvania 17050-1796
www.cvschools.org

Cheryl Gruver is currently an instructional coach for the Cumberland Valley school district. She trains teachers on lesson planning, assessments, and best practices. Her prior teaching experience includes being a dance instructor, French teacher, and school musical director.

I had my first big "ah-ha!" moment my second year of teaching. My first year, I was emergency certified. I had taken education courses eight years ago, and my second semester as an emergency-certified teacher was my student teaching semester. This meant that I did not have any current courses on lesson planning. Nor did I have a cooperating teacher working with me on a daily basis. I was on my own. The assistant principal at the time did give me a tip to use when planning: Plan at least three different activities per lesson.

My first year went fairly smoothly. I was teaching a language survey course that only met for one marking period. This is ideal for a first year teacher. At the end of each marking period, I would reflect on my lessons and find new activities to incorporate. My unit on numbers was (what I thought) my best unit. I had many different activities in the lesson, and the students really seemed to enjoy them. I continued the year reflecting on my lessons and adding to my plans.

At the beginning of the following year, I adjusted my lessons by reviewing my reflection notes in my electronic copies. My lesson was activity-rich, but content-poor. I had some wonderfully engaging activities that reinforced numbers, but the students mastered the content long before the lesson was summarized. I never stopped to assess students formatively and check to see if they mastered the information. I just kept plugging away at the activities because they were in my plan and fun for the students.

This lesson made me stop and think about the learning targets for this unit. How does the lesson meet these targets and what activities best meet the needs of my students? I continued to keep a record of all of the activities in the unit to use when I needed, but I no longer used all of the activities. I identified the three most effective activities and kept them in the lesson, while the rest were filed as reinforcement or differentiated assignments.

I thought to myself, "How did this happen?" After teaching, I reflected immediately on the effectiveness of a lesson. I used the district's lesson plan format. I had three activities. Ah-ha! Were these activities the best ones to move students toward the learning targets, or were they simply fun? It finally occurred to me that I never went back to look at the learning targets and the goals of the lesson when I added activities. I just kept adding and never looked at the lesson as a whole.

What I took away from this moment was that it is necessary for teachers to always start with the end in mind. When reflecting, one should revisit the learning targets to ensure modifications do not affect the end goal. Teachers have a lot of curriculum to cover, so educators need to plan efficient lessons that will accomplish end goals in a reasonable amount of time. Today, I always plan with the end in mind, and as a result, I can cover more information in greater depth. Students retain information better when teachers teach for quality and not quantity. Quality planning and backward design helped me reach more students. They helped me become a better teacher.

ELEMENTS OF A LESSON PLAN

Every teacher has his or her own unique way of teaching. Likewise, each individual has his or her own individual manner of creating lesson plans. A lesson plan is the way in which a teacher organizes his or her method for relaying a specific topic. Lesson plans are required for each day of teaching. They help teachers meet the curriculum set by the school district and state. You will have a general idea of what types of lessons you want to include when you create your syllabus at the beginning of the year. Each lesson plan needs to be carefully written out prior to starting a new unit of study.

Trying to meet the required curriculum goals can be overwhelming, especially for a new teacher, but there are ways to attain the goals without overburdening yourself and your students. While some school districts are very clear about the curriculum you are to follow, other districts are not. If your district is one that clearly expresses what you are required to teach and when you are to teach it, then be sure to get a copy of these materials and follow the set plan they have made for you. When you go to acquire these outlined materials, you will need to ask for the content standards or the educational standards. If they do not have these, you can ask for the grade-level standards or the district curriculum expectations.

There are as many types of lesson plans as there are potential lessons. Certain elements, however, remain standard. Good lesson plans should include the following:

- **Title.** What is the lesson about? Provide a title that is self-explanatory. You may know everything about the lesson now, but you may not remember it in the future.

- **Lesson plan identifier.** Use a date or corresponding text. This number provides you with something for easier organization and identification later on.

- **Curriculum areas (or concepts).** What areas of the curriculum correspond to this lesson plan? What standards can be applied? The course curriculum, or regular course of study, is predetermined by the school district. There are government standards for each grade level. For example, pre-algebra, American history, basic grammar, and life sciences are predetermined to be part of the middle school curriculum. To prepare a lesson plan for one of these math courses, find out the primary learning goals for students completing this course and include them in this area of your lesson plan.

- **Essential question.** This area of the plan relates to the standards and requirements that must be achieved based on school, state, and national guidelines. It was previously stated as the lesson plan objective. Now this information is worded in question form and concerns the big ideas.

- **Pre-assessment (or screening).** Before introducing any new material, you must understand your students' prior knowledge on the subject.

- **Direct instruction.** Plan what information you must provide to the students during the lesson.

- **Student activities.** This area includes detailed descriptions of your specific plans for the students. Include information on the type of activity, such as whole group, small group, or individual activity.

- **Summary or closure activity.** Wrap up the lesson with an activity that reviews what you taught.

- **Materials.** Plan what materials you and the students will need.

- **Homework and testing.** Plan measurable assignments that correlate to the lesson.

- **Assessment.** Provide different types of assessment on each lesson. This ensures that you will have sufficient information from the different types of learners.

"As a first-year teacher, one of the biggest challenges I experience is creating lessons that engage all students to the point where I can determine whether they have learned what I am teaching. In social studies, sometimes it is difficult to teach without lecturing. When I lecture, I believe it becomes important to generate discussion and feedback from the students. For them to become interested, I need to make relevant connections for them. So, when I do my lesson planning, I have to consider these questions:

- How can I make it relevant to students?
- How can I get students actively engaged?
- How will I assess students as I am teaching my content?"

— Mike Lutz, world cultures teacher,
Cumberland Valley High School

Know the requirements

Before you put anything in writing, consider the standards that you must abide by. During your orientation, you will be given information on what the district priorities are in respect to the curriculum. You will also be given information on benchmarks for the national, state, and local criteria that must be met in your course. Whether you are planning for a specific unit or the entire course, you need to factor in the requirements first. You should:

1. Address the standards and requirements and put them in the lesson plan first.
2. Add in the material you would like to cover if you have time.
3. Identify material for enrichment and/or remedial needs in case it is warranted.

If you went to college to become a teacher, you undoubtedly spent hours on the topic of creating lesson plans. One of the biggest complaints new teachers have concerns lesson plans. Many people feel they are inadequately prepared for the reality of lesson planning. Others feel that they cannot use or do not need much of what was taught to them concerning lesson plans, such as the formal lengthy format. The most important thing to remember is to stay calm and not get overwhelmed. Once you get the hang of it, you will be able to create lesson plans simply, quickly, and efficiently. Until then, spend the time writing out all the information and make sure to include all of the required standards.

"Long, written out lesson plans are not helpful. You are almost never able to get it all done and then you just have to write it out again for the next day. It is better and more useful to plan a whole unit at a time; by doing this, you can just pick up where you left off the next day."

— Jen Mulhollen, itinerant learning support
teacher, Cumberland Valley School District,
Mechanicsburg, Pennsylvania

State standards and benchmarks

In order to gain a comprehensive understanding of how to use your curriculum pacing guides and what you are expected to teach your students, you must have a comprehensive understanding of your state's standards and benchmarks. State standards are the criteria your district or state has set in place for your students to meet. In the United States, each and every state must have standards for measuring the benchmarks of student achievement. In fact, the state testing trend is based on whether your students meet the benchmarks your state has set forth for them. Each state has its own procedure for developing standards, and the structure varies widely from state to state, so you will need to focus only on your state's standards. To view your state's standards in comparison to other states standards, refer to the Developing Educational Standards website (**http://edstandards.org/standards.html**).

STEPS TO CREATING YOUR LESSON PLANS

Once you determine the format you will be using and the elements that you want to include, you can start working on the lesson plan itself. To get started, consider the following points:

1. Get to know your students as quickly as possible. Once you understand their individual needs and learning styles, you will be able to incorporate the information into your lesson plan. Planning for your students' individualism creates a better lesson plan and increases your chances for successful students. Remember to consider different learning styles. Everyone learns differently and each person has areas of strength and weakness.

2. Ask yourself: "How does each student learn best? Are they auditory, visual, or kinesthetic learners?"

3. Do any of your students qualify as gifted? (Note: The U.S. Office of Education defines gifted and talented children as those "identified by professionally qualified persons who by virtue of outstanding abilities are capable of high performance. These are children who require differentiated educational programs and service beyond those normally provided by the regular school program in order to realize their contribution to self and society.") These students may have gifted individualized education plans (GIEPs) to provide suggestions for their curriculum enhancements.

4. Do any of your students qualify as special needs individuals? The Individuals with Disabilities Education Act of 2006 defines "special needs" students as children who have been diagnosed with developmental delays, or any child who has been evaluated as requiring special education and related services. These students have Individualized Education Programs (IEPs) to specify any modifications that need to be made to the classroom or their work.

5. Ask yourself: "Do I need to add or subtract anything to the lesson plan to aid in the success of my gifted or other special needs students?" Realize

that this may be more feasible in some environments rather than others. If you have 30 students in every class and have seven periods of different students every day, it may take longer. Do what you can.

6.   Consider the objective. What do you expect to accomplish? What are the school's expectations? Ask the students what, if any, expectations they may have. At the middle school level, the students may surprise you with earnest thoughts on this matter. Finally, make sure you accomplish any required standards.

7.   When you create your daily lesson plan, be sure to include excess material. Include multiple possibilities and activities for relaying the information. Then, prioritize by importance and effectiveness. That way, you will not miss significant subject matter. Planning extra material also provides you with a safety net. It is better to have activities that you do not get to, rather than having a group of preteens with too much free time on their hands because you worked through the material much quicker than you anticipated.

8.   Use specific measurable objectives. Look at the benchmarks included in the standards for this subject at this grade level. You may know what you want to accomplish in the broad sense, but you need to be very specific and concrete regarding the objectives you plan to accomplish. This will be particularly helpful when you need to assess the standards that need to be met. It is also helpful when someone else, such as a substitute, needs to use your lesson plan.

9.   Be sure to include an area of differentiations. These are modifications or adaptations for students. This part of the plan relates any changes that need to be made for special needs students. This includes ideas on enrichment, remediation, and disability adaptations.

10. Specific information regarding materials is also important. It encourages you to obtain the necessary items early. This is also particularly helpful if a substitute is using your lesson plan.

11. Write down succinctly descriptive steps for the lesson. Show exactly how you will reach the objectives with the plan.

12. Include a form of lesson plan closure. This may be a return to your initial anticipated plan. By reviewing the anticipatory set, you will have a better idea about reaching your lesson plan goals. Allow students to do the summarizing by social processing.

13. Finally, write up an assessment stating whether the goals have been met. Every lesson plan may not necessarily warrant an assessment, but it is important to note if the objectives have been met with each lesson plan. Use authentic, meaningful projects, not busy work. Try to use real-life applications where possible.

Important items to consider

In addition to spending time researching the material you are going to teach, review the school's calendar. Dates and activities that are already built into the schedule might cause you to change your lesson plans. It is easier if you obtain this information prior to planning your lessons. The following are a few suggestions for things that you may have to work around when planning your lessons:

- School scheduled events
- Holidays
- Standardized testing
- Assemblies
- Field trips
- Observation days
- Scheduled fire drills

As you plan your daily lessons, you first need to consider the school calendar. School breaks from a normal, daily routine will affect the flow of learning in your classroom. When students are on winter break or spring break, everything they have learned before the first day of break will be lost; therefore, you should plan your lessons around your school calendar.

The calendar your school follows will determine the long breaks in your district, whether it uses a traditional calendar, a single-track calendar, a year-round calendar, or a multi-track year-round calendar. The traditional calendar is the nine-month calendar schools followed for many generations. A single-track calendar is a balanced calendar for a continuous period of instruction. Summer vacation is shortened with additional vacation days scattered throughout the school year. A year-round calendar is for schools that have session all year with long breaks intervening throughout. The multi-track, year-round calendar is used by some schools to alleviate overcrowding and was designed for schools with a shortage of classroom space. Multi-track schools divide teachers and students into groups of approximately the same size, and each group is assigned its own schedule. A four-track year-round calendar school can extend a capacity for 750 students to 1,000 students.

When you determine which parts of the school year are scheduled for the long breaks, you will want to schedule the more in-depth, longer lesson plans between these breaks. In a traditional school, you will have 180 days to teach your class, but on average, you will lose approximately 30 of those days due to assemblies, special events, and/or visits or other interruptions. It may be easier if you organize your lesson plan as a unit plan. Take each unit and break it down into daily lessons by including the following:

- Identify your objectives.
- Determine what materials you will use to teach said objectives.
- Plan alternatives for absent students, especially if your lesson plan can be hard to make up.
- Decide how you will assess your students on these lesson plans.

Consider your calendar with all school breaks marked off, then pencil in when your units of teaching will begin. This way, you will be able to use your calendar when writing your lesson plans in your plan book.

By taking the time to determine the objectives you want your students to learn, you will find you are reaching your set curriculum in a more organized way. Some schools ask their teachers to follow specific guidelines. If this is the case, administrators will let you know during meetings scheduled before school begins. In planning your daily lessons to meet the set curriculum, you will also want to remember the state-mandated testing that takes place in your school.

> "The first year is really difficult. This year, I have had difficulty finding time to plan lessons and grade assignments while having to worry about all of the other small issues that did not pop up while I was a student teacher. Prioritize what needs to be done. I have placed lesson planning as the most important issue that needs to be addressed. Grades will get done when the lessons are planned. Keep your nose to the grindstone in the first year, celebrate the small achievements, and do not let yourself get dragged down by the difficulties you encounter. Everything is a learning experience, and it only gets easier from here."
>
> — Mike Lutz, world cultures teacher,
> Cumberland Valley High School

Putting it into practice

Some school districts require you to list the standards met on every lesson plan you use. This is another good reason to list your objectives for your lesson plans. It is important to become familiar with the material you are teaching your students. You will find that, with all you have to do in one day, there is not nearly enough time to prepare for tomorrow's lesson plan. But your lesson plan does not need to be a long, drawn-out explanation of each step — you can make your lesson plan brief and use your own personal shorthand while doing so. Although the college professors might have taught you that the long, explanatory lesson plan is the proper way, before your first year of teaching is over, you will find yourself thinking it is a waste of valuable time.

Some school districts require their teachers to turn in their lesson plans, and if this is the case for you, you may want to add a few lines of explanation. Most schools do not mind brief plans as long as it is understandable in the hands of a superior.

How you write your daily lesson plans is up to your discretion. The best advice is to write them in the way that works best for you. While some teachers will write out their lesson word for word, others will use one to five sentences and naturally fill in the gaps while teaching the class. Whichever style is best for you is fine as long as you know the material and can answer questions your students ask. It is fine to be surprised by a question you have no answer for and learn the answer to that question with your students, but if you do not know the material and have no answers, you are going to look bad, lose the respect of your students, and be an ineffective teacher.

While you prepare your plans, you will want to decide how you will assess your students to determine whether they have learned the material. When you have decided which method of assessing you will use, whether through testing, an activity, or a recital, you can then look at the lesson plan again and see whether it will prepare the students appropriately. If the lesson does not teach the student the material needed for the assessment, you will need to either change the lesson plan or your material in the assessment. Keep in mind that lesson plans and assessments go hand in hand.

> "Over the course of five years of teaching, I have learned that the best thing you can do is to over-plan until you know how long each class takes with the different activities."
>
> — Rachele Dominick, advanced placement English teacher, Cumberland Valley High School

USING TECHNOLOGY IN YOUR LESSONS

We live in a digital age, and middle-school-aged students are quite knowledgeable about cutting-edge technology. The affluence of your school district might or might not affect how many students own their own technological gadgets. Regardless, for the most part, your students will be aware of the technology. Your best bet for keeping them engaged and out of trouble is to know what devices they are exposed to and to use whatever is available to you in the classroom.

Research the current trends in classroom technology. Many schools have media specialists and technology departments. If your school does not have either, you may want to look into a technology grant. Many websites provide information on applying for specific school grants. The National Education Association (NEA) is one such organization. It lists available grants on its website (**www.nea.org/grants**).

There are many Internet lessons available for teachers who use computers in the classroom. A computer should be used as a tool, not a replacement for the teacher. The following are some of the ways computers can be used in middle school lessons:

- Differentiated lessons allow students to work on the same material at their own pace.

- Self-correcting math lessons continue until the student figures out how to solve the problems, such as Firstinmath and Study Island.

- Interactive field trips coordinate with material when actual field trips are not an option, such as a map and information pertaining to former president Thomas Jefferson's home at Monticello in Virginia.

- Language skill reinforcement programs such as Rosetta Stone help students learn a language.

- Textbook manufacturers sometimes have entire textbooks online so students do not need to worry about taking the books home. Online textbooks also allows students who are absent to keep up with reading and other work. Some even provide interactive study guides for test preparation.

- Word processing programs not only help students with typing skills, but they strengthen spelling and grammar skills by allowing students to see the words and correct their mistakes.

- Computers in the classroom permit teachers to show students where to find information and images, how to use the information appropriately, and how to cite the sources properly. This allows for teachable moments regarding copyright laws and plagiarism.

SMART Boards

For centuries, teachers used chalkboards as the only visual in the classroom. In recent decades, the messiness of writing with chalk and pounding erasers has been replaced by whiteboards. Whiteboards are flat plastic boards of different shapes and sizes that work with special markers called dry-erase markers. Whiteboards can be freestanding or hung on a wall. Up until recently, they were the standard in most classrooms in the United States.

The newest technological advance in this realm is the SMART Board. The SMART Board was invented in 1991 and manufactured by the company SMART Technologies. The term SMART Board comes from the name of a specific brand of what is essentially an electronic whiteboard. It features digital capabilities, is touch-sensitive, works with the school's computer resources, and interacts with the students. For example, a student can walk up to the SMART Board and use either their hand or a special marker to answer questions, fill in charts, or complete problems. Different academic programs can be downloaded from the Internet.

The item has become increasingly popular in the last several years, and although there are other brand names, the term has become synonymous with the type of technology used in an interactive whiteboard. The original SMART Boards must be purchased by authorized resellers. These electronic whiteboards are connected to the school's computer system through the use of purchased software. They allow students and teachers to interact with the boards by using pen-like devices that are programmed with motion sensors instead of ink.

According to the SMART Technologies website (**http://smarttech.com**), these types of whiteboards are currently used in every state and all of the provinces in Canada. Prior to the start of the 2010 to 2011 school year, SMART Technologies estimated that more than 30 million students would be using their interactive SMART Boards in more than 1.3 million classrooms.

COMMON PLANNING ERRORS BY NEW OR INEXPERIENCED TEACHERS

Despite the amount of time spent on lesson planning in college, most new teachers are unprepared for the reality of this type of planning. It takes time, thought, energy, focus, and concentration. Even the most experienced teachers will have lesson plans fall apart for one reason or another. No matter how tedious lesson plans seem to be, there is a set of necessary elements for a reason. First-year teachers often:

1. Forget the importance of writing course, unit, and daily plans in entirety and think they can "wing it" once they get into the classroom.

2. Despite the importance of mandates, ignore or inadequately prepare for national, state, and district standards.

3. Mistakenly prepare only a list of activities instead of a full-fledged lesson plan.

4. Lecture non-stop to the students for the entire lesson and forget to incorporate other elements.

5. Move over the material too quickly and forget that many students need to be taught in different ways.

6. Eliminate elements that provide for different learning styles.

7. Forget to make provisions for adaptations.

8. Spend too much time on one aspect of the lesson or unit and fail to prioritize.

9. Forget to assess the prior knowledge base of class and individual students before starting a lesson. This creates problems if a piece of the necessary knowledge base is missing. It also prevents the teacher from helping the students to make connections with previously learned material. It can

also be a problem if students already know the material and you waste time being repetitive, thus boring the students.

10. Fail to use elements that evoke critical thinking skills from the class.

11. Inadequately prepare the students prior to testing students.

12. Forget to provide sufficient practice opportunities for using the material.

13. Eliminate homework and other assessment opportunities that help students master the material prior to testing.

14. Neglect to prepare required materials ahead of time.

15. Forget to sufficiently fill out lesson plans that a substitute could easily follow.

16. Forget to use formative assessment to guide instruction.

Experienced teachers believe that lesson plans get easier with time. The first year, you will spend an inordinate amount of time on this task. You will make mistakes and learn to adapt the plans accordingly. Be patient and flexible, and learn as you go.

CHAPTER 10:
Making the Grade

The true test of the effectiveness of your lesson plans comes in the form of grading. Grading is the formula teachers use to assess if the students understand the concept.

Grading is the assessment part of your lesson plans. In a perfect world, if you took everything into consideration and taught the unit effectively for all different types of students, the majority of them would succeed on any form of measured testing. It is not a perfect world, however, and no matter how hard you try to incorporate everything you have learned, there is still a good possibility that a percentage of your students will fail to grasp the lesson when they are tested. Why is this? You are taught in college to accept the differences and to plan your lessons accordingly so that no one is left behind. The truth is that you can never plan for all the variables. You can be patient, observant, and sympathetic when you know what the variables are, but you will not always be able to know what they are. Sometimes you may be able to see that there is a problem, but you may not always be privy to the information you would need to help a student. Some students are not forthcoming about what is going on in their lives. For example:

- You may not always know what is going on at home.
- You may not always know if the student is getting enough sleep or adequate nutrition.
- You may not always know if homework is incomplete because the individual did not want to do it, or if there is a valid reason.

"The enthusiasm of middle school students can be a double-edged sword. While it keeps things fresh and interesting, it also can result in trouble making some topics stick. Good teachers should be conscious of the various learning styles, but middle school teachers especially need to repeat important information in multiple formats. Even if something is written on the board or a handout, it should be discussed verbally as well. Middle school students' attention spans can be short. There is a need to literally rein them back in sometimes. I do this by actually saying, 'All right. Stop. Everyone look at me. Are you looking at me?' By doing this before moving on, the students are more likely to understand what I am talking about, instead of repeating something five more times if I did not secure their full attention first."

— Nancie Menapace, sixth grade English teacher, Good Hope Middle School, Mechanicsburg, Pennsylvania

In addition to student variables, some subjects are more challenging than others to grade, as some concepts are less concrete than others. For example, interpretation of art and literature is much more subjective than knowing the elements in the periodic table and what they are used for. Neither is more or less important than the other; they are just different. This chapter provides advice that will help you in assessing your students. It includes information on the following:

- **Learning styles**. Use this information to help plan your lessons. How your students learn will affect how well they understand the lessons and how they do on assessments.

- **Assessments**. Review the types of assessments and how to use them in your classroom. Read a case study of a first year teacher's grading challenges.

- **Rubrics**. Learn how to effectively use this assessment tool.

- **How you are graded as a teacher.** Understand how your students' performance will affect you and how you will be assessed as a first year middle school teacher.

LEARNING STYLES

Lesson planning and assessment are the two main components of teaching. Many college courses cover these topics, but because they are somewhat intangible concepts, they are difficult to grasp until you are teaching in your own classroom for the first time. One factor that helps in the areas of lesson planning and assessment is the concept of learning styles. A learning style pertains to the method of communication that is most effective with an individual. For example, if you need driving directions, how are you most apt to comprehend them? Do you prefer to see a map, have someone tell them to you, or figure it out as you drive? The way you learn or best understand a new concept is your learning style.

There have been many theories and models related to learning styles over the past four decades. Two of the theories are particularly helpful in basic lesson planning. The first of those theories concerns learning styles. The VARK model, which is described below, is the most commonly used model. VARK stands for the four learning styles: visual, auditory, reading, and kinesthetic. It essentially states the way the brain understands new concepts determines where an individual falls into a basic learning style group. For most people, one of these styles is usually dominant and another might be secondary. When you have a student who appears to be struggling, consider the following concepts — perhaps you can modify the way you deliver a lesson or reconsider the way you have been assessing that individual:

- **Visual learners:** These individuals learn best by seeing. They are very aware of nuances in body language and facial expressions. These students enjoy visual displays and are more likely than their counterparts to take copious notes. Visual learners will naturally gravitate to the front of the classroom. As a teacher, you will reach them by using visual aids, such as diagrams, handouts, and overhead transparencies. These students do not have difficulties making up work, because they can pick up the information easily from the textbook, notes, and handouts.

- **Auditory learners:** If you have students that do well in class, but do not appear to take many notes when you are lecturing, they may be auditory learners. They will understand the material better by paying close attention to you, rather than by writing things down. They are very aware of voice pitch and variation in tone of voice and volume. To these individuals, *how* you say something is as important as *what* you say. They will enjoy lectures with class participation. Auditory learners do well when they are in your class, but they may have difficulty making up work if they are absent. Reading over someone else's notes will not be as effective. If you have an auditory student with special needs, it may be beneficial to allow them to use a tape recorder for the lectures. Listening to it again will help them more than studying the material from a textbook. Auditory learners tend to have greater verbal tendencies.

- **Reading/writer-preference learners:** Students with reader/writer preferences learn best by rewriting their notes or copying material from a textbook to study. Rewriting what they read programs the information into their memory. If a few of your students seem to study a lot by reading the material and listening in class, but cannot seem to transfer what they learned at test time, it might be beneficial for them to recopy their notes or make an outline. Write key facts on the board or display information on an overhead transparency for these students to copy.

- **Kinesthetic learners:** These individuals tend to have the most difficulties in a traditional classroom. Kinesthetic learners learn best in a physical manner and do not like to sit still for long periods. They need to move around. They learn best by doing and touching. Sitting in a classroom listening to a lecture for 45 minutes is painful for these individuals. To reach this type of student, incorporate visual aids that can be passed around. They would also enjoy creating a physical project in class or acting out some part of the lesson.

Some students are more obvious in their learning style than others. To help you gauge the learning styles of your students, use this question: If you needed to determine how to get to a friend's house, how would you do it? Would you:

a.   Ask for directions and remember what you were told.

    b.   Find directions online and print off to take.

    c.   Write down the directions and take them with you.

    d.   Follow someone else who is going there.

The way a person answers is a good indication of his or her learning style. Consider the first word in each answer.

    a.   "Ask" indicates an auditory learner.

    b.   "Find" indicates a visual learner.

    c.   "Write" indicates a reader/writer preference.

    d.   "Follow" indicates a kinesthetic learner.

If you listen carefully for keywords in how students would handle a simple task, you might be able to tell what their learning styles are. You can also have the students take a written quiz or an interactive quiz online at the LD Pride website (**www.ldpride.net/learning-style-test.html**). Note: This website addresses issues with learning disabilities, but the learning style quiz is for anyone, not just people with learning disabilities.

Another widely accepted learning style model is the theory of multiple intelligences. In 1983, Harvard University professor Howard Gardner developed the theory as an argument to the accepted manner of assessing people's intelligence. The theory states that there are eight separate forms of intelligence. In other words, if someone does not appear to have a strong inclination in one area, it is not an indication of his or her intellectual capabilities. The following chart illustrates the theory of multiple intelligences.

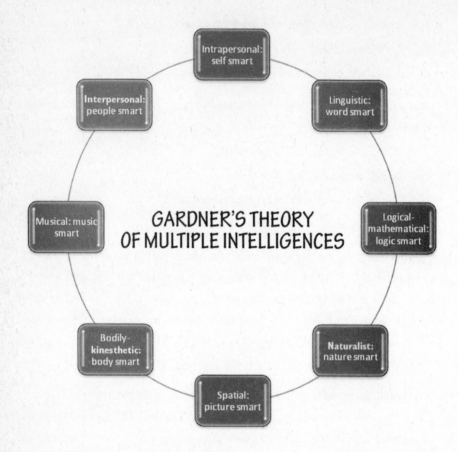

The eight types of multiple intelligence are:

Linguistic intelligence: These individuals are "word smart." They have exceptional vocabularies and speak eloquently. These students will excel at speaking in front of the class, using humor, debating, and remembering information that is told to them.

Logical/Mathematical intelligence: These students are "logic smart." They are skilled in applying logic and reasoning. These individuals will enjoy solving math equations, doing science experiments, and deciphering logic problems.

Naturalist intelligence: People with these capabilities are "nature smart." These students will be most apt to recognize and categorize things in relation to the environment. According to Gardner, this intelligence pertains to "the ability to recognize and classify plants, minerals, and animals, including rocks and grass and all variety of flora and fauna." These students enjoy grouping and categorizing. (Note: This category was not one of the original seven intelligences; it was added later, and some educators dispute the legitimacy of this addition.)

Spatial intelligence: These students are considered "picture smart." Their abilities will include completing puzzles, understanding charts and graphs, and drawing.

Bodily/kinesthetic intelligence: These people are "body smart." They prefer to express themselves by moving. They are very coordinated and excel at sports and other physical endeavors. Projects that allow them to use their hands would be preferable.

Musical intelligence: These are the "music smart" students. Musical learners respond best to music. Memorizing something in song form is very helpful.

Interpersonal intelligence: These individuals are "people smart." They are sensitive to others around them. They are always trying to ascertain everyone else's point of view. They do not like confrontation and do best when everyone is cooperating. These individuals work best in a group.

Intrapersonal intelligence: Students with intrapersonal strength are "self smart." They are more analytical and reflective than others. They might get caught up in their own daydreams and feelings. These students are most effective when they understand the benefit the material has to them.

CASE STUDY: USING GARDNER'S THEORY OF MULTIPLE INTELLIGENCES

Gretchen Pugh
Sixth grade science teacher
Good Hope Middle School
Mechanicsburg, Pennsylvania

Gretchen Pugh has 13 years of teaching experience. She has her bachelor's of science degree in earth and space science and is currently working on completing her master's degree in education.

My education prepared me for the academic side of teaching. I received a solid background in earth and space science. The education-based classes, or "teacher classes" as we called them, allowed us to see how students learn in different ways. Gardner's theory of multiple intelligences touched me the most. His philosophy is that everyone is intelligent in some way. He suggests that you just need to allow them to show you their intelligence in a way that they excel. I try to incorporate his philosophy in my daily teachings.

Through my own personal experiences, I have found that I am not a strong test taker, but given the right outlet, I could show you that I understood the concept. I realize that many of my students may share a similar experience so I need to provide many opportunities for them to show that to me.

The best way for the kids to learn is when they are engaged. I do not always have a hands-on activity that goes with the lesson, but when I can I try to get them to move or interact in some way. When I see them participate, I know they are learning! I also know that I get bored easily, and if I am bored, the kids could be too. I often try to spice up the lesson with a crazy dance, song, or some kind of peer interaction. I often throw in humor during my teaching. I think that helps too.

One lesson plan I use that students seem to particularly enjoy incorporates my love for Gardner's theory of multiple intelligences and pop culture. It was inspired by the TV show *American Idol.* Some students excel in music and this gives them an opportunity for them to shine. Keeping current with what the kids like is really important in keeping their interest too. When I developed the lesson, I knew that many of my students were fans of the show or at least were very interested in music.

The assignment was for them to create a song about minerals and perform it for the class. They had to incorporate at least five mineral facts into their song. They were permitted to work in groups and could put extras in their performance if they wished. Extras could include costumes, props, instruments, and appropriate dance moves. I realized that although some students may excel at this, others may be completely embarrassed to have to stand in front of their peers to sing, so I decided to only grade them on the actual lyrics. The class would vote for the best performance for each class. The winners would earn extra credit and a golden ticket to the auditorium where we would perform the sixth grade *American Idol* finals. The kids had an amazing time and still talk about it years later. The best part is that they even remember the mineral facts because of their songs! Sometimes we have to "trick" them into learning.

Another great lesson that the kids enjoy is for the students strong in the bodily-kinesthetic and musical intelligences. I created dance moves to help them understand the three plate boundaries and three different seismic waves released by an earthquake. It really helped them to remember how the earth was moving during each one of the examples. I made sure I chose some of their favorite songs to dance to. They loved it and they learned the concept.

In addition to learning styles and other unforeseeable student factors, there is the issue of subject matter. Not all subject matter can be graded objectively. For example, an art project must be graded more subjectively than a test on the periodic table of elements. As a new teacher, how should you develop grading policies that will work? First of all, remember you are a new teacher. This is one of the most challenging areas for a new teacher because there is no one concrete formula to follow. Every subject is different and every teacher has his or her own approach to grading. As you will find with most everything else this year, there is a lot of trial and error involved with the first year of teaching. So, where should you start? Begin by understanding the terms and trends in education today.

ASSESSMENTS

Although students, teachers, and parents still refer to the grades on a paper test or project, the term used in education today is "assessment." Assessment is a form of appraisal and evaluation. It is essentially a method for determining the value of the item in question. In the world of education, the value comes from determining whether the student understood the lesson, and to what degree.

As a teacher, you were taught the primary distinctions of assessment. They are:

- Formative and summative
- Objective and subjective
- Referencing formal

Grading, or assessment, is and always has been subjective. In an attempt to keep things fair and equal, there are middle school grading policies. In order to comply with federal and state mandates such as No Child Left Behind (NCLB), public school districts have moved toward standards-based assessments. To use this system correctly, you must understand the difference between formative and summative evaluation and teaching, which are:

- **Formative assessment**: This form of evaluation develops student understanding and mastery of the material. Completed homework assignments, class work, and group interaction fall into this category. Formative assessments, also called educative assessments, continue throughout the lesson plan. For example, this may occur in the form of a teacher providing feedback to the student during the class. If formative assessment is used correctly, the teacher can gauge student progress and offer assistance when and if it is needed. Challenges still arise when some students grasp the material more quickly than others. That is why you need to account for enrichment in your differentiation.

- **Summative assessment**: This method demonstrates the student's individual mastery of the lesson as determined by tests, quizzes, papers, and other projects. Summative assessments evaluate the student's grasp of the concept at the end of the lesson plan.

The point of formative and summative assessment is to have your students' grades truly reflect their mastery of the subject. As a new teacher, it will take time, practice, and a lot of trial and error until you achieve the correct balance of measurement in this area. The following are some suggestions to help you in the meantime. Consider the following:

- The point of grades in using formative and summative assessment is to show mastery. In order to achieve the desired results, you as a teacher need to clearly articulate and document what you consider to be a clear indication of mastery.

- Use rubrics to show the student what is expected for the assignment and how it will be graded.

- Grades are intended to reflect student progress. Along those lines, you should never use grades as a punishment or as a reward.

- Formative assignments are intended to help you gauge the class and individual student's understanding of the topic. Any assignments in this area should only form a very small percentage of the overall grade.

- Summative assessments should comprise the majority of the lesson plan grades, and subsequently the overall grade for the marking period.

- Some teachers include class participation and overall effort into their grades. This is very subjective and cannot be measured objectively. It also does not necessarily indicate mastery. For that reason, this should not be used in this method of grading.

- Since the primary focus of formative and summative grading is to ensure each individual student has understanding and mastery of the subject, group work should not be a portion of the student's overall grade.

- In working toward improving the understanding level of each individual student, test retakes should be allowed within reasonable boundaries that are established up front.

- Formative assignments should be intended for the express purpose of assisting students and allowing them to practice the skills they need to master.

- Anything that you assign as work should be graded to provide feedback to the students on their progress.

- For accurate summative results, you as a teacher have multiple tests, projects, and papers depicting mastery in all the skills that relate to the topics of the unit.

- Final overall grades should be primarily summative. If true mastery is achieved, the grades will reflect consistency.

"Every school has its own report card and grading practices. The school gave a general explanation of the grading policies when I started, and I felt it was sufficient for me. My biggest challenge as a new teacher has been trying to find a consistency in my grading procedures. With all of this material being so new to me, is it difficult to know what I expect as a high quality assignment. Consistency in grading will come in time. Until then, I attempt to make my rubric as specific as possible, so if questions arise about grades, I am able to answer specific concerns."

— Mike Lutz, world cultures teacher,
Cumberland Valley school district

ALL ABOUT RUBRICS

The primary mechanism for grading in the formative and summative assessment methodology is the rubric. The grading tool is a method for clearly stating the teacher's objectives in any given assignment. It explains what grade the student can expect based on how well he or she masters the objectives. The written explanation is written by the teacher and given to the student prior to the paper or project so they know on what they will be graded. The rubric concept is beneficial to everyone. Parents and students see the rubric before the work is completed, making it less subjective.

If you recently graduated from college, you are probably familiar with rubrics. If you are unfamiliar with them, a rubric is a piece of paper divided into blocks. Each block represents a set of criteria and standards pertaining to the assignment. It is actually a very simple tool. It takes opinion and subjectivity out of the equation. Teachers enjoy using rubrics because they take a lot of guesswork out of grading, which saves them time. The grading points are determined prior to the work being completed. The teacher checks off the squares that coincide with the student's work and the grade manifests itself. Rubrics are used for all subjects for any assignment that is graded. *Refer to Appendix E for a sample rubric form.*

Your school might have programs for creating rubrics. If not, there are numerous sites online for creating rubrics. They are all very easy to use. You can start from scratch, or you can find a sample that is for a specific subject or task. The websites post examples for all different subjects at all grade levels, for multiple types of graded assignments. The following are a few teacher recommended sites:

- Rubrics for Teachers (**www.rubrics4teachers.com**): This website provides a large variety of blank rubric templates for multiple subjects and grade levels.

- Teachnology (**http://teach-nology.com/web_tools/rubrics/secondaryrubrics.html**): This website is an online teacher resource for lesson plans, printable worksheets, and rubrics. It assists teachers in creating custom rubrics.

- Makeworksheets.com (**http://makeworksheets.com/samples/rubrics/custom.html**): This website requires you to become a member. Members can access rubric templates or create custom rubrics.

Using rubrics helps students evaluate their own work. It clarifies the teacher's expectations. To use your rubrics in your class, follow these steps:

1. Prepare and show the students good examples of the type of work you expect from them. Create examples depicting poor quality. Let the students compare the quality of the work.

2. After showing the examples, list the criteria that will be used in the rubric. Discuss what qualifies as good work in the highest expectation categories. Ask for student feedback as you go, involving them in the process.

3. Once the criteria for the highest expectations are established, discuss the gradual variations of that quality. In other words, great work includes all aspects of the project and exceeds the expectations; good work meets all the criteria; fair work meets some, but not all, of the criteria; and poor work does not meet any of the expectations of the assignment.

4. To determine if the students understand the assignment and the expectations, ask the students to test the rubric on sample assignments you create. This also allows you to determine whether they thoroughly understand the expectations of the assignment. As the students use the model, have them make any changes to their own work. This step allows you to use formative evaluation to see whether there are student difficulties with understanding the expectations.

5. After they modify their work, ask them to exchange work with another student for peer evaluation and feedback.

6. At this point, students will make additional modifications based on the peer review. Have students revise again based on the feedback they receive.

7. The final step is teacher assessment. This is the summative step. Use the same rubric students used during the revision process and assess their work. If students follow each step, the final product should be much better. The majority of students will at least meet all the expectations, and a number of students will exceed them.

HOW YOU ARE GRADED AS A TEACHER

Students are not the only ones who need to be concerned with assessments. As a student teacher, the cooperating teacher and other student teacher supervisors observed you. As a new middle school teacher, you will again be subjected to observation. Middle school principals, administrators, and department chairs may all perform the evaluations for new middle school teachers. They sit in on classes and observe the teachers at three different points in the year. Depending on the school district, multiple observations generally continue for the first few years of teachers. After that, you will still have observations, but they will be only once a year. As a new teacher, you should ask your principal how frequently you will be observed and in what manner.

There are two types of observations: scheduled and unscheduled. Scheduled observations occur when the principal or other administrator notifies the teacher that he or she is going to be coming into the classroom for an observation visit. These allow the teacher to prepare to be observed. You can plan your lessons accordingly and tell your students what to expect. The other type, unscheduled visits, can create anxiety for even the most seasoned teacher. For a new teacher, the thought of a school administrator dropping in for an unscheduled classroom visit is truly terrifying. After all, everyone has bad days, and there is always a chance for an unexpected visitation to occur on one of those days.

Most schools try to incorporate both types of observation in the evaluation process. By visiting the classroom at both scheduled and unannounced times, the administrators get a more accurate picture of what kind of teacher you are. It shows how you are able to organize and orchestrate a planned lesson; it also depicts how you hold up under pressure when nothing goes as planned. In addition to seeing how you handle yourself and the class, the following are a few of the things administrators are looking at during the observations.

1. **Curriculum**
    - Content quality. To what degree is the subject matter covered accurately?
    - Appropriateness of material. Is the material appropriate for the topic and the grade level?
    - Organization of lessons. Does the lesson plan make sense and is it relayed logically and sequentially?

2. **Instructor effectiveness**

    - Presenting material. Are you presenting the material effectively?

    - Explaining concepts. Are the concepts relayed clearly so that everyone understands?

    - Garnering student interest. Are the students interested and engaged in the lesson?

3. **Students' response**

    - Amount of student participation. Does the lesson allow for student participation? Are the students participating?

    - Quality of student participation. Do you get the appropriate feedback and participation from the students?

The thought of being observed causes some new teachers to panic. If that happens, stop and breathe. You were hired because you had the necessary skills to do the job. You are capable. Take a second to regroup and continue teaching as if no one was in the room to observe you. Continue to teach without getting flustered and you will be more apt to control the environment. If you stay calm, you will get better student participation. If you get nervous, they will get nervous.

BASIC EDICTS OF GOOD TEACHING

Before getting into the technical part of planning a lesson or unit, remember the following fundamental guidelines. These are the intangibles that make outstanding teachers. You will not find them on paper. Simply keep them close to heart when planning.

Expect excellence

First and foremost, expect your students to live up to their potential and accept nothing less. From the first day forward, let your students know mediocrity is simply not accepted. Students should be expected to work up to their highest individual potential in your class. Reinforce this assumption by getting to know your students' abilities and reviewing their work to make sure they are reaching for higher goals.

There are too many students whose biggest difficulty is that they have never been taught to reach for excellence. In middle school, you will find much evidence of students from whom excellence has never been expected. Indeed, there are varying accommodations for students with challenges such as autism, attention deficit disorder, and dyslexia. But the point of accommodations is to groom students to be the best they can be, not to coddle them. There are always challenges in life, and part of educating young people is to teach them that failure only means that they need to try again.

CASE STUDY: MIDDLE SCHOOL STUDENTS ARE SMART COOKIES!

Nancie Menapace
Sixth grade English teacher
Good Hope Middle School
Mechanicsburg, Pennsylvania
nmenapace@cvschools.org

Nancie Menapace has 27 years of teaching experience. She received her bachelor of science degree and her secondary education degree from Millersville University. She also has a master's degree in English language and literature from the University of Maryland.

I am blessed to have a job that I love. I love it every day, even the bad days. There is literally not a day that goes by when I do not get at least one "Wow, that was cool" moment, and that is so rewarding. How many people can say that about their jobs? Even when the overlaps can sometimes tire you out, one little bright moment can immediately make the frustration and the fatigue just melt away. For example, recently on Dress-Down Day, I was wearing a t-shirt that my district designed in 2007 to commemorate and show respect for the students whose lives were lost in the shooting at Virginia Tech. One of my younger students asked about my t-shirt. As I was explaining it, someone asked why the shooter had done that, and I said, "Well, his thinking wasn't right." Another student said, "So, he was like pi?" I looked puzzled, and a second student explained, "He wasn't rational." They had been doing circumference and pi in their math classes that day. I rewarded them with smart cookies.

I used to toss rolls of Smartees candies at students and say, "Smart move!" when they made a particularly keen observation, but when schools started to be more careful regarding unhealthy food, I switched to slips of paper which read, "Mrs. Menapace thinks that I'm a smart cookie." I allow them to use the cookie as a late homework pass or cash it in at the end of the marking period for five bonus points.

During this discussion, a third student related the discussion to our current novel, *Tuck Everlasting*, asking, "Wouldn't the Tucks be like pi too, because they go on forever?" Smart cookie for her! Then from a fourth student, "If a person devoted his whole life to memorizing pi, wouldn't he be like the Tucks? Never getting anywhere, never moving on?" Smart cookie! Finally someone else observed, "You're doing a lot with cookies today" and I joked, "Cookies and pi(e!)" Another student smiled at me and said, "I think you should get one for that."

Every time I share a story like that, I smile and my heart swells a little. I am privileged to work with and direct and appreciate these bright young souls every day.

Insist students earn their grades

Understand the mindset of some middle school students. They might have nothing, not even at home, that motivates them to succeed academically. For these students, it is just as easy to take the "0" than make the effort to succeed. Some students who have barely passed elementary school may not believe they have what it takes to succeed. In order to ensure success among your students, do not make it easy to fail by simply not doing the work. Make earning a decent grade and completing assignments in a timely fashion easier than failing. You can include interventions such as lunch detention, where a student will eat lunch in your class and use the rest of the time to work.

Grading

Some subjects are more challenging than others to grade. As an educator, you will need to learn to grade students for the content of the subject *and* the ability in which they are able to communicate their knowledge. One-word answers to higher-order questions should never be accepted. Questions should be answered in complete sentences. Every student in every subject should be expected to write or type his or her answers clearly and legibly. Think about how a large part of middle school students' lack of success in math is due to careless mistakes from sloppy columns and other handwriting issues. Communicating clearly, whether it be in writing or otherwise, is imperative to success in all aspects of life. If you give credit to students who choose not to accomplish this end, you are cheating them out of the knowledge they need to succeed in the real world.

Real-life lessons

When planning to give examples in your lessons, use illustrations students can relate to. For example, suppose a language arts class is learning internal conflict as experienced by literary characters. Before asking students to apply this literary concept to prose, relate it to something they might have experienced, such as the choice between looking cool in front of their friends or wearing the dorky hat their mother bought them and keeping warm on a snowy day. Or, the internal conflict that might ensue when refusing drugs from a longtime elementary school pal and losing the friendship or making a choice they know in their gut is wrong. Real-life situations will help middle school students begin to understand more abstract concepts.

When using real-life illustrations, students sometimes will get into heated debates. As long as students are respectful of other's opinions, this is healthy. They are learning to synthesize information and form their own beliefs and attitudes. Remember that this is their learning experience. The opportunity to give commentary on a multitude of issues will arise in relation to many of your lessons. Sharing experiences you have had that pertain to the lessons at hand is valuable. This is a subtle reminder that you are human, too, and might have valid life experiences that are worth listening to. You do not need to share the specifics of your personal views, however, especially when it pertains to politics or religion.

CURRICULUM MAPS AND PACING GUIDES

Curriculum maps take on many different forms in United States public education. A curriculum map encompasses the period in which your district or state thinks students should master certain standards or benchmarks. These maps often are accompanied by curriculum pacing guides. Just like any map, a curriculum map charts a course for you and your students to follow throughout the school year and shows you where, should you take a certain road, you should end. Curriculum maps can keep an entire district on target so students can move from one school to another without falling too far behind.

Pacing guides, on the other hand, are developed by you and the rest of the teaching team. They are more detailed and are almost day-to-day guidelines of what you are expected to teach. You can be as creative as you like in the way you present a lesson, but the information your students have absorbed at the end of the day must be the same. Critics say pacing guides do not offer enough time to cover the subjects you need to. Few administrators, however, will fault you for being off a day or two, if you are doing your job well and staying close to the guidelines. At one time, rookies were handed a textbook and, if they were lucky, a generic planning pad to write their plans on and then were told to go teach. Pacing guides are a much more effective way of keeping you up to par on standards and giving you an outline to plan with.

As a result, you need to become familiar with curriculum maps and pacing guides before you begin actually planning your lessons. Your department chair should provide you with this information and you might also be able to find a copy on your district's website. One district with a particularly detailed example is Dade County, Florida (**http://math.dadeschools.net**); click on "Comprehensive Math Plan." Dade County uses maps and curriculum guides throughout all academic areas, and its site gives comprehensive examples of both.

STATE STANDARDS AND BENCHMARKS

In order to gain a comprehensive understanding of how to use your curriculum pacing guides and what you are expected to teach your students, you must have a comprehensive understanding of your state's standards and benchmarks. State standards are the criteria your district or state has set in place for your students to meet. In the United States, each state must have standards for measuring the benchmarks of student achievement. In fact, the state testing trend you often hear about is based on whether your students meet the benchmarks your state has set forth for them. Each state has its own procedure for developing standards, and the structure varies widely from state to state, so you will need to focus only on your state's standards. For example, the following is a sample from the Colorado Model Content Standards for reading and writing. Note that it is generalized for middle grades five through eight. The standard is explained, the rationale is given, and how it will apply to the grades is clarified.

Colorado Model Content Standards
READING AND WRITING
STANDARD 1:
Students read and understand a variety of materials.

In order to meet this standard, students will:

- Use comprehension skills such as previewing, predicting, inferring, comparing and contrasting, re-reading and self-monitoring, summarizing, identifying the author's purpose, determining the main idea, and applying knowledge of foreshadowing, metaphor, simile, symbolism, and other figures of speech;

- Make connections between their reading and what they already know, and identify what they need to know about a topic before reading about it;

- Adjust reading strategies for different purposes such as reading carefully, idea by idea; skimming and scanning; fitting materials into an organizational pattern, such as reading a novel chronologically; finding information to support particular ideas; and finding the sequence of steps in a technical publication;

- Use word recognition skills and resources such as phonics, context clues, picture clues, word origins, and word order clues; reference guides; roots, prefixes, and suffixes of words for comprehension; and

- Use information from their reading to increase vocabulary and enhance language usage.

RATIONALE:

The goal for students at all levels is that they know and can use strategies — various ways of unlocking the meaning of words and larger blocks of text — to become successful readers. The strategies are applied in increasingly difficult reading material at each grade level. At all levels, students should be challenged to read literature and other materials that stimulate their interests and intellectual abilities. Reading from a wide variety of texts, both assigned and student selected, provides experience in gaining information and pleasure from diverse forms and perspectives.

GRADES 5 to 8

As students in grades 5 to 8 extend their knowledge, what they know and are able to do includes

- Using a full range of strategies to comprehend technical writing, newspapers, magazines, poetry, short stories, plays, and novels in addition to the types of reading material mentioned above. Students extend their thinking and understanding as they read stories about people from similar and different backgrounds.

Colorado's structure for benchmarks is equally as simple for all academic areas. The standard is explained so that teachers can easily identify and use them in their planning. Grade levels are clustered so middle school subject areas are easy to locate. You can find benchmarks for all grade levels on the Colorado Department of Education's website (**www.cde.state.co.us**). Click on the "For Parents & Students" tab and then select "Standards/Assessments" under the "Performance & Accountability" heading.

In contrast, other states have a more detailed structure. Florida provides benchmark standards for every grade level. In the following sample, the numbers you see to the left of the benchmark represent the grade level, benchmark, standard, and standard sub-categories in sequence.

Standard 7: Reading Comprehension The student uses a variety of strategies to comprehend grade-level text.	
BENCHMARK CODE	**BENCHMARK**
LA.6.1.7.1	The student will use background knowledge of subject and related content areas, prereading strategies, graphic representations, and knowledge of text structure to make and confirm complex predictions of content, purpose, and organization of a reading selection;

LA.6.1.7.2	The student will analyze the author's purpose (e.g., to persuade, inform, entertain, or explain) and perspective in a variety of texts and understand how they affect meaning;
LA.6.1.7.3	The student will determine the main idea or essential message in grade-level text through inferring, paraphrasing, summarizing, and identifying relevant details;
LA.6.1.7.4	The student will identify cause-and-effect relationships in text;
LA.6.1.7.5	The student will analyze a variety of text structures (e.g., comparison/contrast, cause/effect, chronological order, argument/ support, lists) and text features (main headings with subheadings) and explain their impact on meaning in text;
LA.6.1.7.6	The student will analyze and evaluate similar themes or topics by different authors across a variety of fiction and nonfiction selections;
LA.6.1.7.7	The student will compare and contrast elements in multiple texts; and
LA.6.1.7.8	The student will use strategies to repair comprehension of grade-appropriate text when self-monitoring indicates confusion, including but not limited to rereading, checking context clues, predicting, note-making, summarizing, using graphic and semantic organizers, questioning, and clarifying by checking other sources.

Although there is a colossal contrast in structure between the two states, the content is very similar. You will want to record the standards you are teaching in your lesson plans. Given that their configuration varies immensely from state to state, it is imperative you obtain your own state's benchmarks. They are easy to locate. If you cannot find them on your state's department of education website, call the department or your district and ask for a copy.

CREATIVE PLANNING

Today's students live in a far more fast-paced, entertaining arena than any other generation before them. Teachers are competing with Xboxes, Wiis and iPods, and this is not an easy task, but it is achievable. Fortunately, education has become less stringent over the years and answers more to the needs of our students. Incorporating technology, even cell phones, can help you plan lessons that appeal to tech-savvy adolescents. Yes, even cell phones. It is a slow movement, but some teachers are turning their greatest behavioral bane into teaching technology. Former middle school teacher Liz Kolb established a website, called From Toy to Tool: Cell Phones in Learning (**www.cellphonesinlearning.com**), to encourage discussion and give suggestions about and for using cell phones in the classroom.

Many units and lesson plans, some of which are suggested in this chapter, can help you create innovative activities to keep your students engaged while educating them with the concepts they will need to be successful in high school, college, and beyond.

The first order of business is to know your students' skill levels. You can do this through various assessments. Many schools will do this for you or will have assessment materials you can access if you are a core subject teacher. Additionally, your textbooks often offer supplementary assessments so you can test your students' knowledge of the subject. Larger textbook publishers will provide you with Web pages to help with this. If you would like a preview of the textbooks you may be using, similar to the ones your district has selected for you, check them out at Prentice Hall (**www.phschool.com**) for Prentice Hall textbooks or Holt McDougall (**www.holtmcdougal.hmhco.com**) for Holt McDougall/Houghton Mifflin Harcourt textbooks. You also can review any statewide or norm-referenced tests your students took the previous school year to see where they need to begin and/or what level they are performing at.

> "Middle school students are far more intelligent, clever, and capable of serious thought and analysis than many people realize. When I was a high school teacher, I was guilty of that misconception. I did not think middle school students would really be able to have good, insightful discussions of literature, or really great turns of phrase in writing. In that, I was so wrong! I teach the same two novels every year and there has *never* been a year when a discussion of the book has not turned up at least one student making an observation or asking a pointed question that has never come up in previous years."
>
> — Nancie Menapace, English teacher,
> Good Hope Middle School

Assessing your students is a good policy whenever you begin a new unit. For example, if your curriculum map mandates that you spend three days on addition of fractions, but your students show they have the knowledge they need to move on, go ahead and move on. You can use that extra time in areas where assessments show the students need more focus.

You may be thinking, "OK, assess before each unit. A unit of what?" A unit is a theme in which you teach related concepts or strategies over a period of time. A lesson is simply what you will be teaching in any one given class period. There are several approaches to planning units and lessons. Here are some ideas to explore during your first year. Use them as a foundation and go anywhere in the lesson-planning world you like with them.

Technological grading

Some schools have improved communication between parents and teachers with technology. These schools incorporate online grading systems that parents may access. The programs provide access to student assignments as well as posted grades for tests, quizzes, homework, and papers. This is very effective for parents who want to know what is going on with their children. They can access the information on a regular basis from their own computers at any time of day or night at their convenience. They also offer the ability to click on an e-mail link to contact the teacher with questions and concerns. School districts with technological capabilities have opted to institute these kinds of programs as a means to cut costs by going paperless.

One commonly used application is a website called eSchoolBook (**www. eschoolbook.com**). The program is set up by the school district and is maintained by the technology department. Teachers are expected to enter grades on a weekly basis unless otherwise specified, although parents and students can access them daily to see any updates. In these schools, technology is favored over paper reports. Teachers still have the ability to print hard copies of progress reports when the need arises. For example, if a student does not have a computer in the home, you still have the traditional options:

- Print off a copy to send home with the student.
- Mail a hard copy of the report to the parent or guardian.
- Call the parent or guardian and discuss your concerns.

The eSchoolBook information is password protected so no one else can access your students' information. Currently, the program provides online grading for students in grades six through 12. Additionally, family members are linked, so parents can access all their children's grades with one password. School districts generally require parents to attend a seminar explaining the program. Subsequently, they need to fill out an application and they must produce their driver's license to prove who they are. The application is reviewed before it is submitted to the technology department. This adds an element of safety and security.

Teachers find the technology to be both a blessing and a curse. Because the grades are online, students and parents should be aware of their grades. There should not be any surprises when report cards come out. On the negative side, teachers are expected to grade and update the website on a regular basis. If they are behind on grading, parents and students can get frustrated if they do not have immediate access to the grades.

Schools with available technology can close the communication gap between teachers and guardians. In addition to providing grades online, teachers at many schools have their own class-related websites. These sites include copies of the syllabus and information about the curriculum. They include calendars of upcoming homework, projects, and tests. Cumberland Valley School District in Mechanicsburg, Pennsylvania is an example of a technologically advanced school. The district has a comprehensive school website (**www.cvschools.org**) that allows teachers and parents to communicate freely with each other as often as necessary. The school even posts the daily announcements. Of course, like anything else, it is only as effective as the individuals who take advantage of it. In today's busy times, as we become increasingly dependent on technology, it serves as a positive progressive step towards keeping the lines of communication open.

As a new teacher, you may want to check the teacher's individual websites for the types of information that is provided in this public domain. Check to see if your school has the capacity for this type of program. If not, and if you live in an area where most people are technologically advanced, you still can create your own website for parents to access. You will not be able to post grades, but you can provide a syllabus and calendar for their review. This is helpful if students have computers at home and are able to check assignments.

CHAPTER 11:

Classroom Management 101 — Rules and Discipline

Facilitating appropriate behavior and cooperation is crucial to a successful learning environment. As a matter of fact, it is safe to say classroom management will make or break you as a teacher. Teachers who can create an atmosphere of cooperation and respect will, on most days, go home feeling content and accomplished in their careers, and their students will have learned that day. Teachers who do not master this fundamental foundation of successful learning usually do not last long. If they do, they are easily identified by their attitude of cynicism and crassness in the teachers' lounge. To help you from becoming the latter, this chapter picks up where your college professors might have left off: the basic rules of the classroom, effective ways of enforcing rules, and making your classroom a safe learning environment.

> "There is a rhythm that only comes with experience and really cannot be taught. It involves overlap skills, timing a lesson, and eyes in the back of your head. Much like cooking a meal, you have to do it a few times to get the timing down and to master getting several items ready and hot at the same time. It is very similar with classroom management."
>
> — Nancie Menapace, English teacher,
> Good Hope Middle School

You will find that few teachers and administrators agree on all rules. Most, however, agree on the basic principles of middle school behavior, the rules that are the underlying foundation of good classroom management. For example, a 2009 study by researchers at the Baylor College of Medicine showed that gum-chewing may keep students focused on their work and increase math test scores. Therefore, many teachers are promoting chewing. But you need only look under a desk in a middle school class to see why other teachers will not allow the sticky substance in their classroom. In contrast, it is unlikely you will find a teacher who does not agree that a student who yells out, "You're stupid!" while a peer gives a presentation is behaving in a totally inappropriate manner and requires intervention.

Take some time when deciding what guidelines and consequences you will set for your students. Jot down the answers to the following questions:

- What are your expectations of each student in terms of behavior?

- What does a well-behaved classroom where students are learning look like to you?

- When your students are working in groups, how will you bring their attention back to you?

- What will you do if a student refuses to sign a detention slip or accept other consequences for his or her actions?

- How will you handle a student who consistently comes in tardy? Is there an across-the-board tardy policy in the school, or do you have to establish your own?

Discuss classroom management strategies with other veteran teachers at your school. Be sure when compiling your classroom management plan you:

- **State and list rules in the positive.** For example, instead of saying, "Do not call out in class," state, "Raise your hand and wait to be called on before speaking."

- **Post your rules prior to the first day of school.** Even if you are going to employ single-school culture in your classroom, always have the basic norms conspicuously posted.

- **Keep expectations to one sentence.** Do not get wordy, or the meaning will be lost to your students. Create a draft of your expectations and re-read them for clarity. Take out any unnecessary verbiage.

The teacher message board at the online teacher resource page TeAchnology (**www.teach-nology.com***)* offers helpful suggestions regarding classroom behavior. The website does require a subscription, but it offers many free tools and is worth exploring. After going to the site, type "Classroom Rules" in the search tab and scroll to the bottom of that page. Click the article titled "Classroom Rules - Middle Level." This article offers several sets of suggested classroom rules. The relevant topics include everything from what some teachers do about classroom bathroom passes, to bullying prevention.

Do not, however, depend only on a website for teacher input. Consult with your colleagues before putting your expectations down on paper. What are the expectations and consequences they use in their classrooms? Are these shared norms that you can use with your students? Your colleagues have experience with your particular student population and will know what works and what does not. Ask them questions such as:

- How do they deal with things such as excessive tardies?
- What consequences have they found most effective?
- What preventative measures have helped their class discussions run smoothly?
- How do they let students consult with each other while working in pairs and groups while still maintaining control of the class?
- How have they dealt with issues such as note-passing?

Other teachers can help you anticipate what to expect from your students, which will assist you in deciding what guidelines and consequences will work in your classroom. You are less likely to be rattled if you are prepared for the sometimes-outrageous behavior of middle school students. Maintaining control will also keep students in your classroom and learning instead of in the discipline office waiting to talk to the assistant principal.

SINGLE-SCHOOL CULTURE

A trend found to be effective in numerous school districts around the country is single-school culture. This model of holistic classroom consistency can help you develop a set of expectations that is comfortable for you and respected by your students. Single school culture is an organizational way of establishing shared behavioral standards in a district, school, and classroom. It discourages the idea of teaching as an "us against them" proposition and encourages harmony in the learning process. Its shared norms and values work to encourage respect and success among students, teachers, and administrators.

Although single-school culture is a holistic view of a school's climate and not limited to classroom discipline only, it is a great place to start. If your school and district are working on incorporating single-school culture standards into your population, this information will be included in your new-teacher orientation, professional-development classes on teacher workdays, or your school's faculty meetings. If not, you can still use some of the ideas in your classroom with your students.

The school districts of Philadelphia and Palm Beach County, Florida, have successfully incorporated single-school culture to create a "This is the way things are done around here" atmosphere. Websites for the school district of Palm Beach County (**www.palmbeach.k12.fl.us**) and the school district of Philadelphia (**www.phila.k12.pa.us**) offer information on how they are using this initiative effectively and are a great place for new teachers to gain background information about this trend. There is a PowerPoint presentation on the single-school culture concept located on the Center-School website (**www.center-school.org/profdev/documents/adler-backhus.pdf**).

STRUCTURING BEHAVIORAL EXPECTATIONS FOR THE CLASSROOM

Oftentimes, middle school students see the word "rules" and immediately zone out. In keeping with the spirit of single-school culture, you may want to label your rules as "expectations." "Rules" seem to connote "You better or else," and some middle school students are at that age where they will test the rules simply to see what they can get away with. It is nothing personal, just the nature of the middle school student. "Expectations" work well. They say, "This is what I expect of you, and here is what will happen if you do not meet my expectations. The choice is yours." You accomplish two objectives in this vein: You clearly establish classroom policy, and you share the responsibility for making good choices with your students. They now have part-ownership in the success of their classroom. Many students this age want to be treated as adults. By listening to their input, you allow them to become invested in the classroom atmosphere and learning environment. It will not discourage all the students from breaking the rules, but it will help.

Regardless of what method you choose to use when deciding your behavior-management guidelines, post expectations and enforcers on the wall in large, bold print, where all students can see them — bulletin board size. Keep basic expectations simple and have a maximum of five. It is inconceivable for middle school students to understand and follow an extensive list of restrictions. Your classroom should have a welcoming, safe feel, not a prison-like atmosphere. Moreover, unreasonable expectations and lack of uniformity will render your classroom-management guidelines ineffective.

Expectations should not be wordy, but clearly written. Be specific. For example, a rule such as "Be on time" is open to interpretation. Make your expectations very clear. Figure out what being on time means to you and word your expectation that way. "Be seated and ready to work when the bell rings" is quite clear, leaving little room for interpretation by future contract attorneys.

Suggestions for basic classroom management

No one put it better than sixth-grader Kelly Purdham when she said, "I believe that to be a good teacher you must be nice, but strict. Remember that you are the boss of your classroom." This middle school student drives the point home by adding, "If I could give advice to a first-year teacher, I would say to him or her, 'Be nice, but do not be a pushover, because if you do not take charge in your classroom, your students will not respect you and will think that they can do whatever they want and get away with it.'"

Purdham has a good point. It is all right to involve your students in the rule-making process, but be sure that guidelines for good behavior are in place even before then to ensure the respect you need to keep order during the process.

PREVENTION AND INTERVENTION

Prevention and intervention are far more effective in deterring classroom disruptions than constantly stopping to correct behavior, write detentions, or call home. Your objective in managing your classroom is to have a safe, comfortable environment where your lessons run smoothly and your students are learning. There is nothing more frustrating to a classroom teacher trying to educate students than dealing with constant interruptions. You can use several techniques to minimize disruptions and keep your students on task the entire period. Easily remember and reference them by using the acronym SCURT: strategize, circulate, use, reward, and train. The following are a list of interventions you can use without missing a beat of your lesson:

1. **Strategize your seating.** This is one of the best misbehavior interventions. To begin with, make sure your desks are set up so you can comfortably move around the room. The first week of school, you will want to seat students alphabetically. This will give you the opportunity to learn your students' names and determine which are among the more outgoing — in other words, talkative — in your class. After a time you will see who needs to be separated. Periodically change your seating and make it a privilege for students to choose their own seats. For example, some of the more boisterous students may like to sit in the back of the room; seat them in the front and use the opportunity to move to the back of the room as a reward for good behavior. If well-behaved students would like to stay where they are sitting, leave them there, if possible. Let them know that a good choice brings freedom for more choices. Truthfully, unless a student is unable to see the board or projector, you

can seat them anywhere. For most of your class period, you should be circulating around the room.

2. **Circulate.** Always be aware of what is going on in your class. This is best accomplished by circulating among your students as much as possible during the period. Circulating will cover a myriad of classroom strategies. It gives you the opportunity to observe whether students are correctly completing their assignments and whether they are on task, and you can avert poor choices simply by being nearby. Students will be less likely to pass notes, talk and giggle, and engage in other off-task behaviors and more likely to strive for success if they know you are watching closely.

3. **Use body language and tone of voice.** If you observe a student's disruptive behavior, walk over to where he or she is sitting and stand there for a moment. Perhaps you will need to point to the task he or she is working on to cue them to get back on track. The student will know he or she has been "nabbed," and your presence will be the best deterrent. If gum-chewing is not allowed in your class, simply walk over to a student with the garbage can and have them spit it out. You will not have to say a word. Middle school students know why you are there. There is no need to stop your lesson or break up group work. If you are working with a student and do not want to stop to walk over, often you can simply state their name in a firm voice, and that will do the trick until you have an opportunity to go to the other side of the room.

4. **Train your students by setting up routines and procedures.** Training students on your expectations upfront is more effective than constantly doling out consequences. For example, even the most well-meaning students will call out answers occasionally if they have not learned appropriate participation techniques. The problem is it is not only disruptive, but discourages the quieter children from participating. There is an easy way to make sure everyone has an opportunity to participate. Incorporate a deck of index cards, each with one student's name written on it. For the first weeks of school, instead of having students raise their hands, choose who to call on by rotating through the index cards.

Have the deck of index cards shuffled and ready at the beginning of class discussions. After a couple of weeks, students will develop better listening skills, and you can transition into not using the cards at all. A website with similar strategies worth exploring by anyone engineering a proactive classroom management is The Honor System: Discipline by Design (**www.honorlevel.com**). Once you have entered the site, you will see a table of contents on the left-hand side. Find training ideas under "Proactive discipline." The site also offers a page where teachers write in and discuss techniques that did not work.

5. **Reward.** Spend more time catching students behaving rather than misbehaving. This teaches your class that positive behavior is worth far more than being disruptive. If you see students doing something positive, reward them with a holiday pencil, cool erasers, or stickers for their binders. You can get lots of these items cheaply. For example, department stores sell packs of ten holiday pencils for a dollar. Your closest dollar store will have a plethora of items, including colorful stickers and other favorite stationery items fairly cheap. But beware of praising your students with candy. Yes, students love candy and will do most anything to get it. However, consider this: In a July 2009 report, the Trust for America's Health, a nonprofit organization, estimated that childhood obesity rates are at or above 30 percent in 30 states. Visit the group's website (**www.healthyamericans.org**) to view the whole article. This means it is plausible you will have several students in your classroom who are overweight. You do not want to teach a student struggling with weight issues that food is a reward. Fortunately, there are plenty of alternatives to candy, such as the ones mentioned above. Also, consider making one positive phone call home after school each day. When you notice a student is well-behaved or making good choices, let his or her parent(s) know. A positive phone call to a parent not only makes the parent's day a little brighter, but carries positive reinforcement for the student's behavior from the classroom all the way home.

CASE STUDY: ARE YOU MEANT TO TEACH MIDDLE SCHOOL?

Nancie Menapace
Sixth grade English teacher
Good Hope Middle School
Mechanicsburg, Pennsylvania
nmenapace@cvschools.org

Nancie Menapace has 27 years of teaching experience. She received her bachelor of science degree and her secondary education degree from Millersville University. She also has a master's degree in English language and literature from the University of Maryland.

I actually never intended to teach middle school. In fact, when I first graduated from college, I really was only interested in teaching at the high school level. In fact, I spent several years in the Washington, D.C. area teaching high school English and journalism.

After I had my son, my husband and I decided to return to central Pennsylvania. It made me laugh when people said that subbing was hard, classroom management-wise. I had just completed ten years of teaching in outer urban areas and some of it got quite rough at times, so that was not an issue. Two more long-term sub jobs led to the promise of a permanent position in my current school district. The first opening was a sixth grade position that was offered to me as a temporary situation. My department chair knew I wanted to teach at the high school level, but asked me to work in the sixth grade position for one year. An 11th grade position was going to become available the next year because of a retirement. I accepted the offer.

In October, I called my department chair to say, "Uh, never mind; I'm happy here." He chuckled and said, "I knew that would happen." I truly feel that teaching is a calling similar to religious vocations, law enforcement, medicine, and the military. In the same respect, middle school teaching seems to be an area for which some teachers just have an affinity even if they do not know it! That was me. Luckily, my department chair was wise enough to recognize that.

I had to overcome my own high school snobbery, a notion that the real teaching goes on at that level. I thought teaching middle school was much more basic, that the content was not interesting, and posed no real challenges. Obviously, I was wrong. Middle school students are interesting, engaging, and so responsive! The best part is I can be 100 percent myself right from the beginning. In teaching high school, I had to keep more of a game face on at the start of the year. For example, tenth graders will judge you by their first impression of you. They may not take you seriously if you are silly, or singing, to get their attention. Middle school students are not like that.

Humor and a light touch are a big part of classroom management at this level. There are many instances when a teacher could really yell at a kid, or throw in an automatic consequence. Sometimes, however, it can be more effective and less disruptive to look at a student sternly and say, "Are you sure you want to do that?" For the most part, students at this age still care what you think of them, so that is usually enough.

In general, classroom management at the middle school level is its own unique animal — a tap dance balancing freedom and structure. They come to us from elementary school, where they have their own desks instead of lockers, where they are led in lines from room to room, where they are dismissed by announcements by bus at the end of the day. Here, they learn to take responsibility for what they need each part of the day. They are both capable and incapable of independent work and group work, and to varying degrees — it is essential to always keep your observing eye peeled and to circulate when students are working around a classroom or moving in a herd through the halls.

Middle schoolers are a "touchy" group, in both senses of the word. Their feelings can easily be hurt, there are always dramas with both girls and boys, and they are credulous — hallway gossip is taken as gospel truth and readily passed along. They are also literally touchy, as in physically touching, pulling, and pushing each other. In high school, I would never have had to post a sign in my classroom that says, "If it isn't yours, don't touch it."

Middle schoolers are also, by nature, fans of frontier justice. If someone kicks their desk, their instinctive reaction is to kick back. "But he took my book first" is felt to be a legitimate defense. And their shortsightedness can often manifest itself in their really not thinking about other people, in the immediate moment. For example, I have mastered the one upraised finger or "Wait a moment" sign, which is now to me as natural as breathing, to use when one student comes up to interrupt while another is already talking. They honestly do not mean to be rude; they just do not consider that someone else needs my attention when they do. I am amused when a student will ask, "May I go and ask Mrs. So-and-so a question?" and I say, "She's teaching a class right now," and my student says, "Oh, really?" in genuine surprise, like it really did not occur to him or her that the other teachers are not just sitting alone in their classrooms waiting for that student to come back!

It takes a lot of mental and emotional energy to teach and manage and generally spend the day with middle schoolers. If you are off your game for whatever reason — illness, lack of sleep, preoccupation with out-of-school issues — it can be tough, and it is easy to grow impatient with those kids who just did not listen the first three times you gave an instruction, who ask a question about something you have just explained, who want to tell you a long, drawn-out story while on lunch duty, or who forget a book for class. And this also comes back to my recommendation to always try to see each student as a person. It can go a very long way toward helping you to be patient, and to also enjoy your time with the students that much more.

Middle school students really do have much more fully developed personalities than some might expect. They are clever, funny, affectionate, creative, and often very, very kind. It is an age at which it is still very realistically possible to "turn around" a kid's life path. This is both rewarding and heartbreaking, as our awareness of baggage that students are bearing from their home lives, social situations, etc., can sometimes lead to helplessness when we really are not able to "fix things" for all of them, and we know that, increasingly, those outside or internal problems are going to affect their school performance, their responsibility, and their motivation. We are very aware that, for some students, we or the school are their only stability and support.

It is amazing to observe the changes in students within each school year, and from sixth to eighth grade. In the process, their hormones are all over the place! The same tough guy who was bothering kids on the bus might be crying about a bad test the next day. This is another facet of teaching middle school which differs from high school: Every kid can have emotional mood swings at any age, but there are times when each kid here is just one big walking exposed nerve. Naturally, being aware of this fact and the need to deal with it help build classroom management skills for middle school educators.

Encountering students with non-academic problems

Even the most well-thought-out classroom management plan can have obstacles. Making the rules and consequences for breaking the rules a constant is a good working theory. The variable, however, is that not every situation is that simple. Many times, there are other factors involved that create the behavioral issue to begin with.

There are elements in place to provide assistance to students who need something additional in respect to academics. These individualized plans help gifted students and students who struggle with learning disabilities and chronic medical conditions. Unfortunately, many other students struggle for completely unrelated reasons. In addition to their schoolwork, many middle school students have other serious concerns in their lives. Some might come from broken homes. Others may face tough problems, either with themselves or with their families, such as the following:

- Bullying
- Divorced parents
- Drugs and/or alcohol
- Depression
- Isolation
- Sex and pregnancy
- Anorexia and/or bulimia
- Low self-esteem
- Thoughts of suicide
- Problems at home
- Physical and/or mental abuse
- Poverty
- Gang violence

> "I think the hardest part about being a teacher is dealing with students' home and personal situations when they creep into and affect their school lives."
>
> — Nancie Menapace, English teacher,
> Good Hope Middle School

Negativity, a lack of respect for authority figures, anger, sadness, and a total absence of joy are potential warning signs. Since the school violence tragedies of Columbine and Virginia Tech, schools have been more aware of issues concerning potentially troubled students. These tragedies involved older students, but there were early warning signs that these individuals needed assistance. That is not to say that everything is preventable, but sometimes being there for a student makes a significant difference in the outcome. The hormone-driven middle school years are particularly tumultuous. Not every act of deviance or anger is a major sign of trouble; therefore, it is important to avoid inappropriately labeling individual students. Pay attention to what you see and discuss it with a counselor at the school. It is important to pay attention, but it is just as critical that you not jump to conclusions. The following are some of the warning signs for students who may become violent. These have been identified by school counselors across the country. Look out for students who:

- Exhibit antisocial behaviors or indications of loneliness.
- Show no close bonds or friendships with other students.
- Frequently express an extremist viewpoint.
- Idolize inappropriate figures.
- Depict a sense of hopelessness and despair suddenly for no known cause.
- Display an unexplainable preoccupation with weapons.
- Get caught for carrying some form of weapon.
- Appear to have little, if any, supervision by parent or guardian.
- Appear to have witnessed or experienced an abusive home life.
- Express suicidal thoughts.
- Have threatened or attempted suicide.

- Demonstrate self-mutilating, such as cutting or burning of his or herself.

- Made and or carried out threats to others.

- Exhibit intimidating behaviors, such as invading personal space, inappropriate touching, unnecessary roughness, harassment, or stalking.

- Previously experienced bullying, harassment, and torment from peers.

- Frequently bully or intimidate those who are younger or weaker.

- Openly exhibit violent behavior.

- Express or brag of future plans of violence.

- Exhibit difficulty in controlling his or her anger and other extreme emotions.

- Exhibit constant signs of nervousness and tension.

- Cry often for inexplicable reasons.

- Display consistent signs of clinical depression or have noticeable mood swings.

- Display a sudden decline in work habits, such as excessive procrastination and decreased quality of prepared work.

- Frequently miss school and make no effort to get caught up on missed work.

- Exhibit signs of dependency on adults by hanging around constantly.

- Display signs of listlessness and lethargy, such as frequently falling asleep in class.

- Show a marked decline in maintaining personal hygiene.

- Report of physical assault or recent loss of someone important, such as friend or family member.

- Display signs of low self-esteem.

- Frequently blame others or refuses to take responsibility for his or her own actions.

- Display an inability to be sympathetic toward others.

- Prefer violent media (violent TV shows, movies, and computer games) to all else.

- Repeatedly use themes of violence or hatred in writings and artwork.

- Have a history of disciplinary problems.

- Have a history of substance abuse.

- Express feelings of intolerance or prejudice.

- Exhibit feelings of superiority.

- Openly discuss an interest in or an involvement in gangs.

- Display a blatant disregard for rules and regulations, as if they do not pertain to him or her.

- Exhibit difficulty in coping with a significant life change or failure.

- Exhibit cruelty to animals.

If you encounter students who might be troubled or difficult, try the following approaches:

- **Talk to the student.** Sometimes the individual simply needs someone to talk to. Once you ascertain the problem, you can decide how to get assistance if it is necessary. Do not promise confidentiality. If a student poses a threat to themselves or someone else at school, authorities need to be notified.

- **Talk to the school counselor or school psychologist.** If you believe the issue is beyond your comfort level or requires assistance outside of the school, do not hesitate to ask for help. For example, if there is a concern about violence or criminal activity, it may require intervention by law enforcement. If the situation is more personal in nature, such as pregnancy, depression, or substance abuse, you may need to involve a physician or psychiatrist. There are suicide hotlines and groups for teens living with substance abuse in the family. School counselors have extensive resources on issues pertaining to troubled teens.

- **Talk to the student's parent or guardian.** If you notice a marked change in behavior that is inexplicable, there may be cause for concern. On the other hand, it may be simply a bad time because of a family member's illness or loss of a job. Before approaching the parent or guardian, speak with the school counselor or an administrator about school protocol unless you have already developed a rapport with the parent or guardian.

Bullying

The "bully" label of old used to be relegated to the rough, tough, colossal kid who was waiting on the playground or at the bus stop to pick on, push, or torment his victim relentlessly. The truth is, bullying has come to have a broader definition. It manifests itself in many different ways and is prevalent among middle schoolers. In fact, all of us have probably experienced being on one side or another of a bully relationship, likely in middle school. Bullying incidents are teachable moments that allow you to redirect students on the path of correct and fair treatment of others.

Schools can no longer ignore bullying situations. Situations involving bullying are prevalent in the news. In March 2010, nine Massachusetts teens faced police charges for bullying a 15-year-old girl on Facebook for several weeks, leading up to her suicide. The case culminated in new anti-bullying legislation.

Veteran language arts teacher Penny Martin believes the way to deal with bullying among students is to change the attitude of bullies and recipients. She said, "Bullying is a problem wherever there are living beings. It occurs not only in classrooms, but also in families, workplaces, communities, and the interaction of states and nations. Some would say that it is forever part of the natural world, and others would even say that it serves to build strength in those who survive it." She believes that to deal with bullying, you must "recognize it, understand it, and re-mold the attitudes of both bully and recipient." This three-step approach is a great way for you to prevent and deter bullying problems with your students.

Recognizing bullying

Dan Olweus, author of *Bullying at School: What We Know and What We Can Do*, defines a victim of bullying as someone who is "exposed, repeatedly and over time, to negative actions on the part of one or more other persons, and he or she has difficulty defending himself or herself." He details more specifically the characteristics of bullying as follows:

- Aggressive behavior that involves unwanted, negative actions
- A pattern of behavior repeated over time
- An imbalance of power or strength

This definition will manifest itself in many ways, from your classroom all the way to the cafeteria. Be aware of the indications. The following are some of the specifics that can help you recognize when bullying is occurring:

- **Verbal abuse:** Although you can observe many types of bullying throughout middle school hallways and classrooms, verbal abuse is a more common behavior among adolescents. It includes derogatory comments about the victim or the victim's family or friends, name-calling, and put-downs such as "stupid." Crass or sarcastic remarks veiled as supposedly humorous puns count. In that case, you may find the victim laughing along with the bully or others, but deep down it is a hurtful remark that scars.

- **Deliberate isolation:** This is not particular to groups of adolescent girls, but it is an occurrence more often found among them and often with individuals who were once friends. Students often ostracize another with cruel intent, perhaps excluding the victim from the lunch table, purposefully leaving the victim for last when choosing partners or teams, or setting him or her apart through calculated lies and false rumors.

- **Physical abuse:** Whether to extort money from another student or simply to pick on someone for fun, shoving in the halls, hitting, kicking, and spitting is most certainly bullying. It is not necessarily the most common form, but it is the most recognizable form.

- **Sexual harassment:** If children have not learned appropriate forms of touch, they need to know now. This goes for bullies and their victims. Bullies and possibly the victims who laugh it off may believe otherwise.

A new type of sexual harassment is a growing concern for middle and high school students. The practice of sending and/or receiving sexually explicit texts and pictures via cell phones is known as "sexting." According to a study conducted by the National Campaign to Prevent Teen and Unplanned Pregnancy, approximately 50 percent of the students questioned admitted to sending or receiving sext messages. It is a growing concern. In January 2009, six teenagers were charged with counts of pornography because of sext messages. As a result of the charges, they had to register as sex offenders with the national registry. Given the growing trend and the resulting concern, teachers need to be even more aware of current laws and school policies regarding cell phones.

- **Cyberbullying (via cell phone or Internet):** The website StopCyber-Bullying (**www.stopcyberbullying.org**) is an excellent source for learning about, preventing, and thwarting cyberbullying. The site defines cyberbullying as "when a child, preteen, or teen is tormented, threatened, harassed, humiliated, embarrassed, or otherwise targeted by another child, preteen, or teen using the Internet, interactive and digital technologies, or mobile phones. It has to have a minor on both sides, or at least have been instigated by a minor against another minor."

  Cyberbullying is a growing problem and should not be dismissed. In January 2010, a 15-year-old Massachusetts girl committed suicide because of repeated cruel messages posted by a group of female bullies. According to the ABC morning show *Good Morning America*, one of the messages actually suggested that the student "go hang herself." The issue should not be taken lightly. As of 2010, 41 states had mounted anti-bullying campaigns. Additionally, 23 of those states had specific statutes in place to counteract cyberbullying. Parry Aftab, a privacy lawyer and internet safety expert, told *Good Morning America* that one sign to look for is a child's hesitancy to use the computer and other technology when it did not exist previously.

- **Racism and prejudice:** Bullies can use any of the above strategies to torment someone because of race, religion, sexual preference, size, or peer group. If not redirected in adolescence, this type of bullying can turn into a destructive community issue.

Understanding bullying

Dr. Marlene Snyder's online article "Understanding Bullying and Its Impact on Kids with Learning Disabilities or ADHD" relates that bullies are not necessarily what we once thought: Students with low self-esteem. "Bullies, in fact, may be average students or even classroom or athletic leaders," she says.

Instead, Snyder states that it is usually the victims who suffer from low self-esteem and view themselves negatively. They often consider themselves failures. They feel stupid, ashamed, and unattractive. "They may come to believe that they 'deserve' to be bullied. They are often lonely, friendless, and abandoned at school," she said. These traits also might mean empowering victims is part of the prevention equation. The following are some suggestions for identifying potential victims:

The passive or submissive victim

- Is nonassertive and through his actions may signal to others that he or she is insecure and will not retaliate if attacked or insulted.
- Is cautious, quiet, or anxious.
- Cries easily and collapses quickly when bullied.
- Has few friends and is not connected to a social network.
- Lacks a sense of humor and pro-social skills.
- Might be physically weak.

The provocative victim

- Is both anxious and aggressive.
- May cause irritation and disruption around him or her.
- Is easily emotionally aroused.
- Prolongs the conflict even when losing.

Redirecting attitudes

Given Olweus's and Snyder's research on this subject, regardless of whether the victims or the bullies are the ones with low self-esteem issues, it is important to empower students to value themselves and others. You can do this in numerous ways in the classroom, including:

- Begin with prevention by teaching tolerance twofold: Both a zero-tolerance policy for bullying in and out of the classroom and 100 percent tolerance for diversity in our classrooms, homes, and communities. For ideas, explore the Teaching Tolerance website (**www.teachingtolerance.com**). Much of what the site offers is free, and you can even sign up to receive a complimentary quarterly magazine with articles and ideas on teaching tolerance.

- Use the calendar for teachable moments and relevant lessons. Almost every month in the United States, a different race or ethnic group celebrates its history, whether it be September's Hispanic Heritage Month, February's Black History Month, or April's Yom Hashoah (Holocaust Remembrance Day). This is a great tool for celebrating the diversity that exists in our American middle school classrooms. *See Appendix F for resources with lesson plan ideas.*

- When using group work or pairs in your lesson plans, be sure to choose the groups, especially if you suspect there is a problem. Additionally, it is best if students have an opportunity to work with different individuals instead of always being with the same group or partners. When they complain, and they most likely will, let them know that learning to work with a variety of personalities is excellent real world practice.

- Create a diversity wall or door. Give your students a 5x7-inch card and allow them to draw, write short poems, and cut and paste pictures on a wall to show who they are. For example, members of the school band might want to cut and paste pictures of themselves playing their instrument, or a math student may want to add a picture of himself or herself surrounded by various equations. It makes for a descriptive mural of who your students are. The Diversity Council website (**www.diversitycouncil.org**) offers terrific, thought-provoking anti-bullying activities.

- Join Peaceful Schools International (PSI). Located in Canada, PSI is an organization that supports schools committed to promoting peace. Students can post their ideas, artwork, and poetry on the organization's website (**http://peacefulschoolsinternational.org**). PSI also has a Facebook page (**www.facebook.com/peacefulschoolsinternational**), featuring news updates, photos, videos, and shout-outs from students across the world.

- Immediately report any talk of bullying, including threatening notes, to the assistant principal. If you notice students you do not know being bullied in the cafeteria, hallways, or anywhere in the school, be sure to report that, too, even if you choose to act as peacemaker. You do not want to learn your mediating skills were unsuccessful when one of your students shows up for class the next day with a big shiner and a fat lip. Also, a student may have serious issues that are manifesting themselves through bullying others. Your assistant principal will want to be aware of any events involving this student. Furthermore, in the realm of middle school reality, students will at times attempt to bring weapons on campus. A heads-up to your assistant principal may avert a serious tragedy.

Middle school classroom management takes time. As a new teacher, you will encounter many different challenges that can disrupt the rules of the classroom. For example, you will have to handle learning disabilities, family problems, emotional issues, and bullying on a regular basis. Situations will arise when you least expect them. It is all part of teaching. You are not expected to know how to handle everything perfectly right away. Becoming a seasoned educator takes a great deal of on-the-job training. Find veteran teachers and other administrators you can approach as situations arise.

CHAPTER 12:

Creating a Successful Partnership with Students and Parents

During the middle school years, students are highly unpredictable because of their hormonal changes. Parents and guardians are not as involved with the students as they were in elementary school, but it is still very important to create a sense of partnership with parents and guardians. Despite the fact that many students this age may act tough and aloof, most of them still care what the adults in their lives think of them.

In working with middle school students, you can expect there will come a time when someone or something interrupts the flow of your classroom. Right from the beginning, you need to establish consequences that will deter further classroom disruption and misbehavior. When instituting consequences, your objective should be to deter behavior that interrupts the learning flow in your classroom. Your consequences should increase in severity. Although consequences are designed to teach and not to punish, some should be used absolutely as a last resort. To be effective, behavioral policies, just like your expectations, must be clearly established the minute your students walk into the room and consistently enforced throughout the school year. Post them on the wall in large, bold print where you can refer to them if necessary. Additionally, make sure guardians are aware of policies and consequences by sending home a document with your syllabus on the first day.

Your consequences should send this message: "You have not met my expectations and have hindered your education or the education of others and have chosen poorly. Hopefully, this consequence will help you make better choices in the future." Consequence norms throughout middle school discipline go something like this:

1. **Warning:** Students make mistakes. Give your students a chance to get back on track. Always call attention to the misbehavior and give the student an opportunity to correct it before bestowing consequences.

2. **Phone call home:** Most teachers will agree that for the average student a phone call home is the best classroom-management tool. Parents generally are more than willing to assist their children in achieving educational excellence and know that appropriate behavior in the classroom must be part of that goal. Let the student know you are calling home. You will at times elicit responses such as "My mother doesn't care how I act," "My father will yell at you," or a favorite, "My mother will sue you." Call anyway. Veteran teachers will tell you it is only in rare cases that you find a parent who is not at least open to hearing what you have to say, and it is probably a good estimation to say that 90 percent of parents will back up your assessment of their child's behavior. In most cases, parents will work with you to provide rewards at home for good behavior, or they will threaten a deterrent, such as the loss of a cell phone or computer privileges if poor choices continue. A word to the wise: Call when you have quiet time and can calmly discuss the situation with the parent. It is human to get annoyed with a student who has disrupted your classroom and impeded your objectives to the point where you must call home. Do not, however, call the parent while you are still agitated. Give yourself time to cool down. Additionally, make note of the call. Always keep parent contact records for future reference.

3. **Detention:** When a student receives detention as a consequence, documentation is sent home and placed in his or her file. If you have the option to schedule your own detention, plan detention for early in the day to make it more uncomfortable for the student. You will find middle school students hate to get out of bed any earlier than their normal routine demands. This immediately makes detention an unattractive

alternative to misbehavior. Further ways to make detention unattractive include requiring students to complete any assignments they may have missed as a result of their behavior and limiting their grade to a 75. Not only will this discourage any further class disruptions, it is not fair to allow a misbehaving student the same credit as a student who was on-task and completed the assignment. Students can also write a list of alternatives to the behavior that landed them in detention, a letter of apology for disrupting the class, an essay on how making better choices helps in reaching their goals, or an essay on why it is important to meet classroom expectations and how it encourages learning. Some teachers feel a consequence that includes an essay turns students off to the writing process, but students are aware of the difference between communicating as a consequence and communicating creatively or for a report, just as they are aware of the difference between going to their room for punishment and going to their room to hang out.

4. **Parent conference:** Parent conferences encourage good behavior, and you can use them for prevention and intervention, especially if you see a child who is approaching the point where he or she may end up suspended because of classroom antics. In most cases, you will find parents willing to assist their child in correcting these antics, and they will appreciate the heads-up before a student is suspended. Take notes at the conference and stay solution-oriented. Your objective is to establish a set of tools that can be put into place to encourage better choices. Stay on that vein. Although background information is important to determine the cause of lack of self-discipline, some parents will go on and on making excuses. Simply say, "How can we use that to implement a behavior plan now?" You can leave it to the parents, but be sure you go into the conference with ideas and suggestions.

5. **Referral:** If you have used all the strategies in your toolbox and a student is still so defiant that no interventions will work, your only recourse is to refer him or her to the assistant principal or dean in charge of discipline for the child's grade level. However, if you use prevention and intervention,

this will not happen often and your superiors will thank you for that. Depending on the severity of the distraction, students likely will not be suspended for their first referral. They might have to attend Saturday school, where they will have to sit quietly for three to four hours. There also may come a time when a student is definitely out of control in your class and is resistant to any intervention. You do not want to depend on others to instill order in your class, but if a student has become a danger to himself or another, or her temper is escalating, get the student out of the classroom. Your school should have an intercom system in place to contact the office. Have an administrator escort the student to the office. Use this recourse only when a student is out of control. Refer a student to discipline only when no other options are left.

"Is working with the middle school child difficult at times? Yes, there are attitudes and behavior problems. These kids are at the age when they are deciding who they want to be. They also have the ability to have engaging conversations. Many have a delightful sense of humor. Sure, the student you just had a heart-to-heart conversation with will walk down the hall right past you and pretend they have no idea who you are. That is the nature of the middle school beast. They can make you laugh. They can make you cry. They can make you want to pull your hair out. As a middle school teacher, you might not make any difference at all in a child's life, but you could also make all the difference in the world. These kids are at a point in their lives where they are very impressionable. They might have trouble at home, relationship issues, friend problems, worries about their appearance and their bodies, concerns about extracurricular activities and of course, grades. That is a lot to burden. They need you in their lives to be an encourager, listener, comforter, supporter, and teacher. Sound like a tall order? Absolutely! But it is an extremely fulfilling profession and cannot think of any other that could be more satisfying."

— Sandy Baughman, seventh grade English
teacher, Good Hope Middle School

This chapter has given you some ideas on engineering a plan of expectations and consequences. It cannot be stressed enough to be prepared with whatever strategies you will use for classroom-behavior management from the first day forward. This will facilitate the positive learning environment you want to create. You also will facilitate mutual respect, go home feeling less tired and more fulfilled, and your students will have learned that day.

"College does not prepare you for the day-to-day 'drama' that ensues. I have experienced many things I never expected, from projectile vomiting during state testing to fights in the hallway. You may also have to deal with many serious matters, such as children who may be neglected at home or who may be recovering from the death of a parent. There are so many things that you learn from experience. The hardest part for me is keeping my heart from overpowering my head. Some of my students have experienced horrible tragedy. At those times, I want to wear my 'mom' hat and try to make it better, but I need to remember I am here to teach them and do the best I can to make their time here safe and structured. It is hard, though, when you know a child is going through such a terrible experience. You just want to give them a hug and tell them everything will be OK."

— Gretchen Pugh, sixth grade science
teacher, Good Hope Middle School

THE CHALLENGE OF SUPERVISING TWEENS AND TECHNOLOGY

As our society becomes increasingly dependent on technology, schools must create new policies on its accepted use in the school environment. In particular, computers and cell phone policies are highly debated in different school districts. Some school districts have very strict policies that prevent middle school-aged children from using cell phones. Others have very liberal policies. Most schools in the country are somewhere in between. The important thing to remember as a new teacher is to understand your school's policy and to stick to it.

Cell phone policies

Most schools have relatively strict rules regarding cell phone usage during school hours. Some schools ban them completely. A total ban might be in place so that students cannot use their cell phones for cheating. Other schools might enforce a more moderate approach. Given their use as communication between students and guardians, some schools will allow cell phones as long as they are not seen or used in the classroom. Variations to a total-ban policy exist because there are situations at home, such as domestic violence or medical issues, that might necessitate a form of communication. Ask the principal what the school's policy is concerning extenuating circumstances.

In most cases, it will be a simple blanket policy. As a new teacher, it is important to understand the policy and the consequences for students who break the rules. To avoid misunderstandings, discuss the rules with the students and post them in the classroom. Additionally, it is important to understand the school's policy regarding teacher cell phone usage.

Newer phones allow Internet access, and even phones without Internet access usually have texting and camera capabilities. This is a particular concern in view of sexting and cyberbullying. As these trends continue to grow, lawmakers are being tasked with creating new laws and regulations. As these regulations evolve, they will affect school policies concerning modern technology and its usage in schools.

Computers

Computer technology provides many positives and negatives in an academic setting. New teachers generally embrace the concept of technology. Keep in mind the need for precautions for you and your students. Understand and be willing to discuss the appropriate use of computers and the Internet. Examples of incorrect usage include cyberbullying and viewing inappropriate websites, such as those containing forms of pornography.

On the positive side, computers allow immediate access to information all around the world. The computer has all but replaced many other reference forms, such as a set of encyclopedias that become quickly outdated. The Internet also provides up-to-the-minute updates on current events and emergent situations.

On the negative side, students must be monitored in the usage of this equipment. Communication through Facebook, e-mail, and instant messaging could be used for cheating. Cutting and pasting information from other sources can lead to intentional, or even unintentional, plagiarism when researching. Also, many viruses online can wreck whole computer systems. If students are not monitored, they could inadvertently infect the school's system. Most schools have technology departments that install firewalls and other safety measures to prevent this from happening. Before using computers in the classroom, determine the school's policies on safety measures concerning the Internet.

Given these concerns, most schools have strict computer usage policies that require teachers, students, and parents to sign agreements about appropriate use of the technology. The documentation generally includes the following:

- Rules for acceptable Internet use
- Limitation of liability
- Firewalls and filtering
- Rules regarding computer access, such as who is allowed to use computers and when
- System responsibilities
- What constitutes appropriate material for viewing
- Privacy
- Copyright laws
- Plagiarism
- Personal safety
- Confidentiality
- Illegal activities
- System security issues

- Inappropriate language or photo use
- Consequences for violations to the policies
- Parent responsibility and notification of student violations to policy

Photo use

The ease of accessibility to the Internet creates many challenges. In addition to documented written material, schools must teach students the appropriate use of photos, logos, and other visual images. In creating a report that uses an image found on the Internet, students must cite the appropriate URL.

Other more serious issues involve personal photos that are taken and shared. Schools have additional documentation for parents to sign concerning photos that are taken of students in the context of school, news, and other publicity. If the guardians do not authorize the use of their child's likeness, it is illegal for the school to use it.

A bigger problem surfaces from student photo sharing. Because many cell phones have camera capabilities, inappropriate photos may be used for sexting and cyberbullying. These issues are becoming more prevalent and in the news regularly as lawmakers seek precedents allowing schools to intervene and handle these situations when they arise.

CASE STUDY: ADJUSTING TO MIDDLE SCHOOL

Katie Bialas, 13, eighth grader
Good Hope Middle School
Mechanicsburg, Pennsylvania
School enrollment: 868 students in
grades six through eight

Katie Bialas is an eighth grader at Good Hope Middle School in Mechanicsburg, Pennsylvania during the 2010 to 2011 school year. She attended school in the Cumberland Valley School District for eight years. She is an honor student and participates in multiple clubs and sports. She offers her thoughts on making the leap from elementary school to middle school.

Going from elementary school to middle school is a big adjustment. The biggest difference is the workload. There is a lot more homework given each day. There are also more sports and activities to be involved in and there is a lot more drama between students. I think most middle school students are shocked at the amount of daily homework compared to elementary school.

In elementary school, I had one primary teacher. In middle school, there is a different teacher for each subject. In addition to having to adjust to having many more teachers, there is a huge difference in the workload. The expectations are much greater. It may be to prepare students for high school, but it is a major change from the amount of work given at the elementary school level.

In the lower grades, you would be given an assignment that was due in several days. In middle school, with the exception of projects and tests, most homework is given one day and due the next. There is a lot of material to cover in each class. In order to cover everything, each teacher gives homework in his or her subject every night. Students are often tired in class from staying up late night after night trying to complete all of the daily assignments. There are many quizzes and tests to study for as well.

My friends and I discuss the situation all of the time. We are all staying up late to get our work done. If I had to give advice to a new middle school teacher, I would suggest working on more challenging assignments during class time rather than assigning so many of them on a nightly basis.

STUDENTS WITH SPECIAL NEEDS

All children in the United States are guaranteed a Free Appropriate Public Education (FAPE). Students are identified as special needs if they meet certain state and federal requirements. The identification process involves parents, teachers, the guidance counselor, the school psychologist, and, where needed, the student's doctor. Any student requiring any form of classroom modification will have an individualized education plan (IEP).

Individualized education plans

An individualized education plan (IEP) is a document discussed, formulated, and written by all the individuals involved in the student's education process. Upon completion, the involved parties meet, discuss, and sign the document. This is required for any student requiring modified special education. In most cases, the term IEP is used to refer to all of these plans. In instances of outlining plans for a gifted student, the form is called a gifted individualized education plan (GIEP).

Any student requiring any form of classroom modification will have an IEP. The IEP is developed by a team of individuals associated with the student in question. It includes teachers, parents, the student, the school psychologist, and the guidance counselor. The team will discuss the student's needs and capabilities and take them into consideration for the finalized IEP. All members of the team must sign the plan in agreement. It must include written documentation concerning the following:

- The current level of the student's academic capability
- Any issues or concerns relevant to the student's existing ability to function independently
- Yearly measurable academic goals
- Measurement criteria for the student's attainment of these goals
- A list of available special education services, supplies, and accommodations that will be provided to the student

- Specific written criteria for modifications that will be made for existing curriculum

- A schedule of special education services that will be provided to the student, including how, where, and the length of time services will be provided

- Data concerning the amount of time the student will spend in a regular classroom and a special needs resource area, otherwise known as least restrictive environment (LRE) data

- Information regarding the mandated assessments required to measure the student's academic and functional capabilities

- In cases where the student is 16 years of age or older, a plan for post-secondary school goals and transition

The IEP modifications may be simple, such as stating that a student focuses better when he or she sits in the front row. They might be more complicated, stating multiple modifications for a student with specific disabilities. Either way, you will need to refer to the information when setting up your classroom, and again for each lesson plan. This information is confidential and must be stored accordingly.

CASE STUDY: HOW TEACHERS CAN HELP STUDENTS WITH CHRONIC HEALTH PROBLEMS

Susan Minnich
Care coordinator
Penn State Hershey Children's Hospital
(717) 531-0003

Susan Minnich is the care coordinator for the Children's Hospital at Penn State Hershey Medical Center. She serves as a patient advocate and helps chronically sick children transition back into their regular routines when they leave the hospital. One of the areas she coordinates is school communication. This Case Study discusses the issue of maintaining a student's education under difficult circumstances involving a medical diagnosis.

My responsibilities include assisting medically fragile children. This information is intended to provide teachers with some background information and advice on handling situations involving these types of students.

Discharging medically fragile children to home from the hospital requires coordination of services. Sending these same children to school is a challenge. From age five to graduation, a child's main goal is to complete their education. Most children struggle with this at some point in time. Children who have a chronic medical condition have an added dimension that can complicate an easy schedule or make a heavy schedule seem impossible. Returning to school does not have to be that difficult. The issues that can complicate returning to school differ at each level.

Children in sixth through eighth grade present a different set of challenges. It is most important to be like everyone else. Image is No. 1 priority. A child with a medical condition may draw attention to him or herself. As a teacher, it is important to minimize the attention drawn to that child. For example, children with cystic fibrosis may need to receive IV antibiotics after discharge from the hospital. They have a PICC (peripherally inserted central catheter) placed prior to discharge so that they can administer their medications. The child can return to school with certain restrictions. Knowing the restrictions and allowing the student to follow them without calling attention to him or her in front of the class is important.

Tweens and teenagers are a challenge when they are well; add a chronic diagnosis, new or old, and you really have your hands full. Young people with chronic diseases are known for their poor compliance. They do not want to be different, they do not want to be reliant on medication, and they are rebellious. At this age, they need to know about their disease and their treatment. They should be taking on the responsibility of their own care. Usually they know it all, just choose not to act. Again, not drawing attention to these students is the first priority. For example, Crohn's disease is an inflammatory bowel condition that creates extreme discomfort for those affected. Teens with Crohn's disease have little time to wait when they have to use the restroom. These students should not have to ask permission to have a restroom break. They should be able to go as needed without drawing attention to themselves.

Over the years, I have encountered many different scenarios. The following are a few suggestions for dealing with medically fragile students:

- If possible, learn about the disease that your student has. It may help you understand a lot more about the individual as well.

- Ask the parents questions when you can. If that is not possible, talk to the school nurse. It is important to know what signs to look for to determine whether the student needs help.

- Try to minimize the attention that you draw to that student — both good and bad. More often than not, the individual does not want to have the extra attention, especially if it concerns their condition.

- Be respectful of their right to privacy. If they want to talk about the condition, they will. If they do not want to talk about it, let it go. Being different in any way is difficult for a child. If the issue includes pain or other difficulties, it becomes even more of a challenge.

- Despite needing to understand and perhaps even watch for signs of trouble, it is important to treat these students like everyone else.

FORMS OF COMMUNICATION AND THE PROS AND CONS OF EACH

Partnerships with parents are valuable to a student's education. They will often be your best allies. Learning how to create and nurture these alliances takes time and patience. Veteran teachers can offer suggestions from personal experience. The following are some tips to consider when you are just starting out:

- When you correspond with a student or family member in writing, keep a copy of your correspondence. It is important to save letters, notes, or e-mails in a file in case the correspondence comes into question later.

- Have someone else, such as a mentor or other trusted faculty member, read your written correspondence before you send it. The written word can be perceived multiple ways. Make sure your message is succinct and appropriate.

- When you speak with a family member on the phone, remember that your tone of voice and word choice will set the tone for the conversation. Consider practicing what you will say with a veteran teacher or mentor.

- When meeting in person, remember that tone of voice, facial expressions, and body language all convey your personal feelings about the situation. Be aware of the message you are sending.

During the middle school years, the majority of American children live with parents or other appointed guardians. If the environment includes positive adult involvement, the children have a better chance of a positive outcome later in life. There is no guarantee, but according to most studies, it helps. A study conducted in 2000 under the George W. Bush administration indicated that parents are a vital component of the academic future success of the student. A lack of parental involvement can be a major obstacle in improving student performance. Keep this in mind as you encounter different types of parents. Keeping the lines of communication open offers the best chance for a successful outcome for everyone involved.

Notes

Notes to parents at the middle school level are probably the least effective form of communication. If you send a note home with a preteen or tween, the parent might or might not ever see it. If you mail the note to their house, it has a better chance of reaching the guardian, but this too is not guaranteed. Many students this age are at home alone long before their parents get home from work or elsewhere. If they get the mail, they may prevent the parents from ever seeing it. If you do send home a written note, ask for a signed reply from the parent or guardian indicating that they saw it. This too is not foolproof; many teenagers can forge their parents' signatures.

E-mail

With today's technology, many people communicate via e-mail. It is quick and efficient, particularly if you are lucky enough to have a computer in your classroom. If you do not, and school access is limited, you can do this from home or the library. If e-mail is a viable option for communicating with the student's guardian, it should be listed on their contact information. Not everyone has a work or home computer, so keep this is mind. Additionally, if an issue is time-sensitive, this is not the best option because not everyone checks his or her e-mail on a regular basis.

"If a parent e-mails you with a concern or an issue, do not immediately blame his or her child for the problems they are facing. Be understanding about parent concerns. If you feel strongly about an issue, then stand firmly on it. When communicating via e-mail, always have a colleague check over your e-mail. They will offer you advice and make sure you have worded your comments delicately and appropriately."

— Mike Lutz, world cultures teacher, Cumberland
Valley School, Mechanicsburg, Pennsylvania

Phone calls

When speaking with numerous parents, the majority agree that phone calls are the most effective form of communication, particularly when the issue is serious or time-sensitive. It is the only way you can be sure the message is relayed. Along those lines, if you call and are unable to reach someone, continue to try until you reach the person you need to speak to. Keep track of the number of times you tried to contact someone. Do not assume that a message has been relayed. The school keeps records of the students' guardians and their contact information. Check with the school secretaries to obtain phone numbers. The school nurse is another source. Most schools require emergency contact forms that the nurse keeps on file.

Any time you speak with a parent or guardian, you need to document the conversation. You may need to provide proof at some point that you did everything you could to assist the child under a specific set of circumstances. You can organize your documentation in many ways. Some teachers keep a communication log, while others write individual notes and keep them in the student's file. Do what works for you. Just be sure to do it consistently in order to protect yourself.

Be prepared for resistance. When you need to call a parent regarding an issue concerning their child, it is probably not going to make them happy. Some will handle it better than others, but understand that as unpleasant as it is for you to make the call, it is even worse for parents to receive it. The following are a few situations you might encounter:

- **Denial.** When a parent is overtly dismissive of your suggestion or concern, saying things like, "My child would never do that," the best way to handle the situation is to be quiet until the news sinks in. Let the parent absorb what you have just told them. Wait until they are done venting his or her denial, and explain the entire situation calmly, stating only the facts. Do not pass judgment or allow your tone of voice to convey anything other than a factual recounting of the event or circumstance. Do not allow yourself to be baited. If you encounter yelling or berating on the other end of the line, stay calm and say, "I am sorry you feel that way. I just needed to call you and inform you of the situation." Get off the phone and document the conversation. If further action needs to take place, you can provide documentation of the first notification.

- **Silence.** A parent in denial may get you upset. A silent parent may be even more difficult to deal with, particularly since you are on the phone and cannot see them. You end up doing all of the talking and without seeing any facial expressions, you have no idea what he or she is thinking. Again, let the news sink in, make sure someone is still on the other end of the call and proceed slowly. Articulate all the details and end the call. Most likely, the parent on the other end is disappointed and uncertain what to say. They will most likely address the situation with their child.

- **Unconcerned.** Some parents will listen to what you are telling them and agree without concern, saying things like, "I'm not surprised," or "That's just the way he is." In these circumstances, there is little you can do other than relay the news and document the conversation. If the parent is not concerned and does not find the behavior or performance to be an issue, you probably will not be able to change his or her mind.

- **Overreacting.** On the other end of the spectrum, there will be parents who immediately want to identify and fix the problem, jumping to the worst possible conclusions as to why something happened. Your best bet is to help this parent stay calm by clearly stating the issue and explaining how you want to approach the issue from your standpoint.

Realize that although a phone call may be the most effective and necessary form of communication, it will not always be comfortable. Stay calm and do not let the person on the other end of the phone get the better of your emotions. That sounds easier than it is. Nonetheless, remember the following when delivering bad news over the phone:

- Wait to call when you are able to stay calm.
- Deliver the news simply and stick to the facts.
- Offer your suggestion for how you want to approach the issue.

- Thank the other person for their time and get off the phone as soon as you can.
- Document everything.

Face-to-face meetings

Phone calls for bad news can seem difficult, but you always have the option of getting off of the phone. Sometimes an issue warrants an actual meeting. The thought of discussing bad news with a parent in person is even more daunting than delivering it over the phone.

For serious issues, face-to-face meetings are the most effective. The first challenge might be getting it scheduled. You probably need to make a phone call to get it set up and getting them to agree to a time might depend on their work schedules. Additionally, you will have to use some other form of communication initially to set up the meeting. If you talk to them on the phone, you will need to provide some information up front. Be prepared to answer questions at that time. Remember to use positive word choices whenever possible so you do not put them on the defensive. Most of the time, you will be able to handle the meeting without concerns. Other times, you may have to deal with difficult people.

"Other than the conference, I don't expect a lot of regular communication from the teachers at this level. Students should be taking more responsibility at this point."

— Tracy Katshir, parent of student
at Good Hope Middle School

TIPS FOR DEALING WITH DIFFICULT PARENTS

The following are some effective strategies for neutralizing difficult situations with volatile individuals:

- In situations involving confrontation, always stay at eye level with the other person. If you sit and they stand, they will be looking down at you, allowing them the power in the situation. Ideally, both parties should be seated. In conflict scenarios, a new teacher should plan to have back-up. In delicate face-to-face situations, it is recommended that you have a third party present, such as a principal.

- Remain calm. A calm tone with neutral words is sometimes the best way to diffuse the situation. If you get angry back at some who is angry, all you do is escalate the problem.

- Listen attentively without interrupting. Wait until they are done talking. Sometimes people just need to vent.

- When they are finished, calmly state the facts pertaining to the situation. Do not relay judgment or feelings.

- Respect the people you are talking with and expect them to respect what you are saying. Do not allow yourself to be bullied.

- If the other individual does attempt to bully you, stop the conversation. Calmly state that you do not permit anyone to speak with you in that tone of voice. Allow the person a minute or two to calm down and collect himself or herself. If the person does, continue with the meeting. If they cannot stop yelling, end the meeting. Do this by calmly and quietly walking away.

- It is of utmost importance that you always conduct yourself calmly and professionally. Even if you feel like a bundle of emotion on the inside, never let them see you sweat.

Dealing with parents is probably one of the hardest parts of the job. In particular, having to impart negative information about a student to his or her parent or guardian is not pleasant. On the other hand, it is very rewarding to be able to pass on praise and other positive statements about students. Make sure this is an integral part of your communication. Find ways to praise whenever possible. Doing this makes everyone feel better and it will give more credence to the less than positive remarks if you are not always complaining about student performance and behavior.

CHAPTER 13

Handling the Unexpected

No specific personality profile fits every teacher. You might be an optimistic college graduate excited to take on the challenges of the modern classroom. You might trust that deep down everyone needs and wants to learn. You might be a mid-career professional who is generally cynical about the world in general. You might think you know how middle schoolers think. You might truly believe that you are prepared for anything and that nothing could shock you. Regardless of how prepared you feel, you will be faced with unexpected challenges daily. One piece of advice that resounded from multiple teachers: No matter how much time you spend planning, you need to remember to be flexible.

This profession is not for everyone. Some teachers leave the profession because they feel overworked, underpaid, overwhelmed, and underappreciated. Some teachers have even contacted the National Education Association and/or the U.S. Department of Education regarding concerns about poor working conditions, building issues, and crowded classrooms. Other teachers object to out-of-date textbooks and materials, inadequate planning time, too many unnecessary meetings, and insufficient pay. It might sound dismal, but it is better to prepare for the worst and be pleasantly surprised because it does not live up to the horror stories.

So how do you survive? Talk to veteran teachers who are still passionate about their jobs. If possible, sit in on their classes. Negative energy is contagious, but thankfully, so is positive energy. It is fine to know the potential downside of the job, but also have a plan for revisiting the upside as often as possible. Luckily, the profession is filled with optimists. Surround yourself with as many as you can — and as often as possible. Veteran teachers who have a positive attitude can offer you a wealth of information, as well as inspiration to keep going.

You start the job armed with plans and ideals. You have reviewed your notes from school and believe you are ready for your new career as a teacher. General education programs might differ in specifications, but they all boast preparedness for teaching. Unfortunately, college cannot prepare you for everything. The pages that follow include some of the less than ideal scenarios you may encounter during your first year as a middle school teacher. On the plus side, you will only be new and inexperienced for a short period. In the mean time, remain flexible and positive and never lose your sense of humor.

THE COLD HARD FACTS

Teaching is hard work. Teaching middle school students is especially challenging. Unfortunately, many idealistic individuals leave the profession because their expectations do not coincide with reality. The following are facts you need to know:

- According to the National Center for Education Statistics (NCES), one out of every five first-year teachers leaves the profession within the first three years.

- Each year, 30 percent of new teachers entering the profession will leave after only two years.

- The proportion of new teachers who leave the profession in the first five years remains around 50 percent. This is a statistic that has existed for several decades, according to Barry A. Farber, a professor of education and psychology at Columbia University in New York.

- More than 50 percent will be gone by the end of seven years.

- The statistics for inner-city schools are even worse. Approximately 50 percent of new teachers in urban areas leave the profession within their first three years.

You might have heard these statistics before. There are multiple reasons for these depressing numbers. There are two primary reasons most teachers cite to explain their departures from this noble profession: They receive insufficient earnings and operate in poor working conditions. There is simply not enough money invested in educating the future generations. These are the people who will inherit the country and they are inadequately prepared. This is, however, not a new problem and has been lamented by educators for the most of the last century. These are the facts and you need to be aware of them as you enter the field of education. Times will be tough and the pay is not great. If you embrace this knowledge and keep a positive attitude, you will be able to survive and even succeed as a teacher.

DISCREPANCIES TO EMBRACE NOW

The following are some details educators did not teach you in college or a teaching accreditation course. These are some of the harsh truths concerning your chosen profession. It is a difficult profession, and it is not for everyone. If you can work past these negatives and focus on the reason you wanted to be a teacher, you will be better prepared to reach your students.

The way it is portrayed versus the way it really is

As you complete your first year of teaching middle school, you will discover some common misconceptions regarding the field of education. If you know what to expect, you will be better prepared. The following are a few fallacies you might encounter:

- Your school's student-teacher ratio is very appealing. Actually, student-teacher ratios do not provide a direct measure of class size. The ratio is determined by dividing the total number of full-time-equivalent teachers into the total student enrollment. These teachers include classroom teachers; prekindergarten teachers in some elementary schools;

art, music, and physical education teachers; and teachers who do not teach regular classes every period of the day. Teachers are reported in full-time-equivalent (FTE) units. This is the amount of time required to perform an assignment stated as a proportion of a full-time position. It is computed by dividing the amount of time an individual is employed by the time normally required for a full-time position.

- **Making the difference in the life of even one child makes it all worthwhile**. That sounds great, and you will probably have many rewarding moments along the way. The harsh reality is that daily teaching can be monotonous and at times extremely unfulfilling. It can be equated to parenting. What you are doing is extremely important, but that does not mean you will get a lot of gratitude for what you do. For the most part, many people believe that they work daily in their jobs so their taxes can pay your salary.

  If, on the other hand, you can hold on to those moments where you have truly reached someone for the first time, you will succeed.

- **The teaching profession has preferable hours**. Many individuals enter the profession thinking it coincides with the hours of their own children's schedules, making it easier to both work and be a good parent. Do not be fooled. Teachers work more than 40 hours, just as in many other careers. They must come in early and stay later. Much of the time, they must prepare for lessons on their own time. Holidays and vacations may appear to coincide with students', but teachers work many of the days that students have off. Additionally, having the summer off is an appealing concept, but teachers do not actually have three months off for vacation. Extra time is required at the beginning and end of the terms to wrap up and prepare for the next class. Schools also have numerous meeting and seminars that require mandatory attendance.

  As long as you did not become a teacher for the hours, you will be fine. Most other salaried positions require work beyond 40 hours and all through the summer as well.

- **The freedom to move around throughout the day and talk to multiple people makes the day go by quickly**. There is some truth to this. Some days may go by quickly, but mostly because you cannot seem to finish anything you start because of interruptions. On the other hand, there will be days that seem rather slow and tedious. Either way, there is little time to accomplish the little things you may now take for granted, such as eating and going to the bathroom. Today's teachers complain that there is little or no personal time built into daily schedules. Not only does this make planning time difficult, it also makes taking care of yourself a challenge.

Unfortunately, this is true for most people today, regardless of their chosen profession. The best advice is to take care of yourself outside of the classroom. Eat well, sleep as much as you can, and exercise to combat stress.

Prepare for the following

This chapter might seem negative in comparison to what you have learned in college. If you are prepared for some of the harsh realities, there is a better chance you will survive the first year. Additionally, facing facts is easier to do when you know what to expect. The following are a few possibilities you may encounter as a first-year middle school teacher:

- You will probably have some, if not multiple, students who have been labeled "troubled" or "bad." When scheduling occurs, returning teachers do everything they can to request the students and classes they prefer. New teachers generally get who is left, or the individuals no one wants to work with.

- Your first classroom may be undesirable. This is another issue of seniority. The teachers who have been around the longest will have the best rooms and equipment. You may be stuck with what is left. Quite possibly, you might not have a classroom at all. In some schools, there are teachers who are required to "float" because there are not enough classrooms for each teacher to have his or her own space. Use what you are given to the best of your ability. Things change and people leave. If you can weather the storm early on, you will earn the right to choose your own space later on.

- You do not get to teach the subject you are best at. There is a teaching shortage, and because many teachers leave after a short amount of time, you might be slotted in wherever you are needed. It may not be in the grade or subject matter you have prepared for. Be flexible. You will earn the respect of those you work for and with. They might not express it, but you will have a job. That needs to be enough for now. As in most professions, you need to earn your way up the ladder.

- Expect the unexpected. A lot of teaching deals with Murphy's Law. If and when something can go wrong, it probably will. Even the most optimistic person can become disheartened when things repeatedly go wrong. Just accept it and continue to work with what you have. Eventually you will be able to deal with anything you encounter. On that note, if you cannot handle something, do not let your students know — it will make you vulnerable. Keep your emotions in check.

- Do not expect to win over your students or your peers immediately. Earning respect takes time. Do not be afraid to make mistakes or to ask questions. Remain as positive as you can and learn to deal with each scenario as it occurs. You will not earn anyone's respect by whining about your circumstances.

"What is my best tip or piece of advice to anyone just getting started as a new middle school teacher? Be flexible! Nothing ever goes as planned. You constantly have to punt when situations arise. If you learn to be flexible, it will make things much easier."

— Gretchen Pugh, sixth grade science
teacher, Good Hope Middle School

Compensating for crowds

Be prepared. Overcrowding in schools is a nationwide epidemic. Some school districts tend to mislead incoming teachers on the actual student-to-teacher ratio.

They do this by using relative math. In other words, they count personnel who assist, but are not actual teachers, such as aides and volunteers. There are numerous reasons for this; some might be financial, while others may have to do with state requirements. Whatever the reasons might be, it is something that new teachers need to be aware of.

The problem of overcrowded classrooms is not limited to big cities, as many people believe. The problem persists in suburban and rural school districts as well. Sometimes the overcrowding in rural and suburban schools is even worse than in the big cities. The fact is there are too few classrooms to adequately house and educate all of the students in the country.

With few exceptions, such as a larger lecture-only class, classes with more students are more challenging to teach. If you are trying to teach a larger number of students with different learning styles and ability levels, particularly if there is a hands-on component to your lesson plan, keeping track of all the students may be difficult.

In many cases, there may be more discipline problems. Additionally, noise can be an issue. It is much more difficult to get 40 preteens to calm down and get to work than it is 20 students. Problems and noise tend to escalate at an exponential rate. The following are a few ideas on managing an overcrowded classroom:

- Keep a positive attitude. If the students sense you are unhappy with the situation, their attitudes will be negative as well.

- Be prepared and committed to your lesson plan. Try to stay on topic no matter what. If you veer off course, it will be tougher to get everyone back on track.

- Keep your lessons interesting. Captivate your students and encourage them to interact with the lessons, and this will help maintain a cooperative, enjoyable learning environment.

- Teach common courtesy by using it. Do not allow students to interrupt you, or each other.

- Keep the noise level at a minimum. Loud noise only makes kids want to get louder.

- Pay attention to room arrangement, making it as open and user-friendly as possible.
- Stay on top of grading papers to reduce your stress. If you get behind with a large number of students, it can be overwhelming to catch up.

Students' ability to focus is another problem that comes with overcrowding, especially if there are one or more students who create distractions. New teachers especially find overcrowding frustrating because they are in a learning period of their career. Truth be told, even veteran teachers cannot meet the needs of every child in an overcrowded classroom. This does not mean teachers should not, or do not, try; it simply means it is close to impossible to do. When you have an overfull classroom, it is even more important to know your students individually in order to have a better chance of helping them.

Asking for help is imperative when you have an overloaded class. Ask if it is possible to get a teacher's aide. Peer tutoring and student pairing may help lighten the load, but try not to rely on this too often. It is not fair to expect students to do this frequently. They may become bitter if they are doing some of the teaching and not having the opportunity to learn something new.

Another product of overcrowded classrooms is insufficient supplies. Many schools are finding that there are not enough textbooks for every student. There are a few ways to handle this situation, including:

1. Leave the textbooks in the classroom and have students sign them out as needed. This might work in theory, but it can also create another set of problems. Textbooks can disappear. Additionally, it might be difficult for all of the students to get the reading and other assignments completed on time. Subsequently, studying for tests is an issue if some of the material is only in the text and all the students do not have copies to take with them prior to the test.

2. Make photocopies of the material that you want the students to read. Have students hole-punch it and keep it in their binders. This way, they have it to study from for future tests and quizzes. An even more effective idea is to blank out some of the words and have them fill the information in during class. It encourages note taking and it becomes a better study aid.

3. Check to see whether your textbooks are available online. Some book companies now offer full copies of their textbooks online. Many of them are even interactive for studying. This is great for multiple reasons. Students will not need to constantly carry 50 or more pounds of books back and forth to school every day, and it will help eliminate the "I forgot to take my book home" excuse for not completing the assignment. Of course, this is only viable for individuals who have computers and Internet access in their home.

Another by-product of overcrowded classrooms may be a shortage of desks. If you find yourself in this situation, hopefully, it is only temporary. Talk to the administrative staff to determine whether there are extra desks anywhere in storage or in another teacher's classroom that you can use. If not, find out what you need to do to order additional desks and chairs. In the meantime, find out whether there are tables and chairs you can use.

Overcrowding is a stressful issue for both teachers and administrators. The problems that arise due to overcrowding can become major issues. According to teachers surveyed for a 2008 report by the National Economics and Social Rights Initiative organization, there is a small increase in school violence with overcrowding because students are harder to control. In 2006, a Chicago principal named Martin McGreal was fired when he closed enrollment to prevent overcrowding.

McGreal was faced with burgeoning class sizes. The school roster that fall would have pushed class size beyond 40 students per teacher. They wanted him to add a third shift of classes beginning at noon to handle the situation. This shift would have extended the school day to 6 p.m. Although most of the parents applauded McGreal's decision to put the students first, he was fired anyway. The school ultimately added the students and employed the third shift concept anyway.

Students and teachers sometimes find themselves forced into cramped spaces that were never meant to be classrooms because of overcrowding. Cramped areas plus too many bodies equals health problems. Overcrowding causes more than just the adverse effect on learning; the spread of colds, influenza, skin disorders, and other health issues are more widespread in classrooms that have a large number of students. This also means the teacher is more likely to catch whatever germ happens to be floating around on any given day. Washing your hands as often as possible, exercising, eating right, and reducing stress is the best fight against the germs you will come into contact with daily.

Student overcrowding also affects the bathrooms. Not only does this problem make it harder to keep the bathrooms clean, which causes more germs and health hazards, but it is more difficult for teachers to allow students to go to the bathroom due to an abundance of people in the building.

In 2008, the education department enrollment figures showed some schools in New York were as much as 200 percent over capacity. Many teachers agree overcrowding affects their instructional techniques. Research as far back as 1988 has proven that congested classrooms cause more stress for teachers and leads to more teacher absenteeism due to physical sickness and stress. Early burnout is another effect stuffed classrooms have on teachers, and it is an important point to consider. In a 2008 survey, 76 percent of first year teachers said that reducing class size would be "a very effective" way of improving teacher quality, and 21 percent responded that it would be an "effective" method.

Teachers and students alike feel overwhelmed, discouraged, and disgusted with the space shortage and its consequences for learning due to overcrowding. Students complained their papers were not checked daily and they did not feel comfortable "taking part in class discussions or special projects." The report also stated, "Teachers are deeply disturbed by overcrowding, and staff stress management related to overcrowding." Teachers have also reported overcrowding as the largest threat to safety due to tension and chaos created by sharing a crowded space. The exasperation and frustration teachers experience because of the inability to have good relationships with their students in overcrowded classrooms was another major concern, according to a report by the National Economic and Social Rights Initiative and the Teachers Unite organization.

While overcrowding is a major concern and issue, it is still possible to survive teaching under these conditions. Holding your students' attention is a priority, but once you have that attention you can build a team environment.

Another possible and highly probable scenario is having no classroom at all. Many new teachers are deemed "floaters." These individuals have the added challenge of not only being able to plan what they need for their lessons, but also having to carry materials with them as they go.

ROAMING WITHOUT A DESIGNATED CLASSROOM

Depending on the school, there might be more courses and teachers than applicable classroom space. In these situations, you may be required to share a space with another teacher or staff member. If that happens, be respectful of the other individual. It might be a shock to him or her as well. If a veteran teacher suddenly has to share a space with you, he or she might not appreciate it either. Approach the situation accordingly.

The situation is not ideal, to say the least. Hopefully, it is just temporary. Either way, you need to adjust and find a way to deal with the situation. Many new teachers are faced with similar circumstances each year. Think about your priorities and go from there.

The following tips will help you stay organized without a classroom:

1. Find a school supply cart that you can designate as your own. You will need to have a way to transport your supplies. Ask around to find out how to obtain one that can be assigned to you for the remainder of your time as a roaming teacher. If you do not plan for this in the beginning, you risk having someone take your cart for other purposes when you are not around. Supplies in general are coveted in the school environment. Larger, more expensive items such as carts may be in short supply. You have a valid argument for needing a permanent cart; you just need to find out whom to approach about getting one. Remember, if you are pleasant when you make the request, you will have a better chance of obtaining what you need than if you demand something with an air of entitlement.

2. Locate a safe spot in the building for your personal belongings. There will be times during the day when you cannot pay attention to your cart. That

being said, it is not the best place to store personal items, such as purses, cell phones, and keys. Find a teacher or other staff member you trust and ask if you can have a spot to lock up your personal belongings.

3. Visit and assess the classrooms you will be working in. You will not have the luxury of organizing the furniture to fit your needs. In order to ensure your success, and the success of your class, find a way to work with the environment as is. It does not matter how nice the other teacher is. The person who permanently occupies the space does not want you to reorganize the space to fit your needs.

After you obtain the cart, you need to figure out how to get and keep it organized for all of your classes. The following are a few tips for setting it up to suit your needs:

- Procure a lightweight box to use as a filing system. You can purchase a small filing system from any office supply store. If you are short on funds, consider using a milk crate or square plastic tub. Include hanging folders and manila files to organize handouts and other paperwork you will need daily. For security reasons, do not include paperwork on students that should remain private. Find another location for that information — perhaps a locked file drawer allocated by another teacher or support staff member. Another possibility is to carry a lockable briefcase for any materials that may be questionable.

- Obtain a variety of plastic bins with lids in different sizes. You may also want a box of large plastic bags that zip closed. You will need a place for all of your school supplies. Do not assume that you can use the supplies that belong to the teacher who occupies the classroom. Bring everything you could possibly need. The lids and zip enclosures will help secure items in case of an accident. Do not underestimate the possibility of someone bumping into the cart. You will want to make sure all items are secure and organized. Having to pick up items and put them back in the proper bins takes up too much time. Plan accordingly.

- Carry a small first aid kit. Plan for items you would normally keep in your desk to get through the day. These items are for you, not the students.

You can always send them to the nurse's office. You, on the other hand, will not have time to go to the nurse's office. Your emergency kit should include anything you might need throughout a typical day. For example it might contain ibuprofen, tissues, hand sanitizer, hand cream, bandages, safety pins, and a needle and thread.

- Be creative. Make the cart yours by decorating with items that pertain to the class. You might not have bulletin boards, but you can still find a way to advertise your class. Use the space you have. You may even want to decorate it for the holidays. Some roaming teachers even add flashing colored lights to their carts.

- Above all, maintain a positive attitude and keep your sense of humor. Those two things alone will help you get through the worst of it. If you have the right attitude, you can turn this into a positive experience. For example, you will get more exercise each day than your peers who remain in their classrooms.

OTHER DUTIES UPON REQUEST

Despite such hardships, it should be stressed that teaching can be wonderful and fulfilling. Many believe it is the most important job anyone can ever do — teachers are responsible for teaching every other profession. That being said, it is also exhausting, and at times thankless, work. If you got into this profession because you longed for student hours working 8 a.m. to 3 p.m. five days a week and having three months of vacation in the summer, you will be sadly disappointed.

Teaching is beyond a full-time position. It requires a major commitment, especially when you are first starting out. Plan to work round the clock on lesson plans and grading your first year. Additionally, there might be many other tasks and responsibilities that eat into your time as well. There are four primary categories: School-day tasks, afterschool requirements, extracurricular activities, and meetings. Here are some of the time constraint factors you may not have considered.

School-day tasks

As a teacher, you expect to spend hours planning lessons and grading work. As a new middle school teacher, you will probably teach five or six classes a day. You are prepared for that. You may not realize, however, that the remaining unscheduled hours are not free planning time. Especially in the current economic climate, with huge school budget cuts, you will be expected to handle a number of other responsibilities. These "as needed" tasks include:

- **Covering other teachers' classes:** It is not always easy to get substitutes at the last minute for every class. If a class does not have a scheduled substitute, other teachers will cover during the periods they have open on their schedules. Just remember to have a good attitude and do the best you can. At some point, that teacher might be covering for you.

- **Study hall:** You will probably not sit in an empty room during any of your class-free periods. Study halls need monitoring teachers. The good news is if you have a good group of students, you might be able to get some work done.

- **Clerical jobs:** All schools require a great deal of paperwork. Even if your school has multiple people in clerical positions, on occasion, you will be expected to copy, collate, staple, and or file. You might even need to answer phones or deliver messages. Everyone helps out, and the sooner you accept it, the easier it will be.

- **Hallway monitor:** Some teachers are given hallway or school perimeter detail. In other words, you have to make sure no one is in the wrong place at the wrong time, doing something wrong. Because you are dealing with middle school students, this can be a challenge. You might have to make sure students get back to class. You might need to break up fights and give out detention. In worse-case scenarios, such as with drug and weapon infractions, you might even call for law enforcement back up. Whatever the situation, take it seriously. It might seem like babysitting, but it is really security detail. As such, it is very important, so do not stand around talking to other teachers and students. Stay alert and do a good job.

- **Cafeteria coverage:** Cafeteria detail is similar to hallway and parking lot monitoring in that you are really monitoring the safety of the students. Hopefully, the biggest concerns will be students cutting in line. Nonetheless, pay attention. It might seem like a bothersome task, but it is still important.

Afterschool requirements

There might be times when you are asked to stay after school to monitor students as well. Some of these items, like detention, might be on a rotating basis. Others might just go to the first available person. As the bottom teacher on the totem pole, you will likely get assigned. Take it all in stride. Everything you do earns you experience and respect, and you will not be the new person forever. The following are some afterschool tasks you may encounter:

- **Detention:** Detention is generally not anyone's favorite job. It might require you to come in early or stay late. Additionally, you might be dealing with an unruly group of kids. Take it for what it is and work through it. No assignment lasts forever. One local school district keeps students in line with a scheduled work program. For certain infractions, or for acquiring too many detentions, the students are required to come in on Saturday mornings to clean the school bathrooms. This punishment is very effective.

- **Tutoring:** There are different types of tutoring. There are some instances where you will stay late to run study groups for an upcoming test. There are other times where you might take on an additional assignment as a paid tutor.

Extracurricular activities

Depending on the type and size of your school, it might offer a number of extracurricular activities. Some people volunteer to lead these groups because they have experience in the type of activity. Many others end up being assigned because no one else would do it. First year teachers are frequently assigned these responsibilities. You might feel completely overwhelmed and snowed under with paperwork. Rather than try to avoid the inevitable, show that you are flexible and willing to be a team player. It will benefit you in the end. The following are a few middle school activities requiring teacher involvement:

- **Club advisor:** If there is an activity you would like to be involved in from personal experience or interest, look into that first. If there is an opening, most schools would love to have you share your experience. If not, you will probably be targeted for either a new group or one that no one wants. Student groups are generally not allowed to organize without an adult sponsor. In many schools, students can start a club with as few as five individuals as long as they find a teacher to sponsor the group and attend the meetings. Because you are new, students might approach you to sponsor their new group.

"Some club advisors get compensated, but others do not in public school. It is usually a union issue. When one teacher asked for compensation, she was told to take it up with the union. To be honest, unless you are the football coach or wrestling coach, the financial reward is quite slim. Teachers at our school do not usually get involved with these activities for the money."

— Kathy Heisler, special interest teacher, Cumberland Valley

- **Sporting event assistance:** Most schools have a wide array of sports teams. In addition to coaching, there are many other tasks that need volunteers. Some schools pay teachers a small amount for these tasks, while others do not. These responsibilities include keeping scorebooks and other stats, running scoreboards, helping in concession stands, working at fundraisers, and being an announcer.

- **Other social events:** In addition to clubs and sports, social endeavors require teacher presence. School dances need chaperones. There might be talent shows and plays with faculty members at some schools. Some schools host fun events, such as bingo or casino night, and might recruit teacher helpers.

Meetings

Your presence might also be requested at numerous meetings. Some might be more important than others. Some you absolutely must attend. If you are uncertain, ask a colleague. The following are some of the meetings you will be expected to attend as a middle school teacher:

- **Staff and department meetings:** If the school is having a staff meeting, you must attend. There might be a policy change, or you might be celebrating someone's retirement. Department meetings will be with the chairperson of your department and other staff members who teach in your department. These are also important and will cover department goals, texts, materials, budgets for supplies, and other program specific information.

- **Early-year professional development meetings:** Your district will require you to attend meetings before the start of the school year. These meetings usually will incorporate side meetings for core curriculum areas such as English, social studies, math, and science. In fact, at least one day of events should be held solely for new teachers. Your new-teacher meeting will include mainly human resources information such as insurance and retirement benefits, explanations of sick time, information on using the county's computer networking systems, and information on e-mail and access to student assessment testing scores. Some districts, including Lake County, Florida, hold a week of professional development for new teachers to introduce them to the world of education as it applies in their district. Lake County's meetings provide workshops that help teachers navigate the district's policies while getting to know other teachers on the starting line of their careers.

Lake County's workshops reinforce the vision the district has for its incoming faculty and are often led by successful veteran instructors. In the mornings, interdisciplinary information, such as classroom management, is facilitated in the cafeteria. Teachers attend afternoon workshops that are broken down by the subject areas they are teaching in. Instructors who are seasoned in Lake County's policies and specific subject areas lead these meetings. Most of them are eager to help you get the information you need about curriculum, classroom management, and lesson-plan suggestions. Because the workshops are so small, there is more opportunity for discussion about the numerous questions new teachers have.

Even if your district has only the requisite one-day teacher meetings to fill out forms, each department will have an early-school-year district meeting for the subject you will teach. If you teach math, the math department will have a meeting where you and your fellow math teachers will come together from throughout the district. The curriculum you will teach and the pacing of your units and lesson plans come from your district's office. Curriculum and pacing guides are essential.

- **School board meetings:** As a new teacher, you should attend school board meetings in order to become familiar with how the district facilitates and maintains the integrity of its mission statement. You also will get to know the individuals who comprise the school board, and you will understand how policies are implemented. Districts post meeting schedules on their websites or in their newsletters, and these meetings often are held on the same day of each week or month, during evening hours. They are public forums, and anyone is invited to attend. This is a great way to find out how your district works. Citizens, teachers, and students might share their opinions with prior notification, so meetings tend to be long and drawn-out when controversial issues are on the floor.

You might find everything from subsidy debates to calendar decisions, and perhaps even people protesting the latest teaching trend or funding fiasco. This edification is well worth your time.

- **PTO/PTA:** School-related meetings might require your presence as a representative of the staff. Additionally, you might find they are discussing a topic pertinent to your job or a major change at the school.

PROFESSIONAL DEVELOPMENT

You have spent years in school preparing to teach. You are finally working in your chosen profession and it is going to take a while to get into a routine. It will come. Be patient and flexible and realize you continue to learn as you go. Before you know it, you will be a veteran educator assisting another first year middle school teacher. The next thing you will need to think about is professional development. As you start teaching, you should start thinking ahead to what you need to do in order to plan your professional development. Every state has its own specific guidelines for teacher professional development. Some states require you to accumulate credits in the first few years of teaching.

Some require hours and credits, others do not. There is also a variety in the time frame you are expected to complete the development in. For example, in Pennsylvania, when a teacher receives their Level I teaching certificate, they have six years to teach on their certificate. If you do not begin teaching on their certificate for three years, that time does not count toward time used on the certificate. When a teacher begins teaching on their Level I certificate, they have six years to apply for their Level II certificate. These teachers can apply for their Level II certificate once they meet the minimum of three years teaching on the certificate and attainment of 24 post-baccalaureate credits. For general teaching, there is not a specific time frame required to obtain your master's degree.

Additionally, there may be a time component. In Pennsylvania, educators must meet 180 hours every five years to keep their certificate active. Any way you look at it, you will have to allocate time to attend extra schooling.

Rather than become overwhelmed from waiting too long, check out your state's criteria right away. If you start scheduling it now, in smaller increments, it will be easier to handle. There are a few options for professional development courses including:

- **In-service training**. The good news is it can count toward professional development requirements. The bad news is you will not have time for grading, organizing, and lesson planning on those extra days.

- **Classes on the weekends**. The length of the class could run a couple of hours or longer. This might seem like a convenient option until you have grading that you cannot get done any other time.

- **Classes on the Internet.** These courses do not require you to leave home, which is a big plus. If you schedule them during the school year, however, you could be adding extra stress.

- **Summer classes.** Some people want to leave their summers for fun vacations or spending time with their families. That is understandable. Nonetheless, summer is the easiest time to get professional development completed and out of the way.

Once you have settled into a regular routine, find a mentor and get advice on some of the professional development options in your area. Ask other teachers in your department what they have done and when they accrued what they needed.

CHAPTER 14:

Politics and Education

To understand the rationale behind testing, special needs, and other mandates, new teachers should have an understanding of the laws and regulations behind them. This chapter explains some of the pertinent government policies concerning education. Additionally, it clarifies for the new teacher how those laws affect various aspects of the first year classroom experience.

By this time, you know what the job entails, whom you are working with, and how to teach your class. It seems pretty simple and straightforward. However, you are not quite there yet. Now it is time for you to discover a myriad of truths that no one told you about in school: the factors you have no control over.

WHAT YOU NEED TO UNDERSTAND

Although you report to the schools' administration and have to answer to the school board, there are actually other factions in charge of your job. Educating the youth of America is a very involved process. It is also a costly affair. You have heard that taxpayers pay teachers' salaries, but how exactly does that work?

Control and funding for education in America comes from three places: federal, state, and local governments. Despite being responsible for the allocation of funds, the government is not involved in setting curriculum. This is a very good thing, especially when you consider that there are more than 5,000 employees in the U.S. Department of Education. Dealing with 5,000 ideas for creating curriculum would be an overwhelming task. Nevertheless, the government does impact the amount of funding each school receives by determining how much money each district is allowed to receive from federal funding. The state also has a say in how much funding certain schools receive from the state.

Understanding mandates

A mandate is essentially a law. It is an obligation handed down by some form of government. In terms of education, there are many mandates that affect those teaching in public schools. Although some issues affect all forms of education, most relate only to public schools. This is one of the primary differences between public schools, charter schools, and private institutions. The government essentially provides funding for public schools, and as such, it indicates what outcomes it expects. The mandates appear at three different levels: federal legislation, state legislation, and local regulations. Federal mandates affect all schools. State legislation varies based on the state's interpretation of their education policies and local mandates are regulated by each school district.

Deciphering the principal's data

No matter what their leadership style is, you will find one of the tools principals commonly use to impart their expectations to the faculty is standardized testing data. A principal's goals will be established by the superintendent and the school board to some degree. Currently, however, the greatest driving force behind middle school principal goals in the United States is the No Child Left Behind Act (NCLB), which is a federal mandate requiring students to perform at pre-established levels.

No Child Left Behind (NCLB)

In 2002, under President George W. Bush's administration, the NCLB Act was signed into law and passed with the intention of getting all students' performances up to their grade level or beyond by the year 2014. The act requires assessments in different subjects at certain grade levels. These assessments are to be acquired during specified years set by the government.

NCLB legislation is set up to begin working with students from the early grades. Given that, a large part of NCLB regulations are concerned with grades three through eight, with concentrated testing every year.

The NCLB Act is federal legislation by which all public schools, districts, and states are accountable. The basic premise is that all students will be able to read on grade level by third grade and continue to be proficient in math and reading throughout their education. Students' results and progress are measured by adequate yearly progress (AYP). It is part of your principal's responsibilities to ensure students meet each year's gains — the amount of points they must increase by to reach the goal set for their grade level. In the kick-off days before students arrive, the principal will share the previous year's data with you and will use it as a baseline to construct goals for the coming school year.

One of the benefits of NCLB is that it provides ways to set and use measurable goals. It will help you as a teacher to see where your particular students fit. This is a fine opportunity to be able to coordinate your principal's goals with your student's expected achievements and apply those to your classroom and/or professional development plans.

When your principal is presenting data, if a copy of it has not been provided to you, ask for one after the meeting. This will give you time to decipher the information you need, such as goals and statistics involving his or her expectations for your class and the relevant standardized testing.

NCLB is an exceptional accountability system. The following are some of the facts about the NCLB Act that you need to know in your early days of teaching:

- The NCLB information is based on statewide tests taken by students toward the end of the school year, usually late March or April. The tests are designed in accordance with the federal guidelines set forth in the NCLB Act. Titles of these tests vary from state to state. For example, Maine has the Maine Comprehensive Assessment System, Florida has the Florida Comprehensive Assessment Test, and California has the California Standards Test.

- The statistics most likely will be compared to other schools in your district and state.

- There will be an overall score, which is determined by variables as mandated by NCLB. During your principal's presentation, you will be able to note your overall score compared with those of other schools.

- Scores then are broken down into separate tested areas. There is always math and reading, and in many states, writing and even science and social studies are included.

- The statistics are then broken down again into subgroups. Subgroups can include lower-economic level students, often referred to as "receiving free and reduced lunch." Subgroups are broken down even further into ethnic categories such as African-American, Asian, Hispanic, and Caucasian.

- Gains are how much each student, group, and overall school improved from the previous year. Your school's gains will determine whether it has met adequate yearly progress as determined by NCLB.

From there, your principal will consider the progress made the previous year and present expectations for this year. For example, if your school did fairly well overall, but Hispanic students showed a decrease in math, the principal's goal might be, "Our school goal is to have all students improve 5 percent on reading scores. Hispanic students will increase their mathematics score by 7 percent."

Some principals, knowing that teachers are on the frontlines of student improvement, might distribute the data, break teachers up into department groups (for example math, reading, and English) and then have the department chairs report back with findings, goals, and what the teachers will need to reach their goals.

Finally, a goal will be set for the school year, which will likely be included in your school's mission statement. Many teachers have found that these measurable goals provide more clarity for what they should teach in the classroom. It cannot be stressed enough, however, that these goals are not set so that teachers are required to "teach to a test." It might seem overwhelming when you are creating your lesson plans. Keep in mind that other teachers have been accomplishing the NCLB goals for several years now, so it is possible.

In order to assist your students, you must first accept the importance of these standards. If you do not believe in the standards you are teaching, your teaching skills will be affected. You will not be the most effective teacher you can be, and your students might not do well on the mandated tests.

Although it is a good idea to review standardized test-taking strategies, by the time your students have reached middle school, they know how to fill in the bubbles. Teach students the skills they need to be successful, such as reading instructions carefully and critically thinking their way through math problems, and they will do astonishingly well on their assessments later in the year.

Take note that a percentage of the revenue your state receives from the federal government, which then filters down to your district and school, is either directly or indirectly related to achievement of the NCLB standards. Do not ignore the importance of statistics that your principal presents. His or her job depends on whether you meet the NCLB federal mandate: That *every* student succeeds.

THE INDIVIDUALS WITH DISABILITIES EDUCATION ACT (IDEA)

Mandating standards ensures that baseline criteria are met for students. Some students, however, are either above or below the baseline. What happens to them? There are mandated regulations that provide rights for students with other needs. These laws also protect the rights of parents of special needs children so that they have a voice in their education. The concept evolving from these laws and regulations is now known as "inclusion." In other words, under the current regulations, students with special needs have the right to be included in regular classrooms.

In 1975, Congress enacted the Individuals with Disabilities Education Act (IDEA). The purpose of the legal action was to guarantee the opportunity of appropriate free public education for children with disabilities. Many updates were made to the law before its final regulations were published in 2006.

One of the most important amendments came into fruition in 1997. IDEA was amended and schools were required to educate special needs children in regular classrooms whenever possible. The individual education plan (IEP) requirement for all special needs children was implemented. A team of teachers, administrators, parents, counselors, and outside experts must develop the IEP. The student for which the plan is developed is also part of the IEP team. Together, this team creates a learning plan that stresses the special needs of the child so his or her educational needs are met.

It might seem to some people that the number of students with special needs is minimal, but approximately half the current population of the United States is affected by disabilities, either themselves or through association.

People who create learning programs for teaching degrees are now encouraged to change said programs in order to include inclusion concepts. For example, the inclusion concept could be educating a teacher to know how to deal with an autistic child. Without proper training, the teachers could be at a loss. Teachers who have been successful with inclusion classrooms have stated that resources, time, and training were the determining factors in their accomplishments. With inclusion being the standard in all classrooms, the concepts of teaching and learning must adapt for the benefit of both teachers and students.

SPECIAL EDUCATION LOCAL PLAN AREAS (SELPA)

States provide a minimum basic special education allocation. This funding is based on a per-pupil amount for a district's entire student population. Funds for special education services are distributed through Special Education Local Plan Areas (SELPA). Under certain circumstances, charter schools also receive funds through SELPA.

With budget cuts and slashed funding, it may be more difficult for teachers to find resources to teach special needs students. Regardless of the burden prompted by budget cuts, it is a law by which teachers must abide. From 2005 to 2006, regular education spending totaled less than $10,000 per pupil in elementary and secondary schools. According to the Center for Special Education Finance (**http://csef.air.org**), the average spending on special education students totals between $20,000 and $30,000, depending on the state.

Another special needs area is English as a second language (ESOL) education, for which the U.S. Supreme Court established English Language Learners (ELL) rights by passing the Education Opportunity Act of 1974. School districts are now required to address linguistic deficiencies of language minorities.

In striving to meet all of these state and federal requirements, please keep in mind your administrator is there to help you succeed. Your success is their success, and all of you are working together to achieve the same goal.

NATIONAL ASSOCIATION FOR GIFTED CHILDREN (NAGC)

The NCLB Act and IDEA have permitted great strides in procuring equitable education for all. Yet, some organizations felt that the focus on equality created another problem: a lack of challenging education for gifted students. In 2004, a philanthropic organization called the John Templeton Foundation sponsored a study on acceleration and gifted students. The results were published in a report titled, *A Nation Deceived: How Schools Hold Back America's Brightest Students*. The document suggested that the current educational trends ignored exceptional students. In 2007, Congressman Elton Gallegly of California introduced the Gifted and Talented Students Education Act. The legislation allows the allocation of resources to pay for gifted education.

BUDGET CUTS IN EDUCATION

Despite growing concerns regarding education in the United States, and the mandates that have been put into place to improve student performance, there have been numerous budget cuts in school programs. Education spending is often one of the first things cut in times of an economic downturn. The juxtaposition can sometimes create challenges for administrators and educators. For example:

- In 2006, President George W. Bush made a proposal to cut education spending by more than $3 billion dollars, but at the same time wanted to strengthen math and science programs.

- California once had an educational system touted as a national model. However, since Governor Arnold Schwarzenegger cut the education budget by $1.3 billion in the 2009 school year and $4 billion the following year, California schools have suffered drastically. Since the beginning of 2010, the number of school systems that might be "unable to meet future financial obligations" has increased by 38 percent, according to the state's Department of Education.

- In Florida, a state that already struggles due to lack of funding, administrators were reported to say the budget cuts were "bleeding the education system." Students and teachers all over central Florida rallied together and wore red shirts to represent their discontentment with the massive education budget cut of $100 million in February 2009. Governor Charlie Crist stated he was waiting for a waiver from the Secretary of Education to get the federal stimulus money for education. Last reported, Florida was not eligible to receive the stimulus money because the state does not fund education enough to qualify.

AMERICAN RECOVERY AND REINVESTMENT ACT OF 2009

President Barack Obama's administration is working to find ways to ease the burden for teachers and at the same time improve the quality of education the students receive. Obama is attempting to begin this process through the American Recovery and Reinvestment Act of 2009. The official website of the Department of Education (**www.ed.gov/index.jhtml**) states, "Providing a high quality education for all children is critical to America's economic future." The site goes on to say that Obama is "committed to providing every child access to a complete and competitive education, from cradle through career."

With the American Recovery and Reinvestment Act, there will be:

- $5 billion for early learning programs, including programs for children with special needs
- $77 billion for reforms to strengthen elementary and secondary education, including $48.6 billion to stabilize state education budgets
- $5 billion in competitive funds to spur innovation

With the American Recovery and Reinvestment Act, $77 billion has been earmarked for reform to strengthen elementary and secondary education and is also to be used for encouraging states to "make improvements in teacher effectiveness and ensure that all schools have highly qualified teachers."

The White House's education Web page states, "Teachers are the single most important resource to a child's learning." It vows to ensure "that teachers are supported as professionals in the classroom" and to "use rewards and incentives to keep talented teachers in the schools that need them the most" have been made. This act offers new teachers promise and recognition.

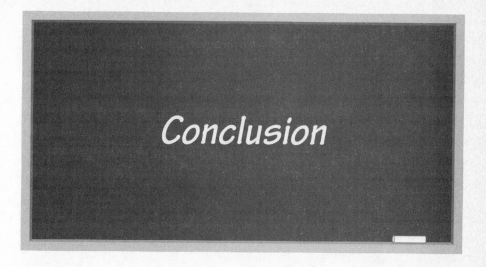

Conclusion

As a new teacher, you will need to juggle paperwork, instructional plans, and administrator and student demands. As time goes on, it will get easier. In the beginning, realize that you will probably make some rookie mistakes. Although you will not always have control of the situation all of the time, the following are some suggestions from veteran teachers. They might help you avoid some common mistakes.

Common mistakes to avoid include:

1. Do not try to bribe your class with treats and prizes. They will get used to this, and it will end up costing you a lot of money.

2. Do not let the boundary slip between teacher and students. You are not their friend. If you forget this, it could end up creating unnecessary problems for you. For example, it might inadvertently cloud your judgment. It might undermine your authority or credibility, or the relationship might be construed as unprofessional.

3. Set class rules and stick to them. If you do not follow through, you will lose credibility.

4. Do not let your students intimidate you. You are the teacher. You make the rules.

5. Do not worry about what the students think about you. Do your job.

6. Always think before you speak. You do not need to be misinterpreted right away.

7. Take a look in the mirror before you teach. Something in your teeth or on your clothes will have your students laughing at you all day.

8. Always have emergency back-up lesson plans.

9. Take your lunch break, and do not let anyone intrude on it.

10. Do not hesitate to ask for help.

"With the exception of my student teaching experience, no other aspect of my college education prepared me for being a teacher at all. That is in no way meant to diminish the jobs done by my college professors in the education department. There just is not a substitute for real life experience."

— Nancie Menapace, English teacher,
Good Hope Middle School

TAKE CARE OF YOURSELF

In addition to trying to avoid rookie mistakes, most teachers cite taking care of themselves as the best advice to give new teachers. Teaching can be a very time-consuming profession and much of the realities surrounding it can be stressful and unpleasant. The bottom line is life is stressful — regardless of the job you take. The important thing is to have a job you enjoy. Find time to relax so that you do not burn out early. The following are a few tips for managing your stress when you are having a bad day.

1. **Talk a walk.** If things are not going well during the day and you can find a way to walk around the building during a break, do it. If you cannot find the time during the day, talk a walk or go to a gym as soon as you leave work. If you are tempted to go home first, you might find you are too tired to go out. If you make the time to do something for yourself before you get home, you will be less stressed and less tired. The exercise will re-energize you, enabling you to grade papers and prepare the next day's lesson.

2. **Call a friend.** Sometimes, a little venting can go a long way. Get your feelings out and then move on. To make sure you do not fall into a pattern

of whining, set a kitchen timer for five to ten minutes. When the timer goes off, you are done venting and it is time to talk about something else.

3. **Get enough sleep.** After school, take a break for a specific amount of time, such as walking for an hour. Make a schedule for getting your evening work done, so you are not up too late. You will be more stressed the next day if you have not gotten enough sleep.

4. **Take a bath.** There is something magical about the healing powers of a hot bath. Give yourself some time to unwind.

5. **Do some yoga.** Yoga and other forms of meditation can help relieve stress. Take a class or put in a DVD at home.

6. **Spend some time outside.** If the weather is nice, work in the garden or sit on a porch swing. If it is winter, take a brisk walk or build a snowman.

7. **Watch a movie.** Watching TV or movies can be a great escape in moderation. Be sure you plan your time accordingly so that you do not end up working late because of it.

8. **Play.** Find someone to laugh with, be it a significant other, a child, or a pet. Do something silly and fun. Nothing relieves stress like laughter.

9. **Listen to music.** Pick music that soothes you. It is different for everyone. For some people it might be jazz, for others it might be country. Whatever you enjoy, turn it up and lose yourself in the music.

10. **Plan a get-away.** When you have a free weekend, find a way to give yourself a mini-vacation. Drive to the beach or visit a friend. Stay at home, turn off your phone, and read all weekend. Whatever the plan, make it just for you.

For effective stress relief, you must be able to disconnect yourself from what is causing you stress. Think it through and then put it aside for as long as you can reasonably allow — whether it is 20 minutes or an entire weekend. Remember, you will be a better teacher when you are in a good frame of mind. Make sure to make time for yourself.

NEVER FORGET YOUR PURPOSE AND PASSION

As you make your way through the pitfalls and triumphs of your first year teaching middle school, keep in mind that you learn from experience. When you find yourself faced with a particularly grueling situation, remember why you got into teaching to begin with. It might not always seem like it, but you are making a difference in many lives.

CASE STUDY: WHAT TEACHING MEANS TO ME

Ruth Hallowell Bortolan
355 Diane Drive
South Windsor, Connecticut

CLASSIFIED CASE STUDIES
directly from the experts

Ruth Bortolan is recently retired after teaching and mentoring in Connecticut for over 40 years. She holds a bachelor of science degree and a master's degree. Over the years, she worked on school certification evaluation committees, state education curriculum committees, and local teacher mentoring programs. She was also published in the New England Celebration of Excellence Project *magazine. She has many memories and stories from her years of teaching. In her opinion, this particular story provides an excellent example of what she loved about teaching and why new teachers should never take for granted the impact they make on their students.*

When I attended St. Joseph College, I took a child development course. The teacher, Sister Mary de Lourdes, taught all of her college prep teachers that the most important thing a teacher can do is greet each student with an honest positive comment each and every day. It is not difficult to find something nice to say, even something as simple as, "You have a nice smile today," or "That's a cool new hairstyle." I remembered that when I became a teacher, and I really tried to use that philosophy often.

During my second year of teaching, I was monitoring a study hall that primarily consisted of ninth grade students discussing the fact that they would quit school as soon as they turned 16. I remember one boy in particular, who was starved for attention and acting out negatively in order to get someone to notice him. One day I politely asked him to move his seat because he was bothering the students near him. He moved to a seat near the window and proceeded to make a hangman's noose out of the cord hanging from the window shade. He then came up to me and announced that he had made the noose especially for me. I told him that I was sorry to have to give him a "pink" pass, the third one from me in about a week. At that time, three pink passes meant he would get two weeks' suspension from school. He took the pass and left the room. I did not really think anything more about it.

A few weeks later, I was wrapping things up to leave my job at that school. I was getting married to a man who was in the military, and we were being transferred to another state. The staff at the school had thrown me a bridal shower that afternoon, and I was one of the last people out of the building that day.

It was snowing and my car was the only one in the front parking lot. As I approached my car, I remember feeling frightened because the boy who had made me the hangman's noose was standing there. Instead of showing my fear, I kept on walking, said "Hello," and asked him how he was doing and why he was out there. He told me he had heard that I was leaving the school, so he was waiting outside in the cold and snow to talk to me before I left. He told me that I was the only teacher who had ever been nice to him and he wanted to thank me. I surely learned something that day! Never underestimate the power of your words or how you treat people.

I was a new bride off to live my life. I have since forgotten the boy's name, but over the years, I have often wondered how he made out in life. It is amazing how many times over the years I have thought of him. When I returned to teaching, I taught for 30 more years, and I always remembered to say something nice to each student as often as I could. This made my teaching job easy and joyful, because the students always treated me the way I treated them.

Treating people well is important at any level, but as a first year teacher, it can help you establish positive relationships that will help you for years. First year teachers in any new position, whether they have experience or not, have tons of work to do. Build a rapport with your students and ask them for help with minor tasks like setting up bulletin boards. It will help you get to know them and give them a chance to feel helpful. This can help build a relationship that is supportive for both of you.

Being a middle school teacher can be very difficult. In order to survive, you will need to be strong, compassionate, and patient. Because of the added challenges brought about by the onset of puberty, it is considered by many to be the most challenging to teach. The following are a few things to consider as you prepare for the challenge:

- You will need to have boundless energy and enthusiasm for your subject.
- You will need to relay the lesson plans in a variety of fun interactive methods.
- You will need to learn to juggle responsibilities.
- You will need to plan for all situations.
- You will need to be flexible in the face of the unexpected.
- You will need to accept the physical, mental, and emotional exhaustion.

If you are willing to confront the demands with a smile on your face, and you do not discourage easily, this is the right job for you. The rigors are great, but the rewards far surpass the obstacles. Watching individuals grow into the adults they will eventually become is extremely gratifying.

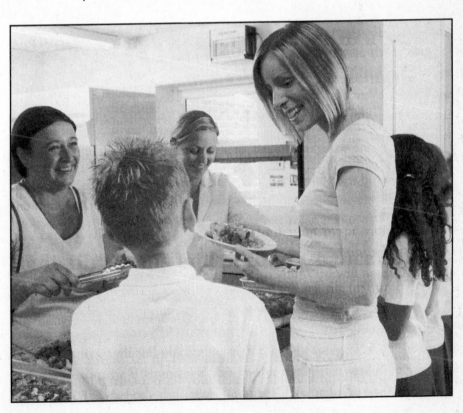

APPENDIX A: SAMPLE CURRICULUM VITAE AND COVER LETTER

MARY ELLEN GRIFFITH
1004 TERRIFIC TEACHER LANE
IMANEDUCATOR, FLORIDA 34736
(555) 111-55555 (home)
(555) 555-1111 (cell phone)
ihopeigetit@e-mail.com

CERTIFICATION

2007–2012   Professional Educator's Certificate, Florida Department
of Education, English Grades 5 – 9, No. 803766.

EDUCATION

2002   Teaching Certificate in English – Florida Atlantic University, Boca
Raton, Florida.

1996 **Bachelor of Social Work – Florida Atlantic University,** Boca Raton, Florida.

1986 **Associate in Arts with a Major in Journalism – Broward Community College,** Pembroke Pines, Florida.

PROFESSIONAL EXPERIENCE

2008–2009: <u>Eighth Grade Writing Composition Teacher</u>
Gray Middle School, 205 East Magnolia Street, Groveland, Florida 34736.

Assisted students in inclusion classrooms encompassing advanced placement, ESE, regular ed., and ESLs on the road to reaching their maximum writing potential. Utilizing differentiated classroom strategies, students were able to achieve the highest gains on FCAT Writes scores in Lake County. Focused on voice, organization, humor, word choice, elaboration, and remedial and advanced conventions. Read and analyzed prolific essayists throughout American history. All teaching tasks and skills included, but were not limited to: creating innovative, high-interest units, and lessons that address various learning levels and styles; keeping computerized plan book, grade book, and classroom calendar on eSembler; parent/teacher/student conferences and regular contact; editing and encouraging student publication.

2003–2008: <u>Eighth Grade English Teacher</u>
Wellington Landings Middle School, 1100 Aero Club Drive, Wellington, Florida 33414.

Encouraged students to explore themselves and the world around them through prose, poetry, and the written word. All teaching tasks and skills included, but were not limited to: creating innovative, high-interest units and lessons; keeping computerized plan book, grade book, and classroom calendar; parent/teacher/student conferences and contact; editing and encouraging student publication.

1998–2003: <u>English Teacher/Intensive Reading Teacher</u>
    Crestwood Middle School, 21 Sparrow Drive, Royal Palm Beach, Florida 33411.

Motivated and encouraged lower-level reading students to reach their full potential, often creating my own high-interest writing as a stepping stone to more difficult texts. All teaching tasks and skills included, but were not limited to: creating innovative units and lessons; keeping lesson plan book and classroom calendar; parent/teacher/student conferences and contact; editing and encouraging publication of student work.

1993–1996: <u>Social Worker</u>
    Seminole Tribe of Florida, Hollywood, Florida.

Liaison to Department of Children and Families under the Indian Child Welfare Act. Focus on tribal preservation. Case management/advocate with duties including, but not limited to: keeping updated case notes and files; home visits; accompanying DCF representatives on Big Cypress, Brighton, and Hollywood reservations; attending family court hearings; working with DCF on suitable child placements within the tribe.

RELATED PROFESSIONAL EXPERIENCE

2008–2009: <u>Gator News</u> — Gray Middle School. Publisher, editor, photographer, graphic artist, and writer for Gray Middle School's primary communication vehicle between parents and the school.

2004–2009: <u>Scrabble Club</u> — Wellington Landings Middle and Gray Middle School. Founded and facilitated the Scrabble Club, wherein students utilize critical thinking, mathematics, linguistics, and spelling skills by competing timed games of Scrabble.

2005–2007: <u>Academic Team Leader</u> — Wellington Landings Middle School. Coordinated and facilitated interdisciplinary units, speakers, and educational team field trips. Responsible for lockers and coordinating parent/teacher conferences. Created student-parent book club during 2006.

2000–2002: <u>Public Relations</u> — Crestwood Middle School. Provided local papers with information on upcoming and newsworthy student events and school, teacher, and student accomplishments.

1995–1996: <u>Assistant to the Dean of the Social Work Department</u> — Florida Atlantic University, Boca Raton, Florida. Assisted Dean Diane Alperne in establishing FAU's Parenting Partnership Newsletter, distributed to social-work colleges throughout the United States.

GRANTS

1995 <u>Indian Child Welfare Grant</u> — Wrote and received a grant to work with adolescents for the Seminole Tribe of Florida. Received a stipend and training in maintaining tribal families under the Indian Child Welfare Act of 1973.

PUBLISHED WORK

Griffith, M.E. (2008, July). "Harry Potter Fans Take over Barnes and Noble." *The Observer News.*

Griffith, M.E. (2001, November). "America the Beautiful." *Parenting Plus.*

Griffith, M.E. (1998, November) "Lilith Fair Rocks South Florida." *Stuart News.*

Griffith, M.E. (1997, November) "Life Guarding Not Just a Kid's 1st Job." *Stuart News.*

Griffith, M.E. (1997, October) "Eagle Academy Opens." *Stuart News.*

Griffith, M.E. (1997, October) "Lake Worth Historic District Refurbished." *Stuart News.*

Griffith, M.E. (1997, August) "Nothing Ever Prepares You for Parenthood." *The Observer News.*

YOUR NAME HERE
1004 TERRIFIC TEACHER LANE
IMANEDUCATOR, FLORIDA 34736
(555) 111-5555 (home)
(555) 555-1111 (cell phone)
ihopigetit@e-mail.com

VIA FACSIMILE TRANSMITTAL

(Including the manner in which you have sent your cover letter with your résumé,
as illustrated above, will help you stand out from others)

December 15, 2009

Julie Administrator, Principal
Successful Middle School
18725 Super School Avenue
Goingsomewhere, Florida 35555

Dear Ms. Administrator,

I am quite interested in a position at Successful Middle School. I am, therefore, sending you my curriculum vitae with the hope that you will review my credentials. ***Insert one or two lines about yourself here.***

If you feel I have the experience and skills necessary to meet the needs of your students, please consider interviewing me should an opening present itself.

Please do not hesitate to contact me at your convenience. Thank you for your time and consideration in this matter.

Sincerely,

(sign here)

Your Printed Name Here

APPENDIX B: FORMS

Returned Forms Checklist

DATE RECEIVED	NAME	PERIOD #														

SUBJECT:

Locker Report Form

DATE	STUDENT NAME	LOCKER #	LOCK SERIAL NUMBER	LOCK COMBINATION

APPENDIX C: SAMPLE SYLLABUS

WELCOME!!!

TO MRS. GRIFFITH'S

6th Grade Language Arts

(555) 111-5555

Griffith-russom@myemailaddress.com

COURSE

SYLLABUS

INTRODUCTION AND TEXTS — Get ready for an exciting first year in Room 707. To begin with, we have brand-new materials with which to explore and learn. Our Prentice Hall textbook, *Language and Literacy*, is supplemented with many technology resources that we will navigate together. Additionally, Prentice Hall has supplemented our literature books with a text of captivating, nonfiction articles called *Reality Central*. Equally thought-provoking is our writing book, Houghton Mifflin's sixth-grade *Write Source Book*. These materials will be accented by lots of hands-on assignments and games.

CONTACT INFORMATION — Please do not hesitate to contact me with any comments, concerns, or questions. I will return your calls or e-mails within 24 hours, if not sooner.

GOALS — Throughout the year, students will be meeting many challenges and accomplishing many objectives. My primary goal, however, will be for each student to achieve their potential by exploring themselves and the world around them, through reading, writing, listening, and speaking.

DAILY TAKE-HOME FOLDERS — These are important! Students are responsible for keeping daily take-home folders (see supply list below). In this folder, you will find the student's individual goals, papers, classroom assignments, homework, etc. Please check your child's folder on Fridays and sign the parent signature sheet in the front. Students who took the initiative to have them signed and bring them to school on Monday will receive ten bonus points to begin their week.

ASSIGNMENTS/HOMEWORK — All assignments and homework will be listed on the board. Students are required to copy these in their take-home folders daily. I will accept late homework without penalty if I receive a written excuse from a parent/guardian or if the child has an excused absence. Missed homework/other assignments will be provided to the student with the new due date clearly listed on that assignment. Students may turn in unexcused, missed homework and avoid work detention if it is turned in before the day of their assigned detention. The assignment grade will be reduced by 10% per day late. I hold work detentions on Thursdays. Any homework/assignments not turned in will be completed in work detention with a maximum score of 75.

GRADING SCALE –   A = 100%–90%
B = 89%–80%
C = 79%–70%
D = 69%–60%
F = DON'T EVEN THINK ABOUT IT!

CLASSROOM EXPECTATIONS – The following is the list of procedures that ensures successful language-arts learning. Should these procedures not be followed, students will first be given a warning. If there is a second infraction, the student will receive a detention. If the behavior continues, the parent/guardian will receive a phone call home and the student can be sent for a time-out to another class if his or her behavior is disruptive. This allows us to work together to create an environment conducive to your child's participation is his/her own education. I will write a referral and send a child to administration if all other interventions fail, especially if these issues are chronic and hinder the student's own education or the education of others. The procedures below are posted on the front wall in the classroom and will be reviewed the first day of class so there is no confusion.

CLASSROOM EXPECTATIONS

1. Be seated, quiet, and ready to learn when the bell rings.
2. Your input is enthusiastically welcome in my class. Please raise your hand and wait to be called on to share.
3. The words "I can't" may not be used in this room. You can, and I will help you. Therefore, you may use phrases such as "I need help" or "I don't understand."
4. Our classroom is a safe zone. We support each other's differences and treat each other with respect. This means: Say what you mean and don't say it mean; hands are for helping, not for hurting; and feet are for walking, not for kicking.
5. Be familiar with the school rules in your student handbook. They all apply in Mrs. Griffith's room.

SUPPLY LIST

I try to keep classroom costs to a minimum. There will be projects throughout the year that may require additional supplies, but I try to make them objects we can find around the house or purchase for a minimal expense. Daily supplies needed are as follows:

1. Daily Folder — three-prong, two-pocket. If you wish to purchase paper folders, you may want to get the five-pack. These folders get lots of use and might wear out quickly.
2. One package of tabbed dividers.
3. College ruled, lined paper.
4. Composition book — any color.

5. One three-pronged, two-pocket folder. These differ from the other folder in that they will be left in class and used as a portfolio for students' work.

6. Black or blue pen.

7. Pencils.

Thank you and I look forward to learning with all of you this year!!!

Please sign below to show you have received and reviewed Mrs. Griffith's course syllabus. Detach this portion and return to me.

_____   _____
Student signature   Parent Signature

APPENDIX D: SEATING CHART

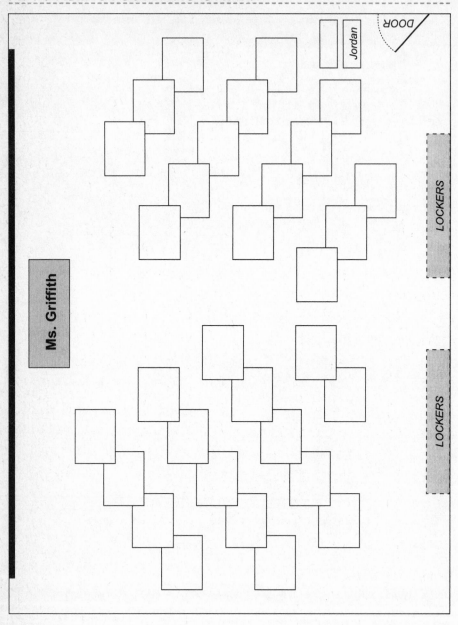

APPENDIX E: SAMPLE RUBRIC FORM

MATH RUBRIC

Name: _____

Grade: _____

Date: _____

Teacher: _____

Criteria	1	2	3	4	Value
Explanation	Misses key points.	Explanation is unclear.	Good solid response with clear explanation.	A complete response with a detailed explanation.	___
Use Of Visuals	No diagram or sketch.	Inappropriate or unclear diagram.	Clear diagram or sketch.	Clear diagram or sketch with some detail.	___
Mechanics	Major math errors or serious flaws in reasoning.	Some serious math errors or flaws in reasoning.	No major math errors or serious flaws in reasoning.	No math errors.	___
Demonstrated Knowledge	Response shows a complete lack of understanding for the problem.	Response shows some understanding of the problem.	Shows substantial understanding of the problem, ideas, and processes.	Shows complete understanding of the questions, mathematical ideas, and processes.	___
Requirements	Does not meet the requirements of the problem.	Hardly meets the requirements of the problem.	Meets the requirements of the problem.	Goes beyond the requirements of the problem.	___
				Total:	_____

TEACHER COMMENTS

APPENDIX F: LESSON PLANS

LESSON PLANS

Week/Date 10/27

Sunshine State Standards
LA (vocab) 6.1.6.1, (nonfiction) 6.2.21 – 6.2.2.3, (research) 6.6.2.1 – 6.6.2.3

	MONDAY	TUESDAY
Objectives	TEACHER WORK DAY	Students will learn academic vocabulary as it applies to analyzing nonfiction text.
Bell Ringer		**P2, 3, 5 & 6** Students will replace everyday language in a given sentence on the board with academic language from their new vocabulary. **P3 & 5** Mr. Jordan will brainstorm with the class about strategies to improve academic progress.
Procedure		Students will be given a brief background on the Salem Witch Trials.
Essential Question		What new vocabulary can I use in my study of nonfiction?

Grade/Subject: Language Arts   **Prepared by Griffith**

Teacher's Goals: Students will begin to comprehend nonfiction, content-area writing. Students will begin to learn research strategies. Students will be able to apply academic nonfiction vocabulary in their reading, writing, and presentations.		
WEDNESDAY	**THURSDAY**	**FRIDAY**
Students will answer a research question using either the Internet or encyclopedia.	Students will collaborate in groups and create a paragraph based on their research using their nonfiction academic language.	Groups will present their written findings to the class.
Students will replace everyday language in a given sentence on the board with academic language from their new vocabulary: Today we will go the library to study stuff about Salem, Massachusetts.	Students will replace everyday language in a given sentence on the board with academic language from their new vocabulary: At the media center yesterday we looked closely at the events and people of the Salem witch trials.	Students will replace everyday language in a given sentence on the board with academic language from their new vocabulary: What kind of stuff was presented in the Salem Witch Trials?
Each student will receive one research question related to the Salem Witch Trials. Students will go to the media center and find the answer to their question. When students return to class, they will be assigned a group for tomorrow's work.	Students will get into collaborative groups and put their research together to construct a paragraph. Students will use their new nonfiction vocabulary.	Groups will share their findings with the class. Class will then view the discovery.com video.
What strategies can I use to answer a research question via the Internet?	Am I able to use my "academic language" to support the presentation of my group's perspective of the Salem Witch Trials?	How can I evaluate information I observe using my background knowledge of a topic?

LESSON PLANS

Week/Date 11/3

Sunshine State Standards: 6.1.7.2, 6.1.6.1., 6.2.2.4.		
	MONDAY	*TUESDAY*
Objectives	Students will understand author's purpose and learn new vocabulary related to tomorrow's text.	Students will be able to determine the author's purpose in the nonfiction short story "Water".
Bell Ringer	Hairy Beast using a word from this week's vocabulary. Students will underline the word and determine the part of speech.	Hairy Beast using a word from this week's vocabulary. Students will underline the word and determine the part of speech.
Procedure	Discuss being aware of the author's purpose. In pairs, students will complete Reading Warm-up B. We will then discuss them as a class.	Students will read "Water" individually. Students will then work in pairs to complete the author's purpose chart. Do vocabulary builder.
Higher Order Questioning	Can you recognize the author's purpose for writing in the selection you are reading?	Can you recognize the author's purpose for writing in the selection you are reading?
Assessment	Completed Assignment – Reading Warm-up A& B	Teacher observation.
Materials	PENCIL/PEN/ PAPER/ TEXT/WB/BR	TEXT/PENCIL/PEN/BR

Grade/Subject: Language Arts **Prepared by M. Griffith**

Notes/Comments: Adjectives and articles are on the selection test, review.		
WEDNESDAY	*THURSDAY*	*FRIDAY*
Students will be able to recognize and name details that indicate author's purpose.	Working in groups, students recognize the author's purpose and narrative.	Students will show mastery over the vocabulary, strategies for finding author's purpose, and a working knowledge of adjectives and articles reviewed during the week.
Hairy Beast using a word from this week's vocabulary. Students will underline the word and determine the part of 'speech.	Hairy Beast using a word from this week's vocabulary. Students will underline the word and determine the part of speech.	Hairy Beast using a word from this week's vocabulary. Students will underline the word and determine the part of speech.
Students will work in groups. Each group will collaborate on completing one of five of the workbook pages. There will be a fifth remedial group. Each group will share their answers with the class for the other students to fill in their workbook pages.	Review author's purpose and narrative and autobiographical essays. Homework: Vocabulary Builder	Selection test. Review as a class.
Can you recognize the author's purpose for writing in the selection you are reading?	Can you understand and use the new vocabulary you learned this week?	Can you show mastery over the vocabulary and author's purpose concepts you have learned this week?
Completed workbook pages and teacher observation.	Completed workbook pages and teacher observation.	Assessment.
WB/TEXT/PENCIL/PEN/	WB/TEXT/PENCIL/PEN/	PENCIL/PEN/PAPER/ TEST

LESSON PLANS

Week/Date   Grade/Subject   Prepared by

Your State's Standards   Notes/Comments

	MONDAY	TUESDAY	WEDNESDAY	THURSDAY	FRIDAY
Objectives					
Bell Ringer					
Procedure					
Higher Order Questioning					
Assessment					
Materials					

Bibliography

"12 Tips for Substitute Teachers." *Why Teach?* Web. 12 Nov. 2009. <**http:// whyteach.wordpress.com/2008/04/24/12-tips-for-substitute-teachers/**>.

"About the Program." Madison Professional Development School Partnership. Web. 28 July 2010. <**http://labweb.education.wisc.edu/magarner/pds/ text.html**>.

"Become a Substitute Teacher." *Teacher World - Education for Teachers and Administrators.* Web. 25 Nov. 2009. <**www.teacher-world.com/ substitute-teacher.html**>.

Become a Teacher - Top Teacher Training Resource. Web. 10 Oct. 2009. <**http:// becomeateacher.info/Certification-Requirements.asp**>.

Brown, Dave F. and Trudy Knowles. *What Every Middle School Teacher Should Know.* Second ed. Portsmouth, NH: Heinemann, 2000. Print.

"Center for Education Reform - K–12 Facts." *Center for Education Reform - Home.* Web. 01 Aug. 2010. <**www.edreform.com/Fast_Facts/K12_Facts**>.

"Developing a Teaching Resume & Cover Letter: A to Z Teacher Stuff." *A to Z Teacher Stuff For Teachers FREE online lesson plans, lesson plan ideas and activities, thematic units, printables, themes, teaching tips, articles, and educational resources.* Web. 25 Nov. 2009. <**http://atozteacherstuff.com/pages/1876.shtml**>.

"Fast Facts." *National Center for Education Statistics (NCES) Home Page, a part of the U.S. Department of Education.* Web. 12 Nov. 2009. <**http://nces.ed.gov/fastfacts/display.asp?id=28**>.

"Format Teacher Resume, Teacher Resume Sample, Teacher Resumes, CV Resume, Educational Resume." *Sample Resumes, Free Sample Resume, Resume Writing Examples.* Web. 25 Nov. 2009. <**www.bestsampleresume.com/teachers-resumes.html**>.

"High School Lesson Plans." *Georgia Educational Technology Training Center.* Web. 15 Nov. 2009. <**http://edtech.kennesaw.edu/intech/hslessonplans.htm**>.

"Inspiring Teachers - Tips - Dealing with Difficult Parents - Empowering Educators Around the World - classroom resources, tips, articles, newsletter, books, webinars, & free web pages." *Inspiring Teachers - Home - Empowering Educators Around the World - classroom resources, tips, articles, newsletter, books, webinars, & free web pages.* Web. 01 Feb. 2010. <**www.inspiringteachers.com/classroom_resources/tips/parent_communication/dealing_with_difficult_parents.html**>.

Job interviews. Free interview questions and answers and job interview tips. Web. 08 Nov. 2009. <**www.best-job-interview.com**>.

Kelley, W. Michael. *Rookie Teaching for Dummies.* New York: For Dummies, 2003. Print.

Kocsis, Anne B. *How to Be Successful in Your First Year of Teaching High School: Everything You Need to Know That They Don't Teach You in School.* Ocala, FL: Atlantic Pub. Group, 2010. Print.

Lambert, Lisa. "Half of Teachers Quit in 5 Years." *The Washington Post* [Washington, DC] 9 May 2006. Web. 15 Nov. 2009. <**www. washingtonpost.com/wp-dyn/content/article/2006/05/08/ AR2006050801344.html**>.

"Lesson Plans." *Teachers Network.* Web. 14 Nov. 2009. <**www.teachersnetwork. org/lessonplans**>.

Linn, Dane. "NGA Center for Best Practices." *National Governors Association.* 24 Jan. 2000. Web. 22 July 2010. <**www.nga.org/portal/site/nga/menuite- m.9123e83a1f6786440ddcbeeb501010a0/?vgnextoid=bb86303cb0b320 10VgnVCM1000001a01010aRCRD&vgnextchannel=4b18f074f0d9ff0 0VgnVCM1000001a01010aRCRD**>.

Lorenz, Kate. "CNN.com - Tricks to remembering names - Jul 22, 2005." *CNN.com - Breaking News, U.S., World, Weather, Entertainment & Video News.* CNN, 22 July 2005. Web. 05 Dec. 2009. <**www.cnn.com/2005/US/ Careers/07/22/names**>.

Mauro, Terri. "What Is a 504 Plan?" *Parenting Special Needs Children.* About.com. Web. 25 Nov. 2009. <**http://specialchildren.about.com/ od/504s/f/504faq1.htm**>.

Mentor: Expanding the world of quality mentoring. Web. 13 Nov. 2009. <**www.mentoring.org/take_action/advocate_for_mentoring/ background_checks/legislative_history**>.

National Association of School Nurses. Web. 08 Dec. 2009. <**www.nasn.org**>.

National Education Association. NEA. Web. 5 Nov. 2009. <**www.nea.org/
home/1704.htm**>.

"NCATE - Public - Home Page." *NCATE - Home Page*. Web. 26 July 2010.
<**www.ncate.org/public/aboutNCATE.asp**>.

"NEA - Grants & Awards." *NEA - NEA Home*. Web. 08 May
2010. <**www.nea.org/grants/grantsawardsandmore.
html?gclid=CNHJxLrBkaICFV_G3Aod92Rljg**>.

Nies, Yunji De. "Mean Girls: Teen Suicide Calls Attention to Cyberbullying
- ABC News." *ABCNews.com - Breaking News, Politics, Online News,
World News, Feature Stories, Celebrity Interviews and More - ABC News*.
Web. 01 Aug. 2010. <**http://abcnews.go.com/GMA/Parenting/
girls-teen-suicide-calls-attention-cyberbullying/story?id=9685026**>.

"IRPA - A Nation Deceived." *Institute for Research and Policy on Acceleration
(IRPA)*. Web. 01 Aug. 2010. <**www.accelerationinstitute.org/
nation_deceived**>.

"NAGC - The History of Gifted and Talented Education." *NAGC: Home*. Web.
01 Aug. 2010. <**www.nagc.org/index.aspx?id=607**>.

Novak, Lauren. "More turn to teaching as a second career." *Adelaide Now*.
The Advertiser, 27 Nov. 2009. Web. 10 Feb. 2010. <**www.adelaidenow.
com.au/news/in-depth/more-turn-to-teaching-as-a-second-career/
story-fn3o6nna-1225803210915**>.

Parks, Jerry L. *Teacher under Construction: Things I Wish I'd Known! : a Survival
Handbook for New Middle School Teachers*. New York: Weekly Reader, 2004.
Print.

Olson, Elizabeth. "The New York Times Log In." *The New York Times - Breaking News, World News & Multimedia*. 14 Oct. 2009. Web. 26 July 2010. <**www. nytimes.com/2009/10/15/your-money/15TEACH.html**>.

Piazza, Elizabeth. "'Sexting' Has School Officials Talking - Farmington Daily Times." *Home - Farmington Daily Times*. 31 July 2010. Web. 01 Aug. 2010. <**www.daily-times.com/ci_15651563**>.

"Resources: 25 Useful Lesson Plan Links | Teaching Tips." *Teaching Tips. com - Online Teacher Certificates - Become a Teacher*. Web. 30 Oct. 2009. <**www.teachingtips.com/library/education-as-a-career-faqs/ resources-25-useful-lesson-plan-links**>.

"Resources for School Counselors." *Welcome to the American Counseling Association*. Web. 07 Dec. 2009. <**www.counseling.org/PublicPolicy/TP/ ResourcesForSchoolCounselors/CT2.aspx**>.

Snyder, PhD, Marlene. "Understanding Bullying and Its Impact on Kids with Learning Disabilities or AD/HD - Social Skills | GreatSchools." *GreatSchools - Public and Private School Ratings, Reviews and Parent Community*. Web. Feb. 2010. <**www.greatschools.org/LD/managing/understanding-bullying-and-its-impact-on-kids-with-learning-disabilities-or-ad-hd.gs? content=823&print=true&fromPage=all**>.

"Society Education." *About the USA*. Web. 01 Aug. 2010. <**http://usa. usembassy.de/society-education.htm**>.

"Teachers—Kindergarten, Elementary, Middle, and Secondary." *U.S. Bureau of Labor Statistics*. Web. 01 Aug. 2010. <**www.bls.gov/oco/ocos318.htm**>.

"Teacher Quotes, Teaching Sayings, Quotations about Teachers." *The Quote Garden - Quotes, Sayings, Quotations, Verses*. Web. 29 Mar. 2010. <**www.quotegarden.com/teachers.html**>.

"Teacher Resume and Cover Letter Examples." *A Resumes for Teachers*. Web. 24 Nov. 2009. <**http://resumes-for-teachers.com/teacher-resume-examples.htm**>.

Teacher Retention and Attrition Information, Questions and Answers. Web. 25 Nov. 2009. <**http://retainingteachers.com**>.

"Teacher." *U.S. Bureau of Labor Statistics*. Web. 21 Mar. 2010. <**www.bls.gov/k12/help01.htm**>.

"What's Possible: Turning Around America's Lowest-Achieving Schools – ED.gov Blog." *U.S. Department of Education*. Web. 27 July 2010. <**www.ed.gov/blog/2010/03/whats-possible-turning-around-americas-lowest-achieving-schools**>.

Wyatt, Robert Lee, and J. Elaine. White. *Making Your First Year a Success: a Classroom Survival Guide for Middle and High School Teachers*. Second ed. Thousand Oaks, CA: Corwin, 2007. Print.

About the Authors

Anne Kocsis worked in the Cumberland Valley school district as a teacher's aide. She is currently a freelance writer and the mother of three children: a son who is a senior in high school, a son in his last year of middle school, and a daughter in fifth grade. This is her third book with Atlantic Publishing Group, Inc. She is also the author of *How to Be Successful in Your First Year of Teaching High School: Everything You Need to Know That They Don't Teach You in School*

Mary Ellen Griffith lives in Florida where she has been teaching English for 11 years and writing for local newspapers and magazines when time allows. She lives happily with her daughter Lexi and their two dogs, Maxine and Charlie.

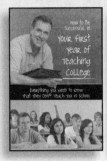

Index